DIVIDED UNION

A VOLUME IN THE SERIES

CORNELL STUDIES IN SECURITY AFFAIRS

edited by Robert J. Art, Robert Jervis, and Stephen M. Walt

A full list of titles in the series appears at the end of the book.

DIVIDED UNION

*The Politics of War in the Early
American Republic*

To Will,

Happy reading.

Scott A. Silverstone

CORNELL UNIVERSITY PRESS

ITHACA AND LONDON

First published 2004 by Cornell University Press

Printed in the United States of America

Library of Congress Cataloging-in-Publication Data

Silverstone, Scott A.

Divided union : the politics of war in the early American
republic / Scott A. Silverstone.

    p. cm. — (Cornell studies in security affairs)

  Includes index.

  ISBN 0–8014–4230–3 (alk. paper)

  1. United States—Foreign relations—1801–1815. 2. United States—
Foreign relations—1815–1861. 3. United States—History, Military—
19th century. 4. United States—Politics and government—
1783–1865. 5. Federal government—United States—History—19th
century. 6. Politics and war—History—19th century. I. Title.
II. Series.

  E338.S56 2004

  973—dc22

                                                      2004001487

Cornell University Press strives to use environmentally responsible
suppliers and materials to the fullest extent possible in the publishing of its books. Such materials include vegetable-based, low-VOC
inks, and acid-free papers that are recycled, totally chlorine-free, or
partly composed of nonwood fibers. For further information, visit
our website at www.cornellpress.cornell.edu.

Cloth printing   10 9 8 7 6 5 4 3 2 1

CONTENTS

PREFACE

This book was written during a time of unprecedented U.S. power, measured not only in terms of the material resources the United States can marshal to project influence abroad but also, and perhaps more important, by the absence of any significant external constraints on how it might use that power. Under these conditions, it is fair to argue, constraints on how the United States uses its power in the international system will depend on limits operating within its own domestic political system. The nature of those internal constraints and the actual effects they might have on U.S. behavior should be of great interest to any contemporary observer of American foreign policy and international relations.

This book is about domestic constraints on state power, more specifically, constraints on the use of military force produced by the political institutions of democratic states. While this topic has been the subject of substantial research in recent years, it was also a major preoccupation of the founders of the United States, who thought carefully about the relationship between domestic institutions and military force as they wrestled with the great constitutional questions of their period. How to create a more peace-prone republic in a competitive anarchical system was a problem they addressed explicitly, yet in a way that students of U.S. foreign policy since the founding have failed to appreciate. The purpose of this book is to present a fresh perspective on American political institutions and war that connects with the contemporary debate on the sources of constraints on state power. It does so by focusing on the fact that the United States was created as a federal union, an institutional innovation for republican government that the founders believed would have a direct effect on America's propensity to resort to force in its foreign policy. The book shows just how federal union mattered in U.S. foreign policy before the Civil War—a period in which the United States was involved in a series of militarized international crises that brought it to the brink of war with foreign adversaries. Like federal union, this time period has been largely ignored by contemporary scholars of international relations and U.S. foreign policy, yet it is rich in insights for those interested in the domestic politics of military conflict.

A number of people have been instrumental in the development of this book. I owe my greatest intellectual debt to Daniel Deudney, who is the most creative and energetic scholar I have had the privilege to work with. Not only did he prompt me to ask the kinds of questions that I pursue in this work, he also served as a tireless mentor, critic, and sounding board as the project grew in theoretical and historical scope. I thank John Ikenberry, who asked hard questions and made important suggestions as I developed these ideas, and Douglas Verney, who carefully read every chapter and provided a wealth of important insights and advice. Robert Jervis provided substantial feedback on the complete manuscript and helped me improve the rigor of the theoretical and empirical dimensions of the book. I also thank editor Roger Haydon of Cornell University Press, who throughout the publication process has been a conscientious and professional advocate for this project. I express my gratitude to other scholars who over the past several years have helped me develop this work by critiquing my ideas: John Owen, Miriam Fendius Elman, Norrin Ripsman, Deborah Avant, Peter Onuf, Chris Harth, Nicholas Onuf, Ian Lustick, Avery Goldstein, Walter McDougall, David Hendrickson, Rey Koslowski, Jonathan Isacoff, and Joseph Mink.

This book is dedicated to my wife Lisa and my children Ian and Norah, who bring perpetual warmth and energy to my life; to my mother Barbara Silverstone, for teaching me the love of reading; and to my father Arnold Silverstone, whose boundless curiosity about this world has always been an inspiration.

SCOTT A. SILVERSTONE

West Point, New York

DIVIDED UNION

BACK FROM THE BRINK

Why Do States Avoid Military Conflict?

During the first sixty years of the nineteenth century, two notable events in U.S. foreign relations immediately draw our attention: the War of 1812, initiated by the young republic to compel British respect for the right of the United States to trade with continental Europe and sail unhampered on the high seas; and the Mexican-American War, initiated by the United States in 1846 against its North American neighbor in a quest for territorial expansion. Despite the fact that the United States was separated geographically from the highly competitive European state system, these conflicts demonstrate that the new republic was not a complete aberration in a system characterized by recurring interstate warfare. While our attention is naturally drawn to these two wars initiated by the United States, another important observation about U.S. foreign relations in this period is largely ignored: the United States was involved in a much larger set of "near miss" international crises, disputes in which the use of military force was a serious option, yet which were resolved short of armed conflict. The general causes of these U.S. crises—great power war and the security problems they create for peripheral states, territorial expansion into regions claimed or held by other states, international border disputes, and political instability in neighboring states—have been common in the broader history of international relations. In this light, the United States does not appear to depart radically in its early foreign policy from the norm of competitive international behavior so familiar to the Europeans.

What makes this set of international crises particularly noteworthy, however, is the fact that in each case it was the United States that backed down, preventing the disputes from escalating to the use of force, or otherwise limiting the degree to which military force decided the outcome. The cases include crises in 1807 and 1809 with Great Britain over the same issues that produced war in 1812. In 1807 the U.S. frigate *Chesapeake* was fired on and seized by the British warship *Leopard*. When news reached the United States a widespread war fever gripped much of the country. While President Jefferson ordered preparations for war and carefully considered this option when the British refused to make amends for the attack, the crisis eventually passed with no U.S. military response. In 1809 a group of prominent Republican legislators collaborated with incoming President James Madison in an effort to replace the U.S. embargo against Great Britain, imposed to force Britain to lift its ban on American trade with continental Europe, with a declaration of war. Despite wide agreement that the embargo had failed to change Britain's policy on neutral trade rights, the United States avoided escalating the dispute from a nonviolent embargo to any form of military confrontation. In another case, from 1811 to 1813 President Madison and Secretary of State Monroe supported a covert then an overt military effort to seize East Florida from Spain. United States officials feared that Spain would turn East Florida over to its British ally and that the colony would serve as a staging area for British assaults on the United States from the south. East Florida was also a haven for Native American tribes that raided along the southern U.S. border and served as a refuge for runaway American slaves. Despite the great advantage enjoyed by the U.S. military forces assembling for the final assault on the Spanish colonial capital, the United States abandoned this military initiative in 1813. In early 1846 America and Great Britain stood on the brink of war over possession of the Pacific Northwest. President Polk had initiated a diplomatic effort, backed up by the implicit threat of force, to take the entire Oregon Territory and thus deny Britain any territory on the Pacific coast of North America. As Britain prepared a force to defend its claim, the president never wavered in his insistence on the right of the United States to "All Oregon," despite the risk of war. The crisis ended, however, with a negotiated settlement and the United States backing down. In 1853 the United States again faced war with Mexico, this time over the disputed Mesilla Valley along the southern border of New Mexico. Despite mobilization for war by both sides and overwhelming military superiority that would permit the United States to dictate the outcome, President Pierce ordered American political and military leaders involved in the dispute to go to great lengths to avoid crisis escalation and resolve the question through negotiations. In 1853 to 1855 the United States was also involved in a long-running dispute with Spain over an effort to obtain Cuba. When Spain refused to sell its colony, ardent expansionists in the executive branch and Congress initiated an effort to use U.S. military force to seize the island. Despite provocations by Spain that could have provided a pretense for U.S. military action, President Pierce refused to actually use military force and the effort to obtain Cuba died. By the end of the 1850s the United States once again faced the prospects of using force against Mexico, this time in response to political instability within Mexico and along the border. This crisis was made more serious by the prospects of European intervention in Mexico's civil dispute, and the likelihood of a European monarch being placed on a Mexican throne. Despite three separate attempts by President Buchanan to obtain congressional approval for U.S. intervention, the effort ended with no U.S. military action. In summary, while the United States did go to war twice in the half-century before the Civil War, in a much larger number of cases we find a clear pattern of constraints on the use of military force to resolve international crises.

While these events are interesting from an historical perspective, the purpose of this book is to examine what this pattern in U.S. conflict behavior can teach us about a critical question in the broader field of international relations: what constrains the use of military force among states? Paraphrasing Rousseau, Kenneth Waltz once observed that interstate war is possible simply because there is nothing to stop it.[1] Waltz was highlighting what has become a truism in the study of international relations: the international system is anarchic, that is, there is no formal system of governance among or above individual states to constrain violence and maintain peace. At a minimum, anarchy creates a permissive environment in which states can use military force against one another for any number of reasons, ranging from achieving physical security, accumulating material wealth, and promoting an ideology or religion to aggrandizing the stature of state leaders or a ruling party.[2] Given the cataclysmic role of interstate vio-

---

[1] Kenneth Waltz, *Man, the State, and War* (New York: Columbia University Press, 1959), 182–83, 232.
[2] For the classic explanation of the effects of anarchy among states, see Thomas Hobbes, *Leviathan* (London, 1651), chap. 13. See also Kenneth Waltz, *Theory of International Politics* (Reading: Addison-Wesley, 1979).

lence in human history and the increasingly destructive potential of
warfare over time, it should be of little surprise that the causes of competition and war have been a dominant concern in the field of international relations.

Despite this literal possibility of endless war described by Waltz,
scholars of various theoretical stripes have also recognized that states are
not perpetually lunging at one another in a violent quest for security, material interests, or ideological objectives. States rarely rush into war, even
when engaged in dangerous, militarized disputes. It has even been observed that statistically war is a relatively rare event in world politics.[3]
While competition may be an inherent feature of politics in both domestic and international systems, this competition does not inevitably produce actual violence. According to a widely accepted claim in the field,
violence in the domestic realm is held in check by a central government
strong enough to enforce law and maintain order.[4] In the international
system, however, no such mechanism exists to keep states in check. This
presents students of international relations with an enduring puzzle:
how can we explain general patterns in which the use of violence is limited in world politics? What is it that prevents conflicts of interest in specific cases from escalating into violent clashes? More specifically, under
what conditions are states less likely to use military force against one another, even during periods of intense competition or open disputes?

In recent years, the most active debate on this question has pitted
scholars who point to constraints operating *within* the states involved in
an international dispute, that is, in the realm of domestic politics,
against realist theorists who argue that state violence is held in check
most often by the international distribution of power *between* states. A
large and diverse research agenda pursues the basic claim that the internal characteristics of democratic politics may impose strong constraints
on the use of military force, regardless of how power is distributed
among the states involved in a particular international conflict. Most

---

[3] Jack S. Levy, *War and the Modern Great Power System, 1495–1975* (Lexington: Univer-
sity Press of Kentucky, 1983), chap. 6; David E. Spiro, "The Insignificance of the Liberal
Peace," *International Security* 19 (fall 1994), 50–86; James Lee Ray, *Democracy and Interna-
tional Conflict: An Evaluation of the Democratic Peace Proposition* (Columbia: University of
South Carolina Press, 1995), 203; Michael W. Doyle, "Kant, Liberal Legacies, and Foreign
Affairs, pt. 1 ," *Philosophy and Public Affairs* 12 (summer 1983), 205–35.

[4] Waltz, *Theory of International Politics*, 112–13; Helen Milner, "The Assumption of Anarchy in International Relations Theory: A Critique," *Review of International Studies* 17
(January 1991), 67–85.

contemporary scholars trace this claim about democracy back to Immanuel Kant, who in 1795 argued that republican states, those that separate legislative and executive power, have a representative legislature with the authority to declare war, and a citizenry with little to gain by going to war would exhibit a "great hesitation" in the use of military force.[5] In the early twentieth century, President Woodrow Wilson championed the notion that democracies are less war prone than nondemocracies. Like many of his contemporaries after World War I, Wilson argued that the European security system, rooted as it was in the balance of power, had failed to keep the violence capacity of the European states in check. Instead of producing a prudent moderation in state behavior and deterring war, the fixation on power in the system provoked war.[6] For Wilson, an important part of the solution to this problem was to be found in democratic politics, a system of governance that he believed would represent and advance the natural public interest in peace. In a large body of recent literature on democracy and war, scholars have revived the argument that democracy matters when it comes to conflict decision-making because democracy creates self-imposed limits on how military force is used and against whom. Certain variants of this argument advance the notion that the liberal political values that underpin democratic governance shape conflict decision-making in a way that prevents war among democracies and even limits the use of certain kinds of military force against any other state.[7]

Other democratic peace arguments, which this work is most interested in, focus on institutional features such as divided government and electoral accountability, characteristics of democracies that may impose political impediments to mobilizing the degree of domestic support necessary for using military force against other states.[8] In a democratic system that institutionalizes competition among numerous political actors

---

[5] Immanuel Kant, *Perpetual Peace: A Philosophical Sketch* [1795], ed. Hans Reiss, trans. H. B. Nisbet (Cambridge: Cambridge University Press, 1970), 100–101.

[6] Woodrow Wilson, *Woodrow Wilson's Case for the League of Nations*, ed. Hamilton Foley (London: Oxford University Press, 1923); Inis Claude, *Swords into Plowshares* (New York: Random House, 1964), 36–50.

[7] Ray, *Democracy and International Conflict*; Bruce Russett, *Grasping the Democratic Peace: Principles for a Post-Cold War World* (Princeton: Princeton University Press, 1993); John M. Owen IV, *Liberal Peace, Liberal War: American Politics and International Security* (Ithaca: Cornell University Press, 1997); Doyle, "Kant, Liberal Legacies, and Foreign Affairs."

[8] For useful general discussions of both normative and institutional versions of the democratic peace argument, see Miriam Fendius Elman, ed., *Paths to Peace: Is Democracy the Answer?* (Cambridge: MIT Press, 1997); Michael E. Brown, Sean M. Lynn-Jones, and Steven E. Miller, eds., *Debating the Democratic Peace* (Cambridge: MIT Press, 1996).

who have access to the policy process, we might expect key leaders to have greater difficulty generating consensus on using military force to pursue particular external objectives or in response to particular crises than leaders in a more centralized political system. Simply put, the more open the political system is to alternative views on questions of war and peace, the greater the chance that some source of opposition will emerge that might moderate the use of military force or block it altogether.[9] In addition to direct competition over policy that divided government can facilitate, an executive who faces some form of competitive elections for office, and thus is accountable to the opinions of the electorate, must be mindful of potential opposition to the use of military force in foreign policy. Unlike divided decision-making authority, electoral accountability has an indirect role as a constraint on the executive's freedom of action because it is important only to the degree that it impacts the executive's incentives for selecting among alternative policy choices. The executive is not directly constrained by other political actors or institutions. Rather, he or she is expected to exercise a self-imposed constraint out of concern that certain aggressive acts or the possibility of a foreign policy failure may jeopardize his or her tenure in office.[10] It is fair to argue that if these characteristics of democracy have any effect on the conflict behavior of democracies as a general type of state, the logic of democratic constraints

---

[9] Susan Peterson, *Crisis Bargaining and the State: The Domestic Politics of International Conflict* (Ann Arbor: University of Michigan Press, 1996), 5–6, 25–27; T. Clifton Morgan and Sally Howard Campbell, "Domestic Structure, Decisional Constraints, and War: So Why Kant Democracies Fight?" *Journal of Conflict Resolution* 35 (June 1991), 191–93; T. Clifton Morgan and Valerie L. Schwebach, "Take Two Democracies and Call Me in the Morning: A Prescription for Peace?" *International Interactions* 17 (1992), 305–20; David R. Mares, *Violent Peace: Militarized Interstate Bargaining in Latin America* (New York: Columbia University Press, 2001), 4–5; 11, 22–23; R. J. Rummel, "Libertarian Propositions on Violence Within and Between Nations: A Test Against Published Results," *Journal of Conflict Resolution* 29 (September 1985), 420; Daniel Geller, *Domestic Factors in Foreign Policy: A Cross-National Statistical Analysis* (Cambridge: Shenkman Books, 1985), 63; Bruce Russett, *Controlling the Sword* (Cambridge: Harvard University Press, 1990), 141.

[10] David L. Rousseau, Christopher Gelpi, Dan Reiter, and Paul K. Huth, "Assessing the Dyadic Nature of the Democratic Peace, 1918–88," *American Political Science Review* 90 (September 1996), 513. See also Kurt Gaubatz, *Elections and War: The Electoral Incentive in the Democratic Politics of War and Peace* (Stanford: Stanford University Press, 1999); Dan Reiter and Allan C. Stam, *Democracies at War* (Princeton: Princeton University Press, 2002); Bruce Bueno de Mesquita, *The War Trap* (New Haven: Yale University Press, 1981), 22–23; John M. Owen IV, "How Liberalism Produces Democratic Peace," *International Security* 19 (fall 1994), 89; Bruce Bueno de Mesquita and David Lalman, *War and Reason: Domestic and International Imperatives* (New Haven: Yale University Press, 1992); Bruce Bueno de Mesquita and Randolph M. Siverson, "War and the Survival of Political Leaders: A Comparative Study of Regime Types and Political Accountability," *American Political Science Review* 89 (December 1995), 841–55.

should have an effect on the United States, which is widely considered the prototypical liberal democracy with highly divided political institutions and robust electoral competition.

In response to these claims about democracy and international conflict, contemporary realists argue that restraints on state behavior have little to do with the characteristics of states themselves.[11] According to this view, domestic political institutions and norms of political practice do little to mitigate the pressures of ensuring survival and autonomy in an anarchical world. Any state that was unable to meet these challenges because of a particular normative or institutional foundation at the domestic level would not be expected to survive in the long run.[12] Instead, states must base their decisions about using military force on the power of their potential adversaries relative to their own. According to realist theory, while conflict is the natural condition of politics within an anarchical system, states must also carefully weigh the potential costs and benefits of using violence as the means to secure their interests. Simply put, states tend to forgo the use of military force if the risk of paying unacceptable costs is considered too high.[13] According to this view, "One who knows that pressing too hard may lead to war has strong reason to consider whether the possible gains are worth the risk entailed . . . . The possibility that conflicts among states may lead to long and costly wars has . . . sobering effects."[14] According to Geoffrey Blainey, the more pessimistic state leaders are about the prospects of achieving their goals with threats of violence or its actual use, the more likely they are to exercise self-restraint, avoid crisis escalation, or seek accommodation.[15] To explain U.S. behavior in the "near miss" cases of international conflict at the heart of this book, realism would suggest that the United States backed down because

[11] John Mearsheimer, "Back to the Future: Instability in Europe After the Cold War," in *The Cold War and After: Prospects for Peace*, ed. Sean M. Lynn-Jones and Steven E. Miller (Cambridge: MIT Press, 1994), 148; Christopher Layne, "Kant or Cant: The Myth of the Democratic Peace," *International Security* 19 (fall 1994), 5–49; Kenneth Waltz, "The Emerging Structure of International Politics," *International Security* 18 (fall 1993), 44–79.

[12] Waltz, *Theory of International Politics*, 118.

[13] Michael Howard, *The Causes of Wars* (Cambridge: Harvard University Press, 1984), 265–84; Edward Gulick, *Europe's Classical Balance of Power* (New York: Norton, 1955); Stephen Walt, *The Origins of Alliances* (Ithaca: Cornell University Press, 1987); Patrick M. Morgan, *Deterrence: A Conceptual Analysis* (Beverley Hills: Sage, 1977).

[14] Waltz, *Theory of International Politics*, 114.

[15] Geoffrey Blainey, *The Causes of War* (Free Press, 1988), 35–56.

American leaders calculated that they were at a power disadvantage relative to their British, Spanish, and Mexican adversaries, and therefore faced unfavorable strategic circumstances for armed conflict.

This dichotomy between "democratic peace" and realist explanations for constraints on military force is not limited to the theoretical debate but is also evident in recent empirical studies of key cases in the democratic peace literature. For example, John Owen argues that the normative affinity between liberals in the United States and Great Britain, combined with institutional constraints imposed by the Senate on President Polk, kept the Oregon crisis of 1845–1846 from escalating to the use of military force. In contrast, Stephen Rock contends that the United States made the strategic decision to back down against a much stronger adversary in a dispute over territory of marginal value.[16] What prevented Britain and France from going to war over the Fashoda region of the Sudan in 1898? Michael Doyle suggests that it was shared liberalism as a feature of their domestic regimes, and James Lee Ray points to mutual expectations of peaceful conflict resolution, rooted in democratic values, as an important moderating variable in the conflict.[17] According to Christopher Layne and Raymond Cohen, however, France simply backed down in the face of British military superiority.[18] In a third case, why did Great Britain back down from war in the 1898 Venezuela border crisis with the United States? For Bruce Russett it was a spirit of accommodation and peaceful conflict resolution driven by popular and elite notions that the United States and Britain shared homogeneous political and cultural values and institutions. For Layne, Britain backed down because the distribution of naval and economic power favored the United States in the Western Hemisphere.[19]

As in these cases, the question posed in this book about constraints on U.S. conflict behavior in the early nineteenth century goes to the heart of the debate between advocates of democratic peace theory, who would look for answers in the democratic politics of the United States, and realists, who would anticipate that U.S. behavior must have been the result of prudent policy choices to avoid the costs of war under unfavorable

[16] Owen, *Liberal Peace, Liberal War*, chap. 4; Stephen R. Rock, "Anglo-U.S. Relations, 1845–1930: Did Shared Liberal Values and Democratic Institutions Keep the Peace?" in *Paths to Peace*, 106–12.

[17] Doyle, "Kant, Liberal Legacies, and Foreign Affairs"; Ray, *Democracy and International Conflict*, 191–92.

[18] Layne, "Kant or Cant," 32–33; Raymond Cohen, "Pacific Unions: a Reappraisal of the Theory that 'Democracies Do Not Go to War with Each Other,'" *Review of International Studies* 20 (1994), 219.

[19] Russett, *Grasping the Democratic Peace*, chap. 1; Layne, "Kant or Cant," 27–28.

strategic circumstances. The objective here, however, is not simply limited to comparing international and domestic level explanations for
these specific cases. As discussed in greater detail below, the core question to be addressed is exactly *how* democracy might have reduced the
frequency with which the early United States engaged in armed conflict.
In doing so, this book advances two main arguments. First, strategic calculations by key leaders of the distribution of power and the likely costs
and benefits of war did not produce the pattern of constraints we find in
U.S. behavior across this diverse set of international crises. This does not
mean that power calculations were irrelevant in conflict decision-making
by the United States. For some political actors within the U.S. system,
power calculations were clearly a dominant motive for opposing the use
of military force in particular situations. Yet in no way did U.S. decision-
makers converge on a common perception of the interests at stake in a
given conflict, on the distribution of power between the United States
and its adversaries, or on the likely costs and benefits of war. Moreover,
U.S. decision-makers did not agree that power calculations were the
most important variable that should determine whether the United
States resorted to force or not. As a result, each crisis produced a highly
competitive domestic decision-making process as political opponents
tried to leverage their positions within U.S. institutions to either promote
or hamper the use of force or shape what objectives the United States
would pursue through force. Kenneth Waltz, a dominant figure in the realist school, has made a similar point about domestic politics. Despite the
central role of the international distribution of power in Waltz's work, he
concedes that in order to explain the behavior of states in particular circumstances, that is, to explain the choices they make that constitute their
foreign policies, we must also include domestic-level variables.[20] As
Waltz might expect, U.S. behavior in this period cannot be explained

[20] "The bothersome limitations of systemic explanations arise from the problem of
weighing unit-level and structural causes . . . . [International] structures shape and
shove. They do not determine behaviors and outcomes, not only because unit-level and
structural causes interact, but also because the shaping and shoving of structures may
be successfully resisted." Kenneth Waltz, "Reflections on *Theory of International Politics*:
A Response to My Critics," in *Neorealism and Its Critics*, ed. Robert O. Keohane (New
York: Columbia University Press, 1986), 343. In *Man, the State, and War*, Waltz argues,
"Whether or not [an] attack occurs will depend on a number of special circumstances,"
including "type of government." If states "fight against each other it will be for reasons
especially defined for the occasion by each of them . . . . These immediate causes of war
are contained in the first and second images," or at the domestic and individual levels of
analysis (p. 232). See also Andrew Moravscik, "Introduction: Integrating International
and Domestic Theories of International Bargaining," in *Double-Edged Diplomacy: International Bargaining and Domestic Politics*, ed. Peter B. Evans, Harold K. Jacobson, and Robert
Putnam (Berkeley: University of California Press, 1993), 6–7.

without understanding the domestic politics of crisis decision-making within the distinctive institutional setting of the early American republic.

The second argument pursued in this book is that *federal union* was the most important institutional feature shaping domestic competition over questions of war and peace in the United States at this time. The American founders recognized that federal union was the new republic's most distinctive institutional feature. Its effects, they believed, would not be limited to domestic issues; federal union was expected to have a decisive impact on conflict decision-making as well. Despite the importance attached to federal union at the founding, it has been completely ignored by contemporary scholars of U.S. foreign policy and international relations theory. The purpose of this book is to develop the logic of political constraints produced by America's federal union and to demonstrate how this logic provides a valuable framework for explaining U.S. conflict behavior across a diverse set of militarized disputes. In this way, this book departs most significantly from previous works on democracy, U.S. foreign policy, and war.

American Democracy and Conflict Behavior

Consistent with the broader debate in international relations theory about the sources of constraints on the use of military force, this book takes a fresh look at how U.S. domestic politics affected the use of military force and its broader conflict behavior. More specifically, did the structure of U.S. institutions actually produce any discernible pattern of constraints on the use of force or on the objectives the United States pursued through the use of force? Clearly, the study of American democracy and armed conflict is not in itself novel. Long before the democratic peace became a coherent research agenda in the field of international relations, students of U.S. foreign policy were highlighting the importance of democracy as a source of constraints on its use of military power. Perhaps the best-known early work on this topic is de Tocqueville's. Writing in the 1830s, de Tocqueville described a cultural predisposition against warfare in the United States as rooted in the "mildness of manners" produced by the social equality of democracy.[21] More recently, many scholars have examined the persistent tension between the presi-

---

[21] Alexis de Tocqueville, *Democracy in America*, vol. 2, ed. Phillips Bradley (New York: Vintage Books, 1945), 279.

dent and Congress over war powers and control of foreign policy,[22] the effects of public opinion and electoral accountability on U.S. leaders' willingness to pursue high-risk or costly foreign policies,[23] and the limited capacity of the American state to extract resources from society to support armed conflict.[24] In terms of America's place in broader international relations theory, few states seem to fit as readily into the study of democratic peace as the United States does. According to the most commonly used comparative measures of democracy, the United States is consistently ranked among the "most democratic" of states, primarily because of the broad distribution of power built into its political institutions.[25] Additionally, the United States is widely treated as the primary example of a democratic state that is often guided in its foreign policy by the liberal values embedded in its domestic political system.[26] It should be of little surprise then that the United States has been the subject of more theoretical and empirical inquiry in the democratic peace literature than any other democratic state.[27]

What is surprising, however, is that despite the impressive volume of research on U.S. democracy and its foreign policy, few studies attempt to determine whether the institutional structure of the United States actually reduces its propensity to use military force. In other words, we know little about whether the constitutional distribution of political authority in the American system tends to "push toward

[22] For a small sample, see Thomas E. Mann, ed., *A Question of Balance: The President, Congress and Foreign Policy* (Washington, D.C: Brookings Institution, 1990); Louis Fisher, *Constitutional Conflicts Between Congress and the President* (Princeton: Princeton University Press, 1985); Cecil V. Crabb, Jr., and Pat M. Holt, *Invitation to Struggle: Congress, the President, and Foreign Policy* (Washington, D.C.: Congressional Quarterly Inc., 1984); David Gray Adler and Larry N. George, eds., *The Constitution and the Conduct of American Foreign Policy* (Lawrence: University of Kansas Press, 1996).

[23] John Mueller, *War, Presidents and Public Opinion* (New York: Wiley Press, 1973); Ole Holsti, *Public Opinion and American Foreign Policy* (Ann Arbor: Michigan University Press, 1997).

[24] Fareed Zakaria, *From Wealth to Power: The Unusual Origins of America's World Role* (Princeton: Princeton University Press, 1998).

[25] In the widely used Polity database, the United States receives a perfect score on the democracy scale and the lowest score on the autocracy scale. Theodore Gurr, Keith Jaggers and Will Moore, *Polity II Handbook* (Boulder: University of Colorado Press, 1989).

[26] For example, see Doyle, "Kant, Liberal Legacies, and Foreign Affairs"; Owen, *Liberal Peace, Liberal War*.

[27] For other examples see John M. Owen IV, "Perceptions and the Limits of Liberal Peace: The Mexican-American War and Spanish-American Wars," in *Paths to Peace*; Ido Oren, "The Subjectivity of the 'Democratic' Peace: Changing U.S. Perceptions of Imperial Germany," in *Debating the Democratic Peace*, 263–300; William R. Thompson, "Democracy and Peace: Putting the Cart Before the Horse?" *International Organization* 50 (winter 1996), 141–74.

peace,"[28] reducing the *frequency* with which the United States would otherwise use military force if it had a more centralized political system. The democratic peace literature on the American case is of little help on this question. With few exceptions, these studies focus on the normative dimensions of U.S. conflict decision-making, specifically, on how American liberal values might act as a constraint on using military force against other liberal democracies. These studies say little to nothing about U.S. institutions and conflict decision-making.[29] But what about the volumes of research on the separation of war powers in the United States? The separation of legislative and executive powers is the most visible institutional feature of the U.S. system directly connected with claims about the proper allocation of political authority over war and peace. It is the only formally constituted mechanism that defines and circumscribes this authority, which implicitly declares that war-making power must be controlled in some way because it is a power that is most dangerous if abused. From this perspective, the fixation on the separation of powers among students of domestic politics and U.S. conflict behavior is understandable. Those who lament the presidential eclipse of congressional authority over armed conflict since World War II borrow from the American founding the implicit assumption that concentrated power is likely to produce a greater tendency for the use of force in foreign affairs.[30] On one level, the American founders clearly considered executive power more war prone than the allegedly more deliberative législature, which, they assumed, would avoid rash, arbitrary, or vainglorious military exploits. President Johnson's escalation of the war in Vietnam and President Nixon's widening of the conflict into Cambodia and Laos are the key historic referents for those concerned with abuses of presidential authority

---

[28] Morgan and Campbell, "Domestic Structure, Decisional Constraints, and War," 189–90.

[29] The most obvious exception is Owen, who argues that both liberal norms and political institutions work together to hold the use of force by the United States in check. See *Liberal Peace, Liberal War*. While Owen provides an important reminder that democratic institutions matter in decision-making, the logic of constraints in his argument ultimately still hinges on liberal norms. See also David P. Auerswald, "Inward Bound: Domestic Institutions and Military Conflicts," *International Organization* 53 (summer 1999), 469–504; Miriam Fendius Elman, "Unpacking Democracy: Presidentialism, Parliamentarism, and Theories of Democratic Peace," *Security Studies* 4 (summer 2000), 91–126. Neither of these studies, however, attempts to establish whether there is a pattern of institutional constraints on America's use of military force across cases.

[30] Gordon Silverstein, *Imbalance of Powers: Constitutional Interpretation and the Making of American Foreign Policy* (New York: Oxford University Press, 1997).

that take the form of a greater propensity to use military force.[31] If the president must have congressional approval before engaging in armed conflict, it is reasonable to expect that this authority will be withheld now and then, producing over time a reduction in the frequency of the use of military force in U.S. foreign policy. This expectation, however plausible, remains largely untested. The bulk of the institutional research on war powers is devoted to either descriptive studies of the changing roles of Congress and the executive branch in foreign affairs,[32] or to the long-running debate over the legal scope of the president's authority to send U.S. troops into combat and whether war powers are rightly reserved for Congress.[33] As extensive as the research on war powers is, it fails to address directly whether, or why, a more activist Congress and greater fidelity to the principle of the separation of powers will actually produce constraints on the use of force.

The purpose of this book is not simply to correct any deficiencies in the literature on the separation of powers, or to test whether this specific mechanism produces any pattern of constraints on the use of force by the United States. Instead, the book pushes beyond the separation of powers, reaching deeper into America's institutional structure to examine another feature of the U.S. political system—federal union—that the founders realized would greatly enhance the potential for constraints on the use of military force. As James Madison carefully pointed out in

[31] Arthur M. Schlesinger, Jr., *The Imperial Presidency* (Boston: Houghton Mifflin Company, 1973); Jacob K. Javits, *Who Makes War: The President Versus Congress* (New York: Morrow, 1973); Louis Fisher, *Presidential War Power* (Lawrence: University of Kansas Press, 1995); John Hart Ely, *War and Responsibility* (Princeton: Princeton University Press, 1994).

[32] Abraham Sofaer, *War, Foreign Affairs, and Constitutional Power: The Origins* (Cambridge: Ballinger, 1976); Henry Bartholomew Cox, *War, Foreign Affairs, and Constitutional Power: 1829–1901* (Cambridge: Ballinger, 1984); Robert Dahl, *Congress and Foreign Policy* (New York: Harcourt, Brace, 1950); David Deese, ed., *The New Politics of American Foreign Policy* (New York: St. Martin's Press, 1994); David M. Abshire and Ralph D. Nurnberger, eds., *The Growing Power of Congress* (Beverly Hills, Calif.: Sage, 1981); Barbara Hinkly, *Less than Meets the Eye: Foreign Policy Making and the Myth of the Assertive Congress* (Chicago: University of Chicago Press, 1994); James M. Lindsay, *Congress and the Politics of U.S. Foreign Policy* (Baltimore: Johns Hopkins University Press, 1994).

[33] A few examples of this massive literature include Schlesinger, *The Imperial Presidency*; Fisher, *Presidential War Power*; Edwin S. Corwin, *The President: Office and Powers, 1787–1957* (New York: New York University Press, 1957); Francis D. Wormuth and Edwin Firmage, *To Chain the Dog of War: The War Power of Congress in History and Law* (Dallas, Texas: Southern Methodist University Press, 1986); L. Gordon Crovitz and Jeremy A. Rabkin, eds., *The Fettered Presidency: Legal Constraints on the Executive Branch* (Washington, D.C.: American Enterprise Institute, 1989); Gordon S. Jones and John A. Marini, eds., *The Imperial Congress: Crisis in the Separation of Powers* (New York: Pharos, 1988).

Federalist 51, the U.S. Constitution did not simply create a "single republic" with but one level of government divided into separate departments. The Constitution created a "compound republic" that merged multiple geographically defined political units—the states—into a "republic of republics."[34] According to Madison, while the Americans borrowed the principle of representation from Europe, "America can claim the merit" of discovering how to make a geographically "extensive republic" possible through federal union.[35] Building on the foundation of thirteen original states, new territory was added to the United States and organized politically through the process of incorporating new geographically defined subunits. Each new federal subunit was then integrated into the national level political system through the internal structure of the legislature and the presidential electoral college. Federal union, therefore, provided the deep institutional structure of this new, distinctive, and expanding political system and the building blocks of national institutions. The founders of the United States knew that the creation of a federal union, and not simply a "single republic" that separated executive and legislative authority over war powers, had profound implications for U.S. foreign policy. Since the founding, however, not a single study of U.S. foreign policy has systematically examined how this institutional innovation may affect conflict behavior in theory, or whether federal union actually had an impact on the use of military force by the United States. This book takes on that task.

Some might question the relevance of federalism in foreign affairs. According to the classic definition of federal government, a study of federalism should focus on the behavior of state-level governments as separate political actors within the larger federal state, and the relationship between the states and the national government.[36] The U.S. Constitution assigns the general government exclusive authority over foreign affairs, while the individual states are denied the right to engage in foreign affairs as independent political actors.[37] According to John Jay, "the safety of the people" in a competitive international system depended on union under "one government, watching over the general and common inter-

[34] James Madison, *Federalist 51*, in *The Federalist Papers*, ed. Clinton Rossiter (New York: Mentor Books, 1961), 323.

[35] Madison, *Federalist 14*, 100–101. For an extended treatment of the importance of union to the founders, see Rogan Kersh, *Dreams of a More Perfect Union* (Ithaca: Cornell University Press, 2001).

[36] William H. Riker, *Federalism: Origin, Operation, Significance* (Boston: Little, Brown, 1964), 11.

[37] United States Constitution, Article 1, Section 10.

ests and combining and directing the powers and resources of the whole."[38] A leading scholar of federalism argues that the first "yardstick" for judging whether a political system is federal in character (and not simply confederal) is that the national government must exercise "exclusive control over foreign relations."[39] Like most students of federalism, Ivo Duchacek emphasizes that this constitutional arrangement does not allow for power sharing over foreign affairs between subunit governments and the national government. According to Duchacek, "in a federation it is the national (federal) government in whose hands lies the ultimate control over the major issues in foreign policy and the conduct of peaceful or violent international relations. The tasks of both the diplomatic service and the armed forces mirror the preoccupations, interests, and goals of the federal nation rather than those of the nation's territorial components."[40] And Riker is correct to assert that the states as distinct political actors "lost their voice" in foreign affairs as the importance of state militias in national defense declined after the War of 1812.[41] The effects of federal union on conflict decision-making highlighted in this book, however, *do not depend on the actions of state governments.* Of interest here is the *federal character of the national government itself.*

It is important here to note clearly that this book employs a broader conception of the federal features of U.S. democracy than the classic conception described above. Students of federal government acknowledge that "there is no generally accepted, satisfactory, or simple definition of federalism."[42] But what this term best captures is the territorial organization of a system that enhances the political impact of diverse, geographically distributed constituencies and societal interests. The American states were preserved in the constitutional arrangement of the new republic not only because they had distinct political identities forged during the colonial period and sustained under the Articles of Confederation.[43] The founders also acknowledged the social reality of

---

[38] John Jay, *Federalist 4*, 49.

[39] Ivo D. Duchacek, *Comparative Federalism: The Territorial Dimension of Politics* (New York: Holt, Rinehart and Winston, 1970), 208.

[40] Ibid.

[41] Riker, *Federalism*, 57–59.

[42] Ivo D. Duchacek, *The Territorial Dimensions of Politics: Within, Among, and Across Nations* (Boulder: Westview Press, 1986), 93; Arthur W. Macmahon, ed., *Federalism: Mature and Emergent* (Garden City: Doubleday, 1955); S. Rufus Davis, *The Federal Principle* (Berkeley: University of California Press, 1978), 150, 156; Douglas V. Verney, "Federalism, Federative Systems, and Federations: The United States, Canada, and India," *Publius* 25 (spring 1995), 81.

[43] James Brown Scott, *The United States of America: A Study in International Organization* (Oxford: Oxford University Press, 1920).

economic, cultural, and geographic diversity across the different regions of the United States, differences that would produce diverse and
often conflicting interests in domestic and foreign affairs.[44] On one
level, these diverse "territorial communities" within the United States
are respected and protected by state-level governments. Yet at another
level, the Constitution formally grants these territorial communities
institutional access to national-level decision-making. Many different
kinds of nation-states may be characterized by similarly diverse geographically distributed social interests, yet the federal character of the
national government in the United States provided leverage for these
diverse territorial constituencies to influence national decision-making in ways that may simply be unavailable to similar groups in a
more centralized political system. If our understanding of U.S. federalism is limited to the role of state governments, we miss the fact that the
internal structure of the U.S. Congress and the presidential electoral
system are both organized along federal lines. In other words, the
basic components of the national government directly engaged in foreign affairs, the Congress and the president, derive their authority and
face political accountability in a system structured by federal union.

The individual territorial communities that made up the Union
were guaranteed direct access to national-level decision-making
through representation in both the Senate and the House of Representatives.[45] Because senators were selected by state legislatures, and
members of the House of Representatives depended on direct election
by even smaller geographic constituencies, the political incentives
produced by this system guaranteed that members of Congress had to
remain focused on the interests of their electors back home. As a result,
competition over policy *within* Congress and *between* Congress and the

[44] Peter Onuf and Nicholas Onuf, *Federal Union, Modern World: the Law of Nations in an
Age of Revolutions, 1776–1814* (Madison, Wis.: Madison House, 1993); Peter S. Onuf,
"Constitutional Politics: States, Sections, and the National Interest," in *Toward a More
Perfect Union: Six Essays on the Constitution*, ed. Neil L. York (Provo, Utah: Brigham
Young University, 1988); David C. Hendrickson, *Peace Pact: The Lost World of the Ameri-
can Founding* (Lawrence: University Press of Kansas, 2003).

[45] The House of Representatives is not a purely "federal" institution because individual members of the House are elected by popular vote and not by state legislatures as in
the case of U.S. senators (until the Seventeenth Amendment to the U.S. Constitution of
1913. The Seventeenth Amendment instituted direct popular vote within each state for
U.S. senators). Also, the states are not equally represented within the House; total population, which varies widely among the states, determines representation in this body.
But like the Senate, the House of Representatives reinforces the territorial organization
of the U.S. Congress by establishing a direct link between smaller scale territorial constituencies and the national decision-making process.

president could take on a distinctly territorial character and thus reflect a diverse array of political perspectives that make it difficult for
the president or congressional leaders to control the policy agenda or
generate consensus on the use of military force. While the separation
of powers may highlight how Congress could impede presidential initiatives, it says nothing about the conditions that produce opposition
in Congress to the use of force in the first place. Separation of powers
alone does not define how the legislature is internally organized, it
does not describe the kinds of interests represented there, or whether
the legislature centralizes or decentralizes decision-making. These features are crucial for understanding the role the legislature may play in
conflict decision-making and its relationship with the executive in
matters of national security. As discussed in chapter 2, there is nothing
about a separation of powers system that makes opposition to using
military force more likely than support for the use of force. Without
looking within Congress and appreciating the territorial character of
the political incentives federal union produces, it is impossible to understand the competitive dynamics that emerge among members of
Congress, why certain members of Congress support or oppose the
use of force, or the coalitions that form to produce certain legislative
outcomes.

Through federal union, distinct territorial communities also have a
key role in electing presidents. While it is common to point out that the
president is elected by a "national" constituency, unlike individual
members of Congress, this national constituency is actually an aggregate of individual territorial constituencies organized at the state level.
As a result, the president faces a federally organized electoral system
that demands he pay close attention to how foreign policy problems
are perceived across the geographically extended American republic.
The president must be concerned with the political ramifications of antagonizing certain regions or states within the Union. The prospects of
losing political support within a particular region may be enough incentive for the president to avoid using military force in particular
cases. Moreover, federal union reduces the president's ability to control
the policy agenda through his political party. In the best of circumstances, when the president's party controls both houses of Congress,
party unity on policy questions might bridge the institutional divide
created by the separation of powers. Yet the political incentives created
by federal union undermine the president's ability to discipline members of his own party and line up support for his preferred policy
choices. In summary, federalism means that the numerous, often

conflictual, political interests of the various territorial communities within the Union were given the *institutional leverage* necessary to engage in a domestic struggle over foreign policy, even over questions of war and peace, through legislative action and electoral pressures on the president. Only federal union provides a broad enough institutional perspective to explain the common link between congressional behavior, presidential political incentives, and the role of parties, and to establish a common domestic politics link among the various cases of constraints on military force that we find in pre-Civil War U.S. foreign policy.

Contributions to Theory and History

The next chapter presents the logic of "federal democratic peace," which links the institutional features of federal union with constraints on armed conflict. To put this logic to the test, chapters 3 through 6 examine fourteen cases between 1807 and 1860 in which U.S. political leaders faced decisions on whether to use military force and the gains to be made from the use of force during an international crisis. In eleven of the fourteen cases there is a clear pattern of constraints on U.S. expansionist initiatives, its ability to initiate and prosecute war, and its ability to take full advantage of available gains from war.[46] Most important, this book argues that this pattern is best explained by the internal competitive dynamics of federal democracy. This case set not only lets us examine the theoretical basis of U.S. conflict behavior, it sheds light on a period in U.S. foreign relations that has been largely, but unjustifiably neglected in international relations literature,[47] in

---

[46] Steve Chan makes the important argument that democratic peace research should not be limited to simply examining the propensity of democratic states to engage in war. "War is just one extreme segment of a long spectrum of organized violent activities." Democracy may also have an important impact on "the *scope, severity, and duration* of wars." Chan, "Democracy and War: Some Thoughts on Future Research Agenda," *International Interactions* 18 (1993), 207; emphasis in original.

[47] According to the prevailing characterization of U.S. foreign policy prior to the end of the nineteenth century, the United States was most concerned with remaining isolated from the corrupting system of power politics dominated by European states. Henry Kissinger, *Diplomacy* (New York: Simon and Schuster, 1994), 20; Thomas A. Bailey, *A Diplomatic History of the American People* (Englewood Cliffs: Prentice-Hall, 1980); Paul Schroeder, "Historical Reality vs. Neo-realist Theory," *International Security* 19 (summer 1994), 101–48. Aside from the Monroe Doctrine of 1823, international relations scholars rarely consider the significance of North American international relations in their study of the field.

democratic peace research,[48] and in diplomatic history.[49] The most common assertion about the early U.S. republic is that it was largely isolated from the competitive international system by the blessings of geography and prudent policy. President Washington's famous warning in 1796 about the perils of "permanent alliances," which advised future American statesmen to avoid being dragged into the war-prone European system, and President Monroe's doctrine of 1823 that announced the intent of the United States to resist European efforts to transplant this competitive system to the Western Hemisphere, stand as the rhetorical high points of America's efforts to set itself apart from the normal mode of intercourse in international affairs. In practical terms, the demand by the United States that it had the right to be treated as a neutral state in the long-running struggle between France and Great Britain is seen as the clearest manifestation of a state not fully integrated into normal international politics.[50] Some scholars seek to demonstrate the limited potential for U.S. engagement in the competitive international system by pointing to the fact that the United States avoided building a large standing army. This is said to have created a basic impediment to the vigorous use of military force as an option in U.S. foreign policy.[51] Of course, the United States did pursue an external territorial thrust across the North American continent in the nineteenth century on a scale unprecedented in history.[52] Most scholars, however, treat westward expansion not as foreign policy, but simply as one dimension of the internal development of the United States.[53] It is not until the Spanish-American War of 1898 and

[48] The only pre–Civil War cases currently examined in the democratic peace literature are the War of 1812, the Anglo-American Oregon crisis, and the Mexican War. See Rock, "Anglo-U.S. Relations, 1845–1930"; Owen, *Liberal Peace, Liberal War*; Elman, "Unpacking Democracy."

[49] William Earl Weeks, "Historiography: New Directions in the Study of Early American Foreign Relations," *Diplomatic History* 17 (1993), 73–96; Kinley Brauer, "The Great American Desert Revisited: Recent Literature and Prospects for the Study of American Foreign Relations, 1815–61," *Diplomatic History* 13 (summer 1989), 395–417; Bradford Perkins, "Early American Foreign Relations: Opportunities and Challenges," *Diplomatic History* 22 (winter 1998), 115–21.

[50] Onuf and Onuf, *Federal Union, Modern World*, 8, 93, 159.

[51] James M. Lindsay, "Cowards, Beliefs, and Structures," in *The Use of Force After the Cold War*, ed. H. W. Brands (College Station: Texas A & M University Press, 2000), 140.

[52] Donald W. Meinig, *The Shaping of America: A Geographic Perspective on 500 Years of History*, vol. 2 (New Haven: Yale University Press, 1993).

[53] For a useful discussion of this point, see John Mack Faragher, "Introduction" in Frederick Merk, *Manifest Destiny and Mission in American History: A Reinterpretation* (Cambridge: Harvard University Press, 1963), ix.

the U.S. assertion of a global role at the beginning of the twentieth century that most students of U.S. foreign policy accept that the United States finally entered the ranks of "normal" states caught up in the competitive struggle for international power.[54]

From this traditional perspective, the United States before the Spanish-American War seems to offer little case material to investigate the relationship between democracy and war, aside from the War of 1812 and the Mexican War of 1846–1848. But this perspective is fundamentally flawed, and our understanding of democracy and war is compromised as a result.[55] While the United States certainly did limit its role in the power politics of the European continent during the first half of the nineteenth century, any subsequent claim that the United States hid from competitive international relations altogether is false.[56] Moreover, when considered from the perspective of the democratic peace debate, which focuses on international crises that *could have, but did not*, produce armed conflict,[57] the early nineteenth century presents a rich and varied set of crises involving the United States and others on its periphery in North America, including Great Britain, Spain, Mexico, and France. As noted at the beginning of this chapter, except for the two clear cases of war in this period, each of the other crises involving the United States did not produce armed conflict, despite the fact that war was openly considered among the choices available to resolve each.

---

[54] For an excellent critique of this view see Richard W. Van Alstyne, "The Significance of the Mississippi Valley in American Diplomatic History, 1686–1890," *Mississippi Valley Historical Review* 36 (September 1949), 229.

[55] A few works on U.S. democracy and foreign policy do include chapters on pre–Civil War foreign relations. Melvin Small, *Democracy and Diplomacy: the Impact of Domestic Politics on U.S. Foreign Policy, 1789–1994* (Baltimore: Johns Hopkins University Press, 1996); Michael D. Pearlman, *Warmaking and American Democracy: the Struggle over Military Strategy, 1700 to the Present* (Lawrence: University Press of Kansas, 1999).

[56] For a similar assessment, see Walter McDougall, *Promised Land, Crusader State* (New York: Houghton Mifflin, 1997), 50–51.

[57] While Layne is a critic of all variants of democratic peace arguments, he makes the important point that strong tests of democratic peace propositions must include "near miss" cases. Layne, "Kant or Cant," 6. The absence of war alone is not enough to validate either realist or democratic peace explanations for this observation. Raymond Cohen argues that the absence of war among any given set of states may be simply the result of the absence of opposing interests or the inability to project power against the other state's interests. Under these conditions, the absence of war is unsurprising. Cohen, "Pacific Unions," 214. In contrast, "near miss" cases, those in which two or more states tangled over a particular issue and actually considered the use of force to resolve it, provide the best opportunity to examine the logic of various explanations for the avoidance of armed conflict.

In addition to providing new empirical material for the analysis of democracy and war, the cases from this time period are valuable for democratic peace research in several other ways. First, in most of the cases examined here, the United States backed down from the use of force even though the distribution of power favored the United States. As Legro and Moravcsik note, this leads us to question the suitability of realist theory as an explanation for these cases while supporting explanations rooted in domestic politics.[58] Second, with the exception of the Anglo-American Oregon crisis, these cases involve mixed democratic/nondemocratic dyads, that is, the United States was engaged in a dispute with a nondemocratic state. This is important for democratic peace research because of the relatively few studies on the effects of democratic regime traits in cases where democracies are not dealing with fellow democracies. Harvey Starr notes that the consensus position among scholars seems to be that the democratic peace is a dyadic phenomenon, that democratic states are less prone to use military force only in relations with other democracies.[59] As a corollary, this dyadic line of argument holds that democracies are as war prone as any other regime type in relations with nondemocracies. In contrast, a monadic line of argument would assert that certain regime characteristics of democracies will impose constraints on their behavior toward any other state, regardless of the other state's regime type.[60] The theory of federal democratic peace presented in this book is purely monadic: the political dynamics of federal union should constrain the use of force by the United States whether America is confronting another democracy or a nondemocracy. Third, this book addresses another important shortfall in the democratic peace literature: the paucity of work on democratic institutions and conflict decision-making relative to the more widely researched effects of democratic norms.[61] The case study chapters demonstrate how the distinctive

[58] Legro and Moravcsik contend that the democratic peace claim would be well served by more case studies in which the distribution of power favored that state which deconflicted because of domestic pressure. Jeffrey W. Legro and Andrew Moravcsik, "Is Anybody Still a Realist?" *International Security* 24 (fall 1999), 50.

[59] Harvey Starr, "Why Don't Democracies Fight One Another? Evaluating the Theory-Findings Feedback Loop," *Jerusalem Journal of International Relations* 14 (1992), 43.

[60] On the need for additional research on the monadic effects of democracy, see Ray, *Democracy and International Conflict*, 20; Elman, "Introduction," in *Paths to Peace*, 40.

[61] For a more general discussion of how institutions shape political behavior and outcomes, see James G. March and Johan Olsen, *Rediscovering Institutions* (New York: Free Press, 1989), 18. Stephen D. Krasner, "Approaches to the State," in *Bringing the State Back In*, ed. Peter B. Evans, Dietrich Rueschemeyer, Theda Skocpol (New York: Cambridge University Press, 1985), 228.

organization of the American federal union persistently constrained the use of military force, most notably, *in the absence of any normative constraints* on state behavior.

Moreover, the majority of the institutional democratic peace literature has little to say about how institutional variation among different types of democracies will affect conflict decision-making and the likelihood of constraints on the use of force.[62] The democratic peace research agenda is weakened by the tendency for most empirical and theoretical studies to treat "democracy" as a relatively homogenous regime type. While most democracies divide political power in some way, and all modern democracies hold their political leaders accountable to an electorate, different types of democratic states do so in very different ways.[63] For example, the ability of a president or prime minister to control the decision-making agenda, the ability of opposition groups or parties to influence decisions on war and peace, and the executive's vulnerability to electoral accountability or the confidence of the legislature will vary widely among such subregime types as Westminster parliamentary, coalition parliamentary, and presidential democratic systems.[64] There has been no sustained systematic effort to disaggregate democracy as a general regime type or to investigate particular types of democracies in detail to refine the logic of democratic constraints in particular cases. If we are going to examine the conditions under which democracies are more or less likely to be con-

[62] A few studies of the structural democratic peace give a nod to the importance of institutional variation, for example, Morgan and Schwebach, "Take Two Democracies and Call Me in the Morning"; Morgan and Campbell, "Domestic Structure, Decisional Constraints, and War"; Thomas Risse-Kappen, "Public Opinion, Domestic Structure, and Foreign Policy in Liberal Democracies," *World Politics* (July 1991), 479–512; Joe D. Hagan, "Domestic Political Systems and War Proneness," *Mershon International Studies Review* 38 (1994), 183–207; Elman, "Unpacking Democracy"; Auerswald, "Inward Bound"; Peterson, *Crisis Bargaining and the State.* In an earlier work Waltz focused on the impact of institutional variation among different types of democracies. Kenneth N. Waltz, *Foreign Policy and Democratic Politics: the American and British Experience* (Boston: Little, Brown, 1967).

[63] Arend Lijphart, *Democracies: Patterns of Majoritarian and Consensus Government in Twenty-One Countries* (New Haven: Yale University Press, 1984); Arend Lijphart, ed., *Parliamentary versus Presidential Government* (Oxford: Oxford University Press, 1992); Giovanni Sartori, *Comparative Constitutional Engineering: An Inquiry Into Structures, Incentives, and Outcomes* (New York: New York University Press, 1994).

[64] See Elman, "Unpacking Democracy," for a detailed analysis of the differences. For a broader evaluation of the decision-making effects of institutional variation among and across democratic and autocratic regimes, see Bruce Bueno de Mesquita, James D. Morrow, Randolph M. Siverson, and Alastair Smith, "Political Institutions, Policy Choice, and the Survival of Leaders," *British Journal of Political Science* 32 (2002), 559–90.

strained in the use of military force, we must consider that different institutional arrangements will impose varying degrees of constraint and will operate differently under similar international circumstances.

These cases also provide an opportunity to compare crises that did not produce armed conflict with crises that did. In all cases, from the *Chesapeake* crisis of 1807 with Great Britain to the Mexican Protectorate Treaty debate of 1860, the institutional context for U.S. decision-making remained constant. However, in three key cases these institutional features did not prevent the Union from using substantial military force against an adversary. These cases include the declaration of war against Britain in 1812, President Polk's unchecked unilateral dispatch of U.S. troops into disputed territory between Texas and Mexico in 1845–1846, and the subsequent congressional recognition of a state of war with Mexico shortly after. These three cases provide the chance to ask why federal union did not prevent the use of military force, while it did have a key role in all the other cases. What other variables affected those three cases to overcome the potentially constraining effects of federal democracy? Finally, studying these cases provides an opportunity to compare the institutional dimensions of U.S. crisis decision-making in the early years of the republic with the institutional dimensions of contemporary crisis decision-making. Since the founding, the formal structure of the U.S. political system has changed very little. Despite this institutional continuity over time, it is fair to argue that the importance of federal union in U.S. foreign policymaking, and in conflict decision-making particularly, has changed significantly. The conclusion of this book briefly explores this observation and puts American federal union and foreign policy in a modern context.[65]

The next chapter looks in detail at the logic of federal union in the new American republic, and at the relationship between this distinctive form of democracy and conflict decision-making. It begins with a

[65] It is important to acknowledge here that the best test of this argument on federal union and conflict decision-making might be to compare the United States in the pre-Civil War period, when the strength of federalism was highest, to either a nonfederal democracy or a period after the Civil War when the strength of federalism declined. Variation on the independent variable would offer a chance to look for subsequent variation in the propensity to use military force. The decision to focus on a period of little or no variation in the importance of federal union is justified, however, because it allows me to explore the dynamics of U.S. federalism in detail across a diverse set of policy problems that all raised the prospects of using military force and which show a clear pattern of similar policy outcomes. In addition, the case set contains a number of crises that have been largely or completely ignored in the international relations and U.S. foreign policy literature.

discussion of the *Federalist*'s perspective on international politics, specifically, their thoroughly realist worldview of the causes of violent
conflict. The U.S. constitutional project was motivated not only by the
enduring problem of providing physical security in an anarchical
world but by a strong belief, rooted in the republican philosophical
tradition, that the solution to this problem could be found in the
proper institutional structure of domestic politics. As discussed in
chapter 2, the arguments raised during the founding period on why
the separation of powers might constrain the use of military force
were vague and left largely unexamined. In contrast, the authors of
The Federalist Papers treated the constraining effects of federal union
much more systematically. The main purpose of the next chapter is to
distill this argument from the larger text of the *Federalist* and to put it
in the complete context of contemporary democratic peace arguments
on institutions and constraints on military force.

FEDERAL UNION AND ARMED CONFLICT

Imagining a More Peace-Prone Republic

In the first paragraph of *Federalist 1*, Alexander Hamilton marveled at the opportunity that lay before the individual American states in 1787. The new political order of the United States, he observed, would not be the result of "accident and force," which had forged the political constitutions of most "societies of men." Instead, it would be the product of "reflection and choice."[1] As Hamilton, Madison, and Jay would argue throughout *The Federalist Papers*, the constitutional choices made by the states would have a direct impact on a cluster of critical security issues: preventing both anarchy and tyranny at home, deterring or defending against aggression from abroad, eliminating the possibility of war among the American states, and limiting the role of military force in foreign affairs.

The United States represents the best example available of a modern political system deliberately structured to achieve, as a first priority, multiple constraints on power in both domestic and foreign affairs.[2] This does not mean, however, that the Constitution was meant

---

[1] Alexander Hamilton, *Federalist 1*, in *The Federalist Papers*, ed. Clinton Rossiter (New York: Mentor Books, 1961), 33.

[2] For an extended discussion of power constraint under the U.S. Constitution, see Daniel Deudney, "The Philadelphian System: Sovereignty, Arms Control, and Balance of Power in the American States-Union, circa 1787–1861," *International Organization* 49 (spring 1995), 191–228.

to prevent the republic from taking those military measures necessary—even offensive war—to ensure its survival and prosperity in a
dangerous world. In fact, as Hamilton argued vigorously, the federal
government's ability to use military force "ought to exist without limi-
tation" because "the circumstances that endanger the safety of nations
are infinite, and for this reason no constitutional shackles can wisely
be imposed on the power to which the care of it is committed."[3] Madison joined Hamilton in this view: "If a federal Constitution could
chain the ambition or set bounds to the exertions of all other nations,
then indeed might it prudently chain the discretion of its own government." Because this is impossible, he continued, "It is in vain to oppose constitutional barriers to the impulse of self-preservation."[4]
Once unlimited war powers are provided, however, the problem
becomes one of controlling how this power is used. The *Federalist* is
careful to point out that the structure of political authority within the
republic was designed to prevent the wanton exercise or abuse of that
power. As a result, the United States remains a critical case for evaluating the relationship between democratic institutions and conflict behavior, and more broadly, to shed light on the continuing debate over
international and domestic sources of constraints on the use of military force.

While the framers devised several institutional mechanisms to provide "checks and balances" in the U.S. political system,[5] this chapter
looks closely at one particular institutional feature—federal union—
which has been largely ignored in the study of U.S. foreign policy and
military force. The value of union to better secure the American states
against European aggression has been widely acknowledged among
students of U.S. foreign policy. International relations scholars have
recognized that union would also eliminate anarchy among the American states, and thus remove this dangerous background condition
that would make war more likely in North America.[6] However, when

---

[3] Hamilton, *Federalist 23*, 153.
[4] James Madison, *Federalist 41*, 257.
[5] Madison, *Federalist 51*, 322–23. See also Gottfried Dietze, *The Federalist: A Classic on Federalism and Free Government* (Baltimore: Johns Hopkins University Press, 1960).
[6] Kenneth N. Waltz, *Man, the State, and War* (New York: Columbia University Press, 1954), 237; Deudney, "The Philadelphian System," 201; Daniel Deudney, "Binding Sovereigns: Authorities, Structures, and Geopolitics in the Philadelphian System," in *State Sovereignty as Social Construct*, ed. Thomas J. Biersteker and Cynthia Weber (Cambridge: Cambridge University Press, 1996), 190–239. For the original statement on this see Hamilton, *Federalist 8*, 66.

it comes to institutional constraints on the use of military power by the United States against foreign nations, the discussion typically begins and ends with an assessment of the separation of powers that divides authority over questions of war and peace between the legislature and the executive branch of the national government. The separation of powers is clearly an important feature of U.S. democracy, one that the framers considered essential for checking the use of military force. But a closer look at *The Federalist Papers* reveals that while the founders considered the separation of powers a necessary component in a scheme to control the use of military force, alone it was not sufficient to achieve this goal.

To go beyond the separation of powers alone, this chapter reconstructs the argument introduced in *The Federalist Papers* that federal union was essential for producing constraints on key decision-makers and would create the tendency to "push toward peace." The founders emphasized the fact that the federal basis of the U.S. political system at the national level was best reflected in the internal composition of Congress. As an institution, Congress was not only bicameral in structure, it also guaranteed that the diverse geographic constituencies within the Union—the building blocks of the federal republic—would have direct access to national-level decision-making. To the degree that Congress would ultimately decide on the use of military force, the federal character of this institution was central to how questions of war and peace would be resolved. It is also important to look beyond Congress at executive decision-making and the role of electoral accountability as an incentive for self-restraint by the president. While the founders were committed to the principle that Congress would have the final word over authorizing military force, a "due dependence on the people," in Hamilton's words, meant that popular sentiment would in some way limit the president's actions as well. Practical experience has shown us, and the founders anticipated this, that presidential initiative in foreign affairs can put the question of military force on the agenda in the first place. Presidential initiative might even create what Hamilton called an "antecedent state of things," a diplomatic or military crisis that compels a congressional response and limits the policy options available for avoiding the use of military force.[7] It is important then to consider how the federal

---

[7] Arthur M. Schlesinger, Jr., *The Imperial Presidency* (Boston: Houghton Mifflin, 1973), 19.

structure of the presidential electoral process might produce political incentives for the president to avoid situations that could lead to armed conflict.

This chapter will also consider the relationship between federal union and political parties in conflict decision-making. Despite the importance of political parties to democratic politics, the democratic peace literature has virtually ignored these institutions. In the case of the United States it is important to consider whether the party system could produce solidarity among members of Congress despite the disparate constituencies they represented. In theory, unified parties might nullify the institutional divisions built into this system, bridging the gap between the executive branch and Congress if the same party controlled both, or the division between the Senate and House of Representatives. It will be argued below, however, that the federal structure of the legislative and presidential electoral systems acted as a consistent impediment to party unity, and thus inhibited the centralization of policymaking that might otherwise have been produced by party solidarity. The final section of this chapter introduces the empirical portion of this book. The next section sets the stage for a detailed examination of federal union and conflict decision-making by explaining the founders' views on the causes of international conflict and the Enlightenment debate over solutions to the problem of war.

International Conflict and the Federalist Worldview

While the U.S. Constitution stands as the most sophisticated practical manifestation of republican political theory, the founders were animated in their constitutional project by a thoroughly realist worldview of the causes of violent conflict. This is an important starting point for appreciating the institutional solution they devised to solve the cluster of domestic and international security problems that they believed endangered the American states. In the process of laying out the dangers of war inherent in both human nature and international anarchy, the *Federalist* challenges the common Enlightenment notion that "republics were constituted for peace,"[8] refuting both theoretically and empirically the claim that republics will be less war prone than monarchies.

---

[8] Peter Onuf and Nicholas Onuf, *Federal Union, Modern World: The Law of Nations in an Age of Revolutions, 1776–1814* (Madison, Wis.: Madison House, 1993), 94, 151–52.

The *Federalist* even warns against the belief that republican government will produce a dyadic peace among similarly constituted democratic republican states. Hamilton goes so far as to mock those "visionary and designing men, who stand ready to advocate the paradox of perpetual peace."[9] The *Federalist* ultimately concludes that no single institutional feature—certainly not the separation of executive and legislative power alone—is sufficient to constrain the arbitrary or hasty resort to military force in foreign affairs. As we will see below, however, champions of the U.S. Constitution were careful to explain that the federal character of the U.S. republic, which most clearly distinguishes it from other republics, was the key to reining in the tragic war-prone tendencies that characterized the behavior of other types of states.

Like contemporary realist theorists of international relations, Hamilton, Madison, and Jay fully accepted the logic of anarchy as the background condition for insecurity, militarized disputes, and war. Most significantly, they argued that the individual American states, despite their republican constitutions, would not be immune from the pressures of anarchy and the danger of war with each other if they remained independent sovereign states. In *Federalist 5*, Jay argues against an alternative proposal debated during the Constitutional Convention that the states should be organized into several smaller unions, instead of one union among all the states. Jay was convinced that if political divisions remained in North America, the form of power politics familiar to the Europeans would inevitably plague the Americans as well. He argues, "Like most other *bordering* nations, [the states] would always be either involved in disputes and war, or lie in the constant apprehension of them."[10] In even blunter terms Hamilton declared,

> A man must be far gone in utopian speculations who can seriously doubt that if these States should either be wholly disunited, or only united in partial confederations, the subdivisions into which they might be thrown would have frequent and violent contests with each other. To look for a continuation of harmony between a number of independent, unconnected sovereignties situated in the same neighborhood would be to disregard the uniform course of human events.[11]

[9] Hamilton, *Federalist 6*, 56.
[10] John Jay, *Federalist 5*, 51; emphasis in original. In *Federalist 41* Madison articulates the same concern.
[11] Hamilton, *Federalist 6*, 54.

Drawing implicitly on Thucydides and Hobbes, Hamilton argues that the problem of war in anarchy begins with human nature. "Men are ambitious, vindictive and rapacious," he claims, no less so in republics than in monarchies.[12] Popular assemblies as well as individual political leaders are often driven by "the love of power or the desire of pre-eminence and domination," and neither is exempt from "momentary passion" that produces impulsive and irrational decision-making.[13] Among the specific causes of violent conflict among the states, Hamilton argued, would be territorial disputes, which "have at all times been found one of the most fertile sources of hostility among nations . . . . This cause would exist among us in full force."[14] Commercial competition would also create the specific conditions for war. Hamilton criticizes the notion that "commercial republics, like ours, will never be disposed to waste themselves in ruinous contentions with each other," that "they will be governed by mutual interest, and will cultivate a spirit of mutual amity and concord." Instead, he demands, "Has commerce hitherto done any thing more than change the objects of war? . . . Have there not been as many wars founded upon commercial motives since that has become the prevailing system of nations, as were before occasioned by the cupidity of territory and domination?"[15] In summary, Hamilton, Madison, and Jay shared the belief that republican government within each American state would do nothing to mitigate the security dilemma between the individual republics. It would not eliminate human ambition and rapaciousness, nor would republican institutions constrain prominent political leaders within each republic from manipulating public opinion in support of wars that might serve their own selfish ends. Taken together, this assessment of international politics offers a bleak picture of the external behavior of all states, republican and nonrepublican alike.

Despite this bleak outlook, the founders did not abandon the effort to find institutional mechanisms that would constrain this capacity for violence. As Daniel Deudney points out, the *Federalist* reflects realist insights into the causes of violent conflict "without succumbing to the realist embrace of a tragic world view."[16] The most important step, they

[12] Ibid.; Thucydides, *History of the Peloponnesian War* (New York: Penguin Books, 1954), 80; Thomas Hobbes, *Leviathan* [1651] (New York: Penguin Books, 1968), 185.

[13] Hamilton, *Federalist 6*, 54, 56.

[14] Hamilton, *Federalist 7*, 60.

[15] Hamilton, *Federalist 6*, 56–57, and *Federalist 7*, 60–63.

[16] Daniel Deudney, "Publius vs. Kant: Federal Republican Security vs. Democratic Peace," 45. Paper presented at the Annual Convention of the International Studies Association, Chicago, Illinois, February 21–24, 2001.

argued, was to form a tighter union among the individual states by rat-ifying the Constitution. This would obviously eliminate anarchy among the states and thus eliminate this specific source of war de-scribed so vividly by the Federalists. Once this union was created, how-ever, the new extended U.S. republic would still exist in anarchy with all other foreign nations, so the larger problem of international anarchy, competition, and war would continue to bedevil the United States. In *Federalist 24* Hamilton paints an ominous picture of the security chal-lenges confronting the United States in 1787. While Americans clearly appreciated the security benefits of geographic separation from the Eu-ropean continent, Hamilton reminds his audience of the numerous physical threats to the Union. It is worth quoting Hamilton at length:

> Though a wide ocean separates the United States from Europe, yet there are various considerations that warn us against an excess of confidence or security. On one side of us, and stretching far into our rear, are grow-ing settlements subject to the domination of Britain. On the other side, and extending to meet the British settlements, are colonies and estab-lishments subject to the domination of Spain . . . . The savage tribes on our Western frontier ought to be regarded as our natural enemies, their natural allies, because they have most to fear from us, and most to hope from them. The improvements in the art of navigation have, as to the fa-cility of communication, rendered distant nations, in a great measure, neighbors. Britain and Spain are among the principle maritime powers of Europe. A future concert of views between these nations ought not to be regarded as improbable . . . . These circumstances combined admon-ish us not to be too sanguine in considering ourselves as entirely out of the reach of danger.[17]

For the Federalists, this danger of foreign war was one more pressing reason to ratify the Constitution; union would help the states deter ag-gression or defend themselves against these adversaries if necessary. Union, of course, did not solve the problem of defense against Euro-pean powers. Debate still swirled around the need for other institu-tional features such as a stronger executive and a standing army. Union of all states, however, was clearly a better defense option than independent efforts to provide external security from larger powers.[18]

---

[17] Hamilton, *Federalist 24*, 160–61.
[18] William Riker, *Federalism: Origin, Operation, Significance* (Boston: Little, Brown, 1964), 12–13, 17–20.

But what about the impulse toward war that might come from *in-side* the United States, rather than from external aggression? While international disputes were inevitable, did the founders accept armed conflict as the unavoidable result in every case? Clearly not; the founding documents are infused with the belief that how a state responds to particular foreign policy problems or opportunities remains a matter of choice. The question then for the founders is, would the republican structure of government under the Constitution decrease the likelihood of the United States actually resorting to force to resolve the international conflicts that do arise? Similarly, while the U.S. republic would not be immune from the worst traits of human nature, would the republican institutions of government hold them in check to decrease the likelihood that ambition, greed, or passion would actually drive the United States to war? To address these questions, the next section poses another: did the founders consider the separation of powers a sufficient mechanism for achieving these goals?

The Separation of Powers and Constraints on Military Force

Undeniably, the separation of executive and legislative functions, and the careful apportionment of authority over the use of military force, the raising and regulation of armed forces, and the allocation of money to fund military measures were central to the founders' efforts to control state power. While the U.S. Constitution designates the president as "commander-in-chief" of the armed forces, it reserves the bulk of authority in these areas to Congress. This includes the power to declare war, to authorize limited or "imperfect" war, to raise and support armies and maintain a navy, and to call up the militia both to suppress domestic insurrection and repel foreign invasions.[19] In recent decades, scholars and practitioners alike have devoted a great deal of energy to a debate over the proper balance between presidential and congressional authority over using military force. These arguments typically revolve around issues of expediency and rationality in decision-making, the complexities of using military force in the nuclear age, and the need to maintain fidelity to the republican principles of accountability and dispersed con-

---

[19] On the concept of "imperfect" war and its authorization, see Louis Fisher, *Presidential War Power* (Lawrence: University Press of Kansas, 1995), 18; Brien Hallet, *The Lost Art of Declaring War* (Urbana: University of Illinois Press, 1998).

trol over state violence. In essence, this is a normative debate over whether the United States is better served by allowing the president to exercise a relatively unfettered prerogative in foreign affairs, or by an activist Congress that maintains a substantial decision-making role.

Despite the importance of this debate over the proper allocation of war powers, it does not bring us any closer to understanding the basic question pursued in the democratic peace literature, and which is at the heart of this book: is there a logical link between the structure of the U.S. political system and the *frequency* with which the United States employs military force in its foreign policy? Will the proper allocation of war powers actually produce a tendency for the United States to exercise restraint in its use of military force? Specifically, why might granting war powers to Congress, while preventing concentrated power in the executive, tend to "push toward peace" in U.S. foreign policy? Stated differently, why might Congress decide *less often* in favor of war, compared to the president? In all the scholarship and commentary on war powers in the United States, the answer to these questions remains largely unexamined. A survey of the record from the Constitutional Convention, the state ratifying conventions, and *The Federalist Papers* reveals three basic kinds of arguments linking congressional war powers and constraints on the use of force. These include (1) the tendency of individuals with concentrated power to abuse it; (2) the inherent wisdom of collective deliberation and decision-making that characterizes the work of legislatures; and (3) the difficulty of generating consensus in an institution with multiple autonomous members.

The first general argument on this question is drawn directly from the deep-rooted distrust of concentrated power expressed by the American founders. A strong executive not only posed the threat of domestic tyranny, executive power was widely considered to be, by its nature, more war prone than the legislature. Taking their cue from Montesquieu, as well as the colonies' recent experience with the British crown, the Framers accepted the axiom that "every man invested with power is apt to abuse it, and to carry his authority as far as it will go. . . . To prevent this abuse, it is necessary from the very nature of things that power should be a check to power."[20] Madison warned

---

[20] Montesquieu, *Spirit of the Laws*, trans. Thomas Nugent (New York: Hafner, 1948), 150. In *Federalist 47*, Madison notes his debt to Montesquieu. See also Edward J. Erler, "The Constitution and the Separation of Powers," in *The Framing and Ratification of the Constitution*, ed. Leonard W. Levy and Dennis J. Mahoney (London: Collier Macmillan, 1987), 151.

that due to the potentially terrible consequences of war "the management of foreign relations appears to be the *most susceptible* of abuse of all trusts committed to a Government."[21] Articulating this point more explicitly in an essay on presidential war powers, Madison proclaimed,

> In no part of the constitution is more wisdom to be found, than in the clause which confides the question of war and peace to the legislature, and not to the executive department . . . . War is in fact the true nurse of executive aggrandizement. In war, a physical force is to be created; and it is the executive will, which is to direct it. In war, the public treasures are to be unlocked; and it is the executive hand which is to dispense them. In war, the honours and emoluments of office are to be multiplied; and it is the executive patronage under which they are to be enjoyed. It is in war, finally, that laurels are to be gathered; and it is the executive brow they are to encircle.

Madison concludes bluntly, "The executive is the department of power most distinguished by its propensity to war; hence it is the practice of all states, in proportion as they are free, to disarm this propensity of its influence."[22] This belief explains the strong negative reaction from Elbridge Gerry of Massachusetts and George Mason of Virginia during the Constitutional Convention to the suggestion that war powers be granted to the executive.[23] Gerry exclaimed that he "never expected to hear in a republic a motion to empower the Executive alone to declare war." Mason too announced that he "was against giving the power of war to the Executive, because [he was] not safely to be trusted with it."[24] Alexander Hamilton, despite his enthusiasm for an "energetic" executive, provided an explicit warning about the link between executive war powers and the likelihood that the power would be abused. "An avaricious man," he argued,

[21] In a letter to Thomas Jefferson, May 1798. Quoted in Jack N. Rakove, "Foreign Policy Making—the View from 1787," in *Foreign Policy and the Constitution*, ed. Robert A. Goldwin and Robert Licht (Washington, D.C.: AEI Press, 1990), 18; emphasis added. See also David Gray Adler and Larry N. George, *The Constitution and the Conduct of American Foreign Policy* (Lawrence: University of Kansas Press, 1996), 4.

[22] This appears in an exchange of public essays with Hamilton on whether President Washington had the authority to issue the Neutrality Act in 1793. James Madison, *Letters and Other Writings*, vol. 1 (Philadelphia: Lippincott, 1865), 611, 643.

[23] Pierce Butler of South Carolina argued that both the House of Representatives and the Senate would be burdened by cumbersome deliberations and would act too slowly to be trusted with war powers. James Madison, *Notes of Debates in the Federal Convention of 1787*, ed. Adrienne Koch (New York: W. W. Norton, 1966), 476.

[24] Madison, *Notes of Debates*, 476

might be tempted to betray the interests of the state to the acquisition of wealth. An ambitious man might make his own aggrandizement, by the aid of a foreign power, the price of his treachery to his constituents. The history of human conduct does not warrant that exalted opinion of human virtue which would make it wise in a nation to commit interests of so delicate and momentous a kind, as those which concern its intercourse with the rest of the world, to the sole disposal of a magistrate created and circumstanced as would be a President of the United States.[25]

To the extent that war might actually result from the abuse of authority for personal gain, private preferences, or political interests, preventing any one individual from wielding power over questions of war and peace was one obvious way to reduce the likelihood of war stemming from this particular source.

Beyond this axiomatic claim about avoiding the abuse of personal authority, what did the Framers offer to explain why granting war powers to Congress would actually make war less likely? After all, not all those involved in the U.S. constitutional project agreed with the notion that Congress would be less tempted by ambition and power. Gouverneur Morris, a delegate from Pennsylvania, expressed as much distrust of the legislature as others did of the executive. "The Legislature will continually seek to aggrandize and perpetuate themselves," he argued, "and will seize those critical moments produced by war, invasion or convulsion for that purpose."[26] While the previous argument makes claims about the nature of executive power and behavior, the burden remains to establish the nature of legislative power and behavior when faced with decisions on the use of military force. There were two basic arguments on Congress and conflict decision-making expressed during the founding period. The first rests on the belief that Congress, acting as a deliberative body plumbing the true national interest, will represent a general consensus on the wisdom of avoiding war, unless the objective interests of the people, and therefore the state, made war unavoidable in particular circumstances. In contrast, the second argument rests on the belief that members of Congress, acting not as a deliberative collective body but as individual representatives of diverse constituencies, will often fail to generate consensus on questions of war and peace. This makes it exceedingly difficult to generate majority support for war, thereby reducing its frequency.

[25] Hamilton, *Federalist 75*, 451. See also Jay, *Federalist 4*, 46.
[26] Madison, *Notes of Debates*, 322–23.

The first argument is the most ambiguous and problematic of the two, yet it was championed by several prominent participants in the founding debates, and it is related most closely to the general Enlightenment notion of republican pacifism.[27] This argument rests on the claim that the collective judgment of a legislative body composed of numerous members would produce the "wisdom" necessary to avoid the calamities of war. This claim is further based on the assumption that war is often an irrational act, the product of haste, emotion, or rash decision-making. For many in the founding period, a legislative body was far less susceptible than an executive to these perversions in decision-making. According to Hamilton, "Those politicians and statesmen who have been the most celebrated for the soundness of their principles and for the justness of their views have declared in favor of . . . a numerous legislature." The value of this legislature, they argue, is that it is "best adapted to deliberation and wisdom, and best calculated to conciliate the confidence of the people and to secure their privileges and interests."[28] The "privileges and interests" of the people, particularly in questions of war, could only be discovered through deliberation and collective decision-making. James Wilson, during the Pennsylvania state ratifying convention, argued forcefully from this perspective, "This system will not hurry us into war; it is calculated to guard against it. It will not be in the power of a single man, or a single body of men, to involve us in such distress; for the important power of declaring war is vested in the legislature at large: this declaration must be made with the concurrence of the House of Representatives: from this circumstance we may draw a certain conclusion that nothing but our national interest can draw us into war."[29] In a similar vein Roger Sherman argued during the First Congress, "The more wisdom there is employed, the greater the security there is that the public business will be done."[30] The implicit assumption advanced by Wilson and Sherman is that war, as distressful as it may be, occasionally will be necessary to secure the nation's interests. However, the legislature's role is to guard against rushing into war in all other circumstances

[27] Gerald Stourzh, *Alexander Hamilton and the Idea of Republican Government* (Stanford, Calif.: Stanford University Press, 1970), 149–50.

[28] Hamilton, *Federalist 70*, 424.

[29] Jonathan Elliot, ed., *The Debates in the Several State Conventions on the Adoption of the Federal Constitution*, vol. 2 (Philadelphia: J. B. Lippincott, 1901), 528.

[30] David Gray Adler, "Court, Constitution and Foreign Affairs," in *Constitution and the Conduct of American Foreign Policy*, n. 23.

when it can be prudently avoided. For this role, they believed, the legislature was particularly well suited.

This type of "public interest" argument is most similar to Kant's well-known point about representative legislatures producing a "great hesitation" in the use of military force.[31] Like the American founders, Kant begins his analysis of republican constraints by emphasizing the importance of separating executive and legislative functions of government, and of vesting war powers in the legislative branch. While it is clear from Kant's description of a republican political structure that there is a check on the executive's ability to take his or her state into war, this structural arrangement alone does not explain why the legislature, presumably acting in the interests of the citizenry, would necessarily withhold its consent for war. Kant takes his argument one step further and provides an explanation for domestic opposition to the use of force that relies on assumptions about how citizens of republics perceive their interests in relationship to war. Specifically, Kant argues that the citizens of a republic are reluctant to sanction the use of force because they would bear its full costs and miseries. The citizens of a republic would withhold their consent simply because they have nothing to gain from war, and everything to lose. It is important to note that Kant's argument rests on a unitary conception of the public interest, that is, on *consensus* within the legislature that war must be avoided unless it is absolutely necessary to secure the general interests of the citizenry. The arguments advanced by such U.S. statesmen as James Wilson and Roger Sherman, while not as explicit as Kant's, also depend on the superior ability of the legislature as a collective body to discover the true national interest, which in most cases is best served by peace.

Alexander Hamilton found this argument about the peace-prone character of the public interest and representative legislatures unconvincing. This raises doubts about the sufficiency of the separation of powers alone as a mechanism for restraining the use of military force. In *Federalist 6* Hamilton asks: "Have republics in practice been less addicted to war than monarchies?" No, he answers; in fact, "there have been . . . almost as many popular as royal wars."[32] Hamilton goes on to explain that republics may actually be propelled into conflict by the

---

[31] Immanuel Kant, "Perpetual Peace: A Philosophical Sketch," in *Kant's Political Writings*, ed. Hans Reiss (Cambridge: Cambridge University Press, 1970), 100–101.
[32] Hamilton, *Federalist 6*, 56, 58.

war-prone character of the humans that govern them. "Are not [re-publics] administered by *men* as well as [monarchies]? Are there not aversions, predilections, rivalships and desires of unjust acquisitions that affect nations as well as kings? Are not popular assemblies fre-quently subject to the impulses of rage, resentment, jealousy, avarice, and of other irregular and violent propensities?"[33] Not only are repre-sentative legislatures not immune from perversions in rational deci-sion-making, Hamilton also warns that popular sentiment is subject to manipulation by prominent political figures who may generate public support for military conflict simply because it serves some personal objective. "Men of this class, whether the favorites of a king or of a people, have in too many instances abused the confidence they pos-sessed; and assuming the pretext of some public motive, they have not scrupled to sacrifice the national tranquility to personal advantage or personal gratification."[34] So for Hamilton, there is no popular consen-sus on the irrationality of war and the inherent superiority of peace for the citizenry's best interest. In contrast, popular consensus, expressed through the "cries of the nation and the importunities of their repre-sentatives have, upon various occasions, dragged their monarchs into war, or continued them in it, contrary to their inclinations, and some-times contrary to the real interests of the state."[35] Contemporary critics of the Kantian notion of a unitary popular interest in peace echo Hamilton.[36]

This critique of a public interest in peace brings us to the second general argument expressed during the founding period on Congress and conflict decision-making. In contrast to Kant, this argument on Congress pushing toward peace is not based on a consensus view of the national or public interest. This argument is based on the difficulty of generating consensus within Congress due to the diverse con-stituencies members of Congress represent. In *Federalist 70*, Hamilton anticipated that Congress would have difficulty acting with dispatch,

[33] Ibid., 56; emphasis in original.
[34] Ibid., 54.
[35] Ibid., 58.
[36] James Lee Ray, *Democracy and International Conflict: An Evaluation of the Democratic Peace Proposition* (Columbia: University of South Carolina Press, 1995), 2; Robert O. Keo-hane, "International Liberalism Reconsidered," in *The Economic Limits to Modern Politics*, ed. John Dunn (Cambridge: Cambridge University Press, 1990), 176; John M. Owen IV, *Liberal Peace, Liberal War: American Politics and International Security* (Ithaca: Cornell Uni-versity Press, 1997), 16; Bruce Russett, *Controlling the Sword: The Democratic Governance of National Security* (Cambridge: Harvard University Press, 1990), 35–40.

particularly as the number of representatives in the legislature increased. While criticizing the notion of a divided executive branch, Hamilton argued that "whenever two or more persons are engaged in any common enterprise or pursuit, there is always danger of difference of opinion." Dangerous, perhaps, in the executive, but advantageous in the legislature.

> Upon the principles of a free government, inconveniences from the source just mentioned must necessarily be submitted to in the formation of the legislature . . . . In the legislature, promptitude of decision is oftener an evil than a benefit. The *differences of opinion*, and the *jarring of parties* in that department of the government, though they may sometimes obstruct salutary plans, yet often promote deliberation and circumspection, and serve to check excesses in the majority.[37]

This argument goes beyond the formal separation of powers alone by emphasizing the "checks and balances" *within* both the House of Representatives and the Senate that make consensus generation difficult.[38] As Madison noted in *Federalists 10* and *51*, the "division of society into different interests and parties," represented within Congress, would act as a brake on concerted legislative action.[39] Constraints on state power would not simply rest on "parchment barriers" erected by constitutional design; constraints ultimately would be guaranteed by the competing constituencies found within the geographically expansive American republic. Jack Rakove expresses this point well: "The Constitution does not so much invite struggle as permit it to flourish once it has arisen for other reasons—reasons that are almost invariably rooted in different views of national interests rather that principled notions of how foreign policy should be made in the abstract."[40] From this perspective *both* the institutional organization *and* diverse social context of U.S. politics must work together to reduce the frequency of majority support for armed conflict.

The argument to this point remains incomplete until we recognize that its institutional and social components are both structured by "the

---

[37] Hamilton, *Federalist 70*, 425–27; emphasis added. During the Constitutional Convention George Mason of Virginia made this same point when he argued that war powers were best left to the legislature because "he was for clogging rather than facilitating war." Madison, *Notes of Debates*, 476.

[38] M. J. C. Vile, *Constitutionalism and the Separation of Powers* (Oxford: Clarendon Press, 1967), 154, 157, 160.

[39] Madison, *Federalist 10*, 78.

[40] Rakove, "Foreign Policy Making," 18–19.

federal principle" at the core of the U.S. political system.[41] This federal principle defines the character of its competing interests and provides the institutional mechanisms necessary for the expression of diverse territorial interests at the national level. Social diversity in the United States, and thus the difficulty in generating consensus on national political questions, is a direct function of the geographic extent, the sheer physical size, of the U.S. republic. This is a point emphasized repeatedly by Madison in *The Federalist Papers*. In *Federalist 10* he makes this connection by noting, "Extend the sphere and you take in a greater variety of parties and interests; you make it less probable that a majority of the whole will have a common motive."[42] And in *Federalist 51* he argues, "In the extended republic of the United States, and among the great variety of interests, parties, and sects which it embraces, a coalition of a majority of the whole society could seldom take place on any other principle than those of justice and the general good."[43] To make this argument complete and explicit, the next section looks in detail at the logic of federal union and its effects on conflict decision-making.

Federal Union and Constraints on Military Force

The American founders clearly recognized that federal union is what made their new republic distinctive.[44] In fact, they believed federal union was essential for sustaining republican government across a large-scale territorial expanse. Notable political theorists had previously asserted that republican government could not exist beyond the small-scale polity, and the history of previous republics seemed to bear this out. For the Americans, federal union would solve this problem.[45] But how would the institutional and social features of this "compound republic" reduce the state's propensity to engage in armed conflict? Would the "controls" on political power imposed by

---

[41] Madison, *Federalist 51*, 325; emphasis in original.

[42] Madison, *Federalist 10*, 83.

[43] Madison, *Federalist 51*, 325.

[44] Modern students of federalism acknowledge that the idea of "federalism is derived from one source, the United States." Riker, *Federalism*, xi. See also K. C. Wheare, *Federal Government* (New York: Oxford University Press, 1964), 1; S. Rufus Davis, *The Federal Principle* (Berkeley: University of California Press, 1978), 121; Daniel J. Elazar, *Exploring Federalism* (Tuscaloosa: University of Alabama Press, 1987), 7; Ivo D. Duchacek, *The Territorial Dimension of Politics: Within, Among, and Across Nations* (Boulder, Colo.: Westview Press, 1986), 114.

[45] Deudney, "The Philadelphian System."

federalism actually have an impact on foreign affairs, and more specifically, on the use of military force? As noted previously, for most contemporary scholars of federal government, the very definition of a federal state—one divided into two orders of government (national and state)—naturally leads to the expectation that federalism is largely irrelevant in foreign affairs. This is certainly the perspective advanced by the "intergovernmental relations" approach to the study of federalism, which dominates the literature in this field. This literature is most interested in the scope of political authority retained by the subunit governments within the federal state, and in the legal or political relationship between the subunit governments and the national government. In terms of foreign policy, the U.S. Constitution carefully sets out the respective roles of the national and state governments. It explicitly denies the states, as autonomous political units, the right to "enter into any treaty, alliance, or confederation," and, "without the consent of Congress," the right to "keep troops or ships of war in time of peace, enter into any agreement or compact . . . with a foreign power, or engage in war, unless actually invaded" (Article 1, Section 10). Political authority for directing foreign relations is concentrated in the national government. Under the Constitution, the most important role for the states in military affairs was the right to raise a militia, which could only be called into national service by Congress (Article 1, Section 8). If our approach to the study of U.S. foreign policy is framed by these clear constitutional provisions, which deny any role to the states as autonomous political actors, and which decree that foreign policy is the exclusive reserve of the national government, then it would be natural to conclude that federalism can be ignored. Elazar notes correctly that this emphasis on formal constitutional authority in federal states "establish[es] for external purposes what is, for all intents and purposes, a unitary state."[46] This is a perspective implicitly shared by international relations scholars.[47] It also brings us back to

[46] Daniel J. Elazar, "Introduction," *Publius* 12 (fall 1984), 1.

[47] In the democratic peace literature, only Russett and Maoz refer specifically to federalism as an institutional arrangement that is "distinguishable" from the institutional arrangements found in nonfederal democracies. While they include federalism as one component in a quantitative measure of how democracies differ from one another, they do not explore the distinctive logic of federal democracy and how it may produce constraints on military force. Bruce Russett and Zeev Maoz, "The Democratic Peace Since World War II," in *Grasping the Democratic Peace: Principles for a Post-Cold War World* (Princeton: Princeton University Press, 1993), 79–80.

the separation of powers at the national level as the primary source of potential constraints on military force.

While federalism as a political principle is certainly best character-ized by a division of power between two orders of government, the emphasis on this particular institutional feature draws attention away from the other ways that federal union structures the U.S. political sys-tem. Most important, the two orders of government approach ignores the fact that federalism is the organizing principle of the U.S. electoral system at the national level. According to Wechsler, the "strategic role" of the states "in the selection of the Congress and the President" is "so immutable a feature of the system that [its] importance tends to be ig-nored."[48] Federalism organizes the internal structure of both houses of Congress and the political incentives to which members of Congress re-spond. Federalism structures the process for electing presidents, which imposes particular political incentives that shape executive decision-making as well. Even national political parties, which might serve as centralizing institutions in U.S. politics, are organized and internally divided along federal lines. Each must be discussed in turn.

The Federal Structure of Congress

Among scholars of American foreign policy it is common to treat Con-gress as a unitary institutional actor that, depending on the outcome of its voting, either supports, opposes, or coordinates with the president on various foreign policy initiatives. Rarely does the level of analysis go below the legislature as a whole (or the respective houses of Con-gress) to examine how the *composition* of the legislature affects its role in the policy process.[49] But as James Lindsay notes, Congress is not "a monolithic institution with its own preferences and wants . . . Con-gress is a *'they,'* not an *'it.'*"[50] Political competition *within* Congress, and the bases for this competition, must be treated as an important feature of the decision-making process in order to explain the role that

[48] Herbert Wechsler, "The Political Safeguards of Federalism: The Role of the States in the Composition and Selection of the National Government," in *Federalism: Mature and Emergent*, ed. Arthur W. Macmahon (Garden City, N.Y.: Doubleday, 1955), 98–99.

[49] For an excellent example, see Francis D. Wormuth and Edwin B. Firmage, *To Chain the Dog of War: The War Power of Congress in History and Law* (Urbana: University of Illi-nois Press, 1989).

[50] James M. Lindsay, "Cowards, Beliefs, and Structures," in *The Use of Force After the Cold War*, ed. H. W. Brands (College Station: Texas A & M University Press, 1998), 151.

Congress might play in either sanctioning or restraining the use of military force. Studies that do examine political divisions within Congress typically focus on political party identity and how partisanship affects congressional voting, or on the distribution of "hawkish" or "dovish" opinion on foreign policy questions.[51] While these transitory characteristics may indeed be important, partisanship and hawkishness alone fail to account for the fact that both the Senate and the House of Representatives are internally divided along federal lines. Members of both bodies derive their authority not only from the Constitution, but also from the territorial constituents that elect them to national office.

The Constitution explicitly provides the states with the responsibility for organizing congressional elections. Until 1913, U.S. senators were elected by state legislatures. Members of the House have always been elected by clearly defined territorial constituencies within the individual states.[52] The federal organization of the congressional electoral system creates and sustains strong ties between the interests and perspectives of discrete territorial constituencies within the United States and legislators at the national level. Madison points this out in *Federalist 44*:

> The members and officers of the State governments . . . will have an essential agency in giving effect to the federal Constitution. The election of the President and the Senate will depend, in all cases, on the legislatures of the several states. And the election of the House of Representatives will equally depend on the same authority . . . and will, probably, forever be conducted by the officers and according to the laws of the States.[53]

He reinforces this point in *Federalist 45* by arguing,

> The Senate will be elected absolutely and exclusively by the State legislatures. Even the House of Representatives, though drawn immediately

---

[51] For example see Kurt Gaubatz, *Elections and War: The Electoral Incentive in the Democratic Politics of War and Peace* (Stanford, Calif.: Stanford University Press, 1999); Russett, *Controlling the Sword,* chap. 4; Miriam Fendius Elman, "Unpacking Democracy: Presidentialism, Parliamentarism, and Theories of Democratic Peace," *Security Studies* 4 (summer 2000), 91–126. David P. Auerswald, "Inward Bound: Domestic Institutions and Military Conflicts," *International Organization* 53 (summer 1999), 480–81.

[52] United States Constitution, Article 1, Sections 2 and 3, particularly Section 4. The Seventeenth Amendment to the Constitution, ratified in 1913, enacted direct popular election for U.S. senators.

[53] Madison, *Federalist 44*, 287.

from the people, will be chosen very much under the influence of that class of men whose influence over the people obtains for themselves an election into the State legislature. Thus, each of the principle branches of the federal government will owe its existence more or less to the favor of the State governments, and must consequently feel a dependence, which is much more likely to beget a disposition too obsequiesce than too overbearing towards them.[54]

In this way, "the State governments may be regarded as constituent and essential parts of the federal government."[55] Contemporary students of U.S. politics confirm that in practice this is clearly the case. As David Truman explains, "The risks and sanctions to which most members of Congress are particularly sensitive have their focus within the states and localities. The relationships which the legislator has established and maintained within the constituency are primary and crucial."[56] According to David Mayhew, "The reelection quest establishes an accountability relationship with an electorate. . . . At voicing opinions held by significant numbers of voters back in the constituencies, the United States Congress is extraordinarily effective."[57] As a result, the actions of the national government are not truly separate from territorial interests within the states, but bound to them through representation in the legislature. While the role of the states as autonomous political actors in foreign policy was tightly circumscribed by the Constitution, federalism provides state-level constituencies with a direct institutional outlet for shaping national-level policy questions. The diffusion of authority among territorial representatives means that any collective decision by the legislature, including decisions that sanction the use of force for certain foreign policy objectives, must attract sufficient political support from a diverse group of autonomous

[54] Madison, *Federalist 45*, 291. In *Federalist 39* Madison notes that in contrast to the Senate, which is clearly a federal institution, the House of Representatives is national in character because it derives its power from "the people of America" (p. 244). Yet the broader point established in *Federalist 45* is that "the people" electing members of the House are organized into discrete geographic regions, so the House supports the basic principle of geographic representation that is the essence of federalism. House members are often said to be even more sensitive to local interests because their constituencies are smaller and they stand for election more often. V. O. Key, Jr., *Politics, Parties, and Pressure Groups* (New York: Thomas Y. Crowell, 1952).

[55] Madison, *Federalist 45*, 291.

[56] David B. Truman, "Federalism and the Party System," in *American Federalism in Perspective*, ed. Aaron Wildavsky (Boston: Little, Brown, 1967), 83–84. See also Wheare, *Federal Government*, 184.

[57] David Mayhew, *Congress: the Electoral Connection* (New Haven: Yale University Press, 1974), 6, 106.

political actors. The federal composition of the legislature provides an opportunity for coalitions of representatives to block executive branch initiatives as well as to block the efforts of other legislators, or the individual states, to bring national power to bear for particular objectives. This will be discussed in greater detail below.

The Federal Structure of the Presidential Electoral System

While the Framers believed that the national legislature would present the most potent source of constraints on political power in the United States, this does not exhaust the institutional mechanisms that can inhibit the use of military force. Much of the literature on democracy and war focuses on a second source of constraints, derived from the fact that presidents and prime ministers are accountable to an electorate that might punish them politically for pursuing high-risk or costly foreign adventures.[58] Because electoral penalties can only be imposed after the president initiates an unpopular foreign conflict, *ex ante* constraint on executive action depends on the president exercising *self-restraint* out of concern for expected future political losses. As important, the structure of the electoral system in a particular democratic state is crucial in determining the actual degree of vulnerability of a particular executive to electoral punishment. This will vary from democracy to democracy.[59] In the United States, while the president is the only public figure elected by a national constituency, the electoral process is actually organized at the state level. To the degree that electoral incentives will shape presidential decision-making in foreign

[58] David L. Rousseau, Christopher Gelpi, Dan Reiter, and Paul K. Huth, "Assessing the Dyadic Nature of the Democratic Peace, 1918–88," *American Political Science Review* 90 (September 1996), 513; Owen, *Liberal Peace, Liberal War*; Kurt Gaubatz, *Elections and War*; Kenneth Schultz, "Do Democratic Institutions Constrain or Inform? Contrasting Two Institutional Perspectives on Democracy and War," *International Organization* 53 (1999), 233–66.

[59] Bruce Bueno de Mesquita, James D. Morrow, Randolph M. Siverson, Alastair Smith, "An Institutional Explanation of the Democratic Peace," *American Political Science Review* 93 (December 1999), 791–807; Bruce Bueno de Mesquita and Randolph M. Siverson, "War and the Survival of Political Leaders: A Comparative Study of Regime Type and Political Accountability," *American Political Science Review* 89 (December 1995), 841–855; Daniel Geller, *Domestic Factors in Foreign Policy: A Cross-National Statistical Analysis* (Cambridge: Shenkman Books, 1985), 63; T. Clifton Morgan and Sally Howard Campbell, "Domestic Structure, Decisional Constraints, and War: So Why Kant Democracies Fight?" *Journal of Conflict Resolution* 35 (June 1991), 190–91.

policy, the federal structure of this system of accountability must be central to how we examine this relationship.

In *The Federalist Papers* we find a clear appreciation for the constraining effects of electoral accountability on presidential behavior. Hamilton repeatedly refers to the president's "due dependence on the people" as a check on his behavior. In *Federalist 78* he asks: "Does [the structure of the executive department] combine the requisites to safety, in the republican sense—a due dependence on the people, a due responsibility? The answer to the question . . . is satisfactorily deducible from these circumstances: the election of the President once in four years by persons immediately chosen by the people for that purpose."[60] Interestingly, Hamilton also argues that the president must be given sufficient political autonomy to pursue even unpopular policies. The people, Hamilton contends, are not immune from error, passionate sentiment, or manipulation by prominent public figures. Therefore, the president must be able to resist public pressure when necessary to pursue activities that truly serve the "public good."[61] Four years in office was enough time for the president to pursue his responsibilities with energy and wisdom and to ensure that he would have sufficient time to convince voters that his actions were proper before the possibility of political "annihilation" at the next election. But four years is not so long that the president can truly disregard his dependence on the people.[62] And because the president is "re-eligible [for election] as often as the people of the United States shall think him worthy of their confidence," the president's future political prospects should keep him concerned with antagonizing public opinion.[63]

What Hamilton's comments fail to specify is that for purposes of presidential elections "the people" are organized into state-level constituencies, so the presidential electoral system mirrors the congressional electoral system in its basic federal structure. Madison advances this point forcefully when he notes, "Without the intervention of the State legislatures, the President of the United States cannot be elected at all. They must in all cases have a great share in his appointment, and will, perhaps, in most cases, of themselves determine it."[64] In effect, presidents are elected in a federal process that amalgamates the electoral choices of individual state constituencies. As a result, the policy preferences of particular states or regions remain salient for the presi-

---

[60] Hamilton, *Federalist 78*, 463–64.
[61] Hamilton, *Federalist 71*, 432.
[62] Hamilton, *Federalist 72*, 434.
[63] Hamilton, *Federalist 69*, 416.
[64] Madison, *Federalist 45*, 291.

dent because they are not diluted within one national electorate that could otherwise mute particularistic territorial interests. To compete for votes in individual states the president has an incentive to appeal to or avoid antagonizing strongly held interests within regions that might ultimately penalize the president at the ballot box. The president must not only be concerned with aggregate national opinion on questions of war and peace, but must also be mindful of how that public opinion breaks down along state or regional lines. As a result, the institutional arrangement of the federal system may have a constraining effect on the president's actions even in the absence of overt congressional action.

Why Might Federalism Push toward Peace?

So far, this discussion has described how the federal basis of the U.S. political system divides authority within Congress and produces a territorial dimension to the president's electoral incentives. Having described American democracy this way, there is no reason to then assert that these particular institutional features will necessarily "push toward peace."[65] Divided government and electoral accountability alone simply provide the institutional setting that makes domestic opposition to the use of force politically meaningful. These institutional characteristics tell us nothing about the likelihood of opposition to the use of force, the range of domestic interests actually impacted by a particular policy question, or the range of alternative policy choices that may become subject to domestic debate. As Risse-Kappen notes, "State structures do not determine the specific content or direction of policies."[66] Nor does an open electoral system guarantee that the electorate will actually disapprove of the use of force or that it will punish political leaders for risky or aggressive foreign policy. Scholars have provided a number of reasons why sufficient consensus may form at the elite or popular levels on a particular policy question that might then minimize domestic competition. These might include the widely touted "rally-round-the-flag" effect, external pressures that might produce consensus around a common

[65] Morgan and Campbell, "Domestic Structure, Decisional Constraints, and War," 189–90.
[66] Thomas Risse-Kappen, "Public Opinion, Domestic Structure, and Foreign Policy in Liberal Democracies," *World Politics* 43 (July 1991), 485.

perception of state interests and threats, common political values or national identity, or partisan loyalty.[67]

As noted earlier, the Federalists seemed to recognize that political institutions alone would not guarantee controls on state power. Hamilton, Madison, and Jay explicitly recognized that the territorial diversity of the Union was a key ingredient in the logic of institutional constraints. The *Federalist*, particularly the contributions of John Jay, explains that public sentiment on questions of war and peace in the extended U.S. republic will be routinely divided along regional lines. These regional divisions would frequently impede a common domestic view of possible threats, the character of other nations, the proper relationship to have with other nations, and when and where military force should play a role in U.S. foreign policy. The federal institutional arrangement of Congress and the presidential electoral system serve to enable or magnify these regional perspectives and convert them into the basis for competition within Congress and potential political penalties or rewards for the president. Neither regional diversity nor federal institutions alone can produce constraints as robust as when the institutions and societal features are combined.

The contemporary literature on federal government provides further insight. In federal states, the key feature that converts divided authority and electoral accountability into political competition and constrained decision-making is "federal asymmetry." This dimension of federalism is defined by the degree of social, economic, geographic, or political diversity among the "territorial communities" of a federal state.[68] Tarlton defines an ideal *symmetric* federal system as one that has "political units comprised of equal territory and population, similar economic

---

[67] Samuel Kernell, "Explaining Presidential Popularity," *American Political Science Review* 72 (1978), 506–22; Richard Brody, "International Crises: A Rallying Point for the President?" *Public Opinion* 6 (1984), 41–43, 46; Russett, *Controlling the Sword*, 34–44; Bradley Lian and John R. Oneal, "Presidents, the Use of Military Force, and Public Opinion," *Journal of Conflict Resolution* 37 (June 1993), 277–300; Margaret G. Hermann and Charles W. Kegley, Jr., "Rethinking Democracy and International Peace: Perspectives from Political Psychology," *International Studies Quarterly* 39 (1995), 511–33; David Lake, "Powerful Pacifists: Democratic States and War," *American Political Science Review* 86 (spring 1992), 24–37; Jack S. Levy and William Mabe, Jr., "Winning the War but Losing at Home: Politically Motivated Opposition to War." Paper presented at the International Studies Association Convention, Minneapolis, Minnesota, March 18–21, 1998.

[68] Duchacek defines territorial communities as "aggregates of individuals and groups who are aware of bonds of identification with each other as well as with the past, the present and hopes for the future of their area." Duchacek, *Territorial Dimension of Politics*, 3. Both Livingston and Dikshit point out that while politically the territorial communities

features, climate conditions, cultural patterns, social groupings, and political institutions."[69] The homogeneity across a symmetrical federal system would tend to limit the salience of a territorial division of authority for the politics of this technically federal state. Tarlton asserts that states in a symmetrical federal system, "because of their basic similarity, [would] be concerned with the solution of the same sorts of problems. . . . There would be no significant difference from one state to another in terms of major issues."[70] For example, it is hard to imagine highly divergent and competitive political interests emerging between North and South Dakota.

Conversely, an *asymmetric* federal state is one which is composed of territorial communities that do not share similar social, economic, geographic, or political features, and which subsequently have quite different political concerns or different solutions for the issues facing the whole state. Duchacek points out that "there is no federal system in the world in which all units are even approximately equal in size, population, political power, administrative structure, traditions or relative geographic location (e.g., near to or distant from sources of potential external danger)."[71] As a result, for many political issues, even those concerning war and peace, different territorial communities simply will not share common conceptions of the issues at stake, the value of pursuing particular foreign policy objectives, or the costs and benefits of using force in particular circumstances. Citizens and political leaders from different regions may perceive the international environment in very different ways. Different international challenges and opportunities will have different effects on their interests and goals. While some territorial communities or regions may benefit if force is used in response to a particular external problem, other territorial communities or regions may suffer. Federal asymmetry then enhances the probability of robust competition over policy choices and the difficulty of

---

are defined by the political boundaries of the federal subunits, the "bonds of identification" that distinguish territorial communities may cross political boundaries. In this situation, territorial communities may best be thought of as regional and encompassing more than one political subunit. William S. Livingston, *Federalism and Constitutional Change* (Oxford: Clarendon Press, 1956), 3; Ramesh Dutta Dikshit, *The Political Geography of Federalism: An Inquiry into Origins and Stability* (Delhi: Macmillan Company of India, 1975), 11.

[69] Charles D. Tarlton, "Symmetry and Asymmetry as Elements of Federalism: A Theoretical Speculation," *Journal of Politics* 27 (November 1965), 865.

[70] Ibid.

[71] Ivo D. Duchacek, *Comparative Federalism: The Territorial Dimension of Politics* (New York: Holt, Rinehart and Winston, 1970), 280.

building coalitions and generating the necessary political consensus behind military action.[72]

For the American founders, domestic competition over foreign policy questions was not a dangerous weakness, as a realist might contend, it was a source of security against the aggressive potential of republican government itself, a source of restraint that would prevent the United States from resorting to war too quickly or more often than absolutely necessary to secure the true national interests. Ironically, John Jay implies that because of federal asymmetry the United States might actually be subject to more sources of domestic pressure to pursue aggressive foreign policy than a nonfederal state would. Federal asymmetry is seen as both the seedbed of multiple sources of aggressive external initiatives and the solution to republican aggression, whether originating from regional actors, the president, or members of Congress. Overall, however, federal asymmetry, combined with a federal distribution of political authority, was expected to keep the use of military force by the United States in check.

In *Federalist 37*, Madison observes asymmetry in the "circumstances" of different territorial communities at all levels of the compound republic. "As every State may be divided into different districts . . . which give birth to contending interests and local jealousies, so the different parts of the United States are distinguished from each other by a variety of circumstances, which produce a like effect on a larger scale."[73] During the Constitutional Convention, Hamilton noted strong differences in "the local situation of the three largest states, Virginia, Massachusetts, and Pennsylvania. They were separated from each other by distance of

---

[72] For a similar extended analysis of regional diversity in the United States and its link to American foreign policy, see Peter Trubowitz, *Defining the National Interest: Conflict and Change in American Foreign Policy* (Chicago: University of Chicago Press, 1998), xiii–xiv, 4–5, 10–13, 18–20, 238–39, 241. Trubowitz focuses on the asymmetrical regional distribution of economic interests specifically, while his empirical work focuses on the 1890s, 1930s, and 1980s. See also Richard F. Bensel, *Sectionalism and American Political Development, 1880–1980* (Madison: University of Wisconsin Press, 1984). For an alternative view on American domestic politics and foreign policy in the late nineteenth century, see Fareed Zakaria, *From Wealth to Power: The Unusual Origins of America's World Role* (Princeton: Princeton University Press, 1998). Zakaria's argument stresses the growing internal capacity of the United States to support expansion of its global power, particularly as state capacity was perceived by the executive as the turn of the century approached. However, as Lynn-Jones points out, constraints on U.S. expansion resulted from a lack of political consensus between Congress and the president on how U.S. power should be used in the first place. Sean Lynn-Jones, "Realism and America's Rise: A Review Essay," *International Security* 23 (fall 1998), 157–82.

[73] Madison, *Federalist 37*, 230.

place, and equally so, by all the peculiarities which distinguish the interests of one State from those of another."[74] Elaborating on differences across the Union, Hamilton noted that a "considerable distinction of interests lay between the carrying & non-carrying states," those engaged in maritime commerce and those that did not, "which divides instead of unit[es] the larger states."[75] As Madison explains, territorial representatives were then expected to carry the "local spirit" of this federal asymmetry into the national legislature.[76]

Among the authors of *The Federalist Papers*, Jay most forcefully argues that the contending interests and local jealousies that emerge from this asymmetry would have a direct effect on how the different parts of the Union relate to the outside world. In turn, this will affect how these different territorial communities perceive and act on their particular external interests and on national policy. In *Federalist 5* Jay observes divergent economic conditions across the Union. The expected effect was that "different commercial concerns [among the states] must create different interests and of course different degrees of attachment to and connection with different foreign nations."[77] Because different kinds of economic activity were concentrated in particular geographic regions, the commercial implications of war would be felt differently in different places. On a more dangerous level, Jay asserts, "the temptations to violate treaties and commit international injustices may result from circumstances peculiar to the State[s] . . . such violences are more frequently occasioned by the passions and interests of a part than of the whole, of one or two States than of the Union." For example, he cites conflicts with Native Americans that were provoked by the particular interests of different territorial communities. "Not a single Indian war has yet been produced by aggressions of the present federal government; . . . but there are several instances of Indian hostilities provoked by the improper conduct of individual States, who, unable or unwilling to restrain or punish offenses, have given occasion to the slaughter of many innocent inhabitants."[78]

Federal asymmetry also meant that different regions in the Union were expected to have different perspectives on the Union's relations with European powers that held colonial possessions in North America.

[74] Madison, June 29, 1787, *Notes of Debates*, 154.
[75] Ibid., 216.
[76] Madison, *Federalist 46*, 296–97.
[77] Jay, *Federalist 5*, 53.
[78] Jay, *Federalist 3*, 44.

"The neighborhood of Spanish and British territories, bordering on some States and not on others, naturally confines the causes of quarrel more immediately to the borderers. The bordering States . . . will be those who, under the impulse of sudden irritation, and a quick sense of apparent interest or injury, will be most likely, by direct violence, to excite war with those nations."[79] Bordering states may become the most ardent advocates of military force if they perceive the threat as more acute than those living in other regions, or if they expect a positive outcome from the use of force. Alternatively, they may become the most passionate voices for restraint if their confidence in success at acceptable costs is low. Similarly, a military conflict with a prominent naval component holds much greater risk for coastal regions of the state or for those with maritime interests than it does for regions that are geographically insulated. While the *Federalist* does not address this issue, the territorial communities within this diverse federal state were also distinguished by differences in political culture that shaped how different regions of the United States thought about the use of military force in particular circumstances. Political-cultural differences were particularly acute during the first several decades after ratification of the Constitution, as the United States grappled with the question of whether to support Great Britain or France in the European wars beginning in the 1790s. Not only did culturally derived domestic conflict on this issue generate the first political parties in the United States, it produced a strong division between the Northeast and the South and Northwest on a series of foreign policy problems.

Ultimately, Jay argues, diversity among territorial communities within the Union, made salient within the context of its federal political structure, would tend to constrain regional aggression. Jay contends, "Nothing can so effectually obviate that danger [of regional aggression] as a national government, whose wisdom and prudence will not be diminished by the passions which actuate the parties immediately interested."[80] In other words, "the national government, *not being affected by these local circumstances*, will neither be induced to commit the wrong themselves, nor want power or inclination to prevent or punish its commission by others."[81] While Jay's argument here is part of a larger effort to gain acceptance for the stronger national government established by the U.S. Constitution, his reference in this particular passage to the "wisdom and prudence" of the national government gives the misleading impression

[79] Ibid.
[80] Ibid., 45.
[81] Ibid., 44; emphasis added.

of the government acting as a unified body. If we want to examine the effects of federalism specifically, it is important to emphasize that because other parts of the Union will not share these regional interests, other territorial representatives within the legislature will tend to act against this form of aggression. Jay clarifies this point in another passage: "The prospect of present loss or advantage may often tempt the governing party in one or two States to swerve from good faith and justice [in dealing with foreign nations]; but those temptations, *not reaching the other States, and consequently having little or no influence on the national government*, the temptation will be fruitless, and good faith and justice be preserved."[82] Representatives from other states will thus be "more temperate and cool" when confronted with these potential sources of military conflict, so the "national government will proceed with moderation and candor to consider and decide on the means most proper to extricate them from the difficulties which threaten them."[83] While Jay focuses on how regional military initiatives are held in check by federal asymmetry, we can extend this basic logic to examine arguments for the use of military force that are cast as in the national interest. Madison actually anticipated this argument on the constraining effects of federal union several years before the Constitutional Convention. In a letter to Thomas Jefferson in 1784, Madison examined the dangerous conflict then brewing between the American states and Spain over Spain's efforts to restrict use of the Mississippi River. He argued that if Spain wants to restrict threats from the American states to Spanish interests in North America, it should encourage further westward expansion and an increase in the number of states in the confederation. The states were bitterly divided over whether to press Spain on this issue.[84] As a result, Madison argued, Spain's *"permanent* security . . . lies in the Complexity of our foederal Govt. and the diversity of interests among the members of it which render offensive measures, improbable in Council, and difficult in execution. If such be the case when 13 States compose the System, ought she not to wish to see the number enlarged to three & twenty?"[85]

It is important to emphasize that regional diversity alone does not produce political constraints, it is only part of the argument. Two alternative examples help make this point about the importance of institutions

---

[82] Ibid., 43–44; emphasis added.

[83] Ibid., 45.

[84] Joseph L. Davis, *Sectionalism in American Politics, 1774–1787* (Madison: University of Wisconsin Press, 1977), chap. 7.

[85] James Madison to Thomas Jefferson, August 20, 1784, in *The Papers of James Madison*, vol. 8, ed. Robert A. Rutland and William M. E. Rachal (Chicago: University of Chicago Press, 1973), 106.

as a political outlet for social diversity. For an extreme case, consider the
Soviet Union. Regions across the Soviet empire of the mid twentieth century were arguably more diverse in social, geographic, and economic
features than those in the early United States. Yet because the institutional structure of the Soviet Union produced severe concentration of political authority, primarily through the mechanism of the Communist
party, this regional diversity had little to no impact on Soviet foreign policy.[86] For a democratic example, consider India. India has one of the most
diverse populations of any state, and it also has a federal system composed of states with representation in one chamber of the legislature.
India, however, combines these federative characteristics with a Westminster parliamentary structure used to organize the more powerful
lower house, elect the executive, and produce strong cabinet government. These institutional features serve to centralize decision-making in
the Indian system in a way that would not have been tolerated in the
early United States. Moreover, the Congress party, under the founding
leadership of Nehru, worked assiduously to prevent a splintering of the
Indian party system along territorial lines, and for decades was hege-
monic in Indian politics. Nehru believed that a party of unity was essential to subordinate territorial diversity to a national "consensus culture"
and maintain political stability. The combination of Westminster institutions and a dominant party minimized the role of diverse geographically
distributed groups in Indian politics.[87] The institutional structure of the
U.S. government, in contrast, offered multiple points of access for competing regional interests to impact policymaking directly.

Will National Political Parties Centralize Decision-Making in the American Union?

To this point the discussion has focused on the formal institutional features of U.S. federalism and the social, economic, geographic, and political divisions that characterized the Union. Left unmentioned, however,
is another key institutional feature of democratic politics—political

---

[86] Robert V. Daniels, *The Stalin Revolution: Foundations of Soviet Totalitarianism* (Lexington, Mass.: D. C. Heath, 1972).

[87] Nirmal Mukarji and Balveer Arora, eds., *Federalism in India: Origins and Development*
(New Delhi: Vikas Publishing House, 1992); Douglas V. Verney and Francine R. Frankel,
"India: Has the Trend Towards Federalism Implications for the Management of Foreign
Policy? A Comparative Perspective," *International Journal* (summer 1986), 572–99; Joyot-
paul Chaudhuri, "Federalism and the Siamese Twins: Diversity and Entropy in India's
Domestic and Foreign Policy," *International Journal* (summer 1993), 448–69.

parties. Surprisingly, political parties have been virtually ignored in the democratic peace literature, even though parties can have a decisive centralizing effect on decision-making that may override the formal institutional divisions of a particular democratic system.[88] Duchacek notes that political parties are the "great centralizers or decentralizers of a federal system."[89] No matter how many institutional divisions are built into a particular democratic system, unified political parties may render these divisions nearly meaningless. Conversely, "the existence of a noncentralized party system is perhaps the most important single element in the maintenance of federal noncentralization."[90] In other words, instead of bridging institutional divisions, the party system can reinforce them.

At the most basic level, parties are simply an "organized attempt to get power."[91] To do this, parties must "aggregate" the various political interests or demands of the electorate into a coherent political program that is then presented during competitive multiparty elections. "Interest aggregation" within a diverse social system is the first major function of political parties.[92] According to Lipset and Rokkan, "No party can hope to gain decisive influence on the affairs of a community without some willingness to cut across existing [social] cleavages to establish common fronts with potential . . . opponents" and thus compete successfully for national-level offices.[93] In order to maintain party unity, particularistic regional interests, like other potentially conflicting interests within the party, must be subsumed in favor of a broader agenda on which all members can agree. Any national-level political party in a plural society will have to manage internal tension among the competing interests and loyalties of its members. Party unity clearly is not a given, it varies among different political systems and over time in individual democracies. Just as unified political parties can bridge institutional divisions, reduce the impediments to consensus and ease the constraints on executive action, weak and divided political parties often lack the internal co-

[88] One exception is John C. Matthews III, "Turkish and Hungarian Foreign Policy During the Interwar Period: Domestic Institutions and the Democratic Peace," in *Paths to Peace Is Democracy the Answer?* ed. Miriam Fendius Elman (Cambridge: MIT Press, 1997), 439–71.

[80] Duchacek, *Comparative Federalism*, 329.

[90] Elazar, *Exploring Federalism*, 178.

[91] E. E. Schattschneider, *Party Government* (New York: Holt, Rinehart, and Winston, 1942), 35.

[92] Klaus von Beymer, *Political Parties in Western Democracies* (Aldershot: Goweri, 1985), 11–12; Giovanni Sartori, *Parties and Party Systems: A Framework for Analysis* (Cambridge: Cambridge University Press, 1976), 27.

[93] Seymour Lipset and Stein Rokkan, eds., *Party Systems and Voter Alignments: Cross-National Perspectives* (New York: The Free Press, 1967), 5.

herence to perform this function. Under these conditions institutional divisions are more salient as a source of constraints on decision-making. The question for this book is whether the political party system in the United States, particularly during the early decades of the republic, could serve as a strong centralizing element of U.S. politics that would bridge federal divisions and minimize the impact of a federally divided presidential electoral system.

Despite principled opposition to parties at the founding,[94] political leaders like Madison himself faced the practical problem of integrating and organizing supporters on a national scale to compete for national offices, to win elections, and to build winning coalitions in Congress on a range of policy issues.[95] In other words, political parties were formed in the United States for the very purpose of bridging the institutional divisions created by the U.S. Constitution. The big prize in the U.S. system, of course, was the presidency. Competition for this single executive position forced political leaders to organize on a national level. This not only strengthened the role of the two main parties in this period, it was a potent incentive for the parties to avoid issues that would undermine their cohesiveness. In the United States of the early nineteenth century, important socioeconomic and ideological cleavages cut across territorial lines, which provided a relatively stable basis for the creation of two rival parties that could legitimately claim a national constituency. While each party had its core strength in a particular region,[96] the basic socioeconomic and ideological perspectives that distinguished the Federalist party from the Republicans, then the Whigs from the Democrats, were not manifested exclusively by region but found enough adherents across the country to produce party representation that was relatively well balanced in all regions.[97]

Despite the practical incentives for the creation of political parties, in the U.S. federal system these parties could never escape the logic of Madisonian institutions and the social pluralism of the compound republic. These institutions, as Katz observes, are "hostile to cohesive

---

[94] Sartori, *Parties and Party Systems*, 1, 11.

[95] Gerald M. Pomper, "The Place of American Political Parties," in *A Republic of Parties? Debating the Two-Party System*, ed. Theodore J. Lowi and Joseph Romance (New York: Rowan and Littlefield, 1998), xii.

[96] Key, *Politics, Parties, and Pressure Groups*, 248.

[97] Keith Polakoff, *Political Parties in American History* (New York: John Wiley and Sons, 1981); John Gerring, *Party Ideologies in America, 1828–1996* (Cambridge: Cambridge University Press, 1998), 10–12.

parties."[98] In the United States the federal structure of the electoral system produces a federally organized political party system. Trubowitz argues that "the spatially decentralized structure of political representation in the United States heightens the role of territoriality in national politics by forcing politicians to organize on a geographic basis to compete for political power at the national level."[99] The two parties that dominate the national political scene are most accurately characterized as "federations" or "coalitions" of state-based party organizations.[100] According to Key,

> In a sense there are no national parties. There are only state parties which collaborate in presidential campaigns and elections but maintain an autonomous existence in the affairs of their respective states. Parties owe their legal existence to state legislation. . . . The national superstructure over the state party organizations. . . derives its power from their consent. State parties are building blocks in the formation of national party machinery.[101]

As a result, while most legislators throughout U.S. history have been elected as members of one of two main parties, the national party does not control their electoral fortunes as parties would in many unitary democratic states.[102] The U.S. electoral system establishes a political base of support for each legislator that is autonomous from a national party organization, so individual representatives can support local interests without fear of national party retribution. Moreover, political parties cannot escape what Key has called "electoral differentiation." This is a condition in which the "campaign emphases" that mobilize the electorate in one region are not the same campaign themes that mo-

[98] R. S. Katz, "The United States: Divided Government and Divided Parties," in *Party and Government: An Inquiry into the Relationship Between Governments and Supporting Parties in Liberal Democracies*, ed. Jean Blondel and Maurizio Cotta (New York: St. Martin's Press, 1996), 202.

[99] Peter Trubowitz, "Sectionalism and American Foreign Policy: The Political Geography of Consensus and Conflict," *International Studies Quarterly* 36 (1992), 176.

[100] Carl J. Friedrich, *Trends of Federalism in Theory and Practice* (New York: Frederick A. Praeger, 1968), 47; Elazar, *Exploring Federalism*, 179; Truman, "Federalism and the Party System"; Maurice Duverger, *Political Parties: Their Organization and Activity in the Modern State*, trans. Barbara and Robert North (New York: John Wiley and Sons, 1963).

[101] Key, *Politics, Parties, and Pressure Groups*, 305–6.

[102] In some electoral systems, individual office holders rely on national-level party organizations just to stand for election, so they must remain loyal to the party for their future political success. Pippa Norris, ed., "Introduction: Theories of Recruitment," in *Passages to Power: Legislative Recruitment in Advanced Democracies* (Cambridge: Cambridge University Press, 1997), 2–4; Katz, "The United States," 202.

bilize electorates in other regions. Individual members of a political
party must be most concerned with what mobilizes their own local
constituents, even if this contradicts the national-level orientation of
their party. This weakens the ability of national-level party leaders to
sustain the loyalty of members elected at the state level and to maintain
the coherence of a national-level political program.[103] As a result, even
if the same party takes control of the executive branch and Congress,
individual members may still divide on key issues if their territorial
communities differ from other territorial communities on these issues.
"Without intense party loyalties, regional and state-based issues can be
given priority by members of Congress."[104] Simply put, local considerations and incentives can override party loyalty and eliminate partisanship as a potential source of consensus on using military force.

Asymmetric regional perspectives and interests on particular policy
issues can produce several other effects on political parties. First, party
leadership on a particular issue may come from members representing
states with the greatest perceived stake in that issue, who attempt to
use the party as an institutional device for generating support for their
preferred policies. Second, strong federal asymmetry on a particular
issue creates an incentive for members of both major parties in each region to form an intraregional, cross-party coalition to support policy
choices that best serve the interests of their regional constituents. Because legislators have an autonomous political base in this federal system, they can easily form coalitions that may change from issue to
issue. There are no institutional barriers to keep the policy from being
decided by competition among regional coalitions in which party
membership is virtually meaningless. Third, federal asymmetry on issues that come to dominate national, or at least regional, politics may
alter the relative electoral strength of the main parties. If the parties are
identified with rival positions on an important issue that has asymmetric regional implications, the majority of the electorate in particular regions may come to support that one party that is most closely
identified with the interests of their region. Over several election cy-
cles this may dramatically alter the relative strength of the two parties
in the national legislature, or the strength of the parties in particular
regions. This may ultimately determine whether one party controls

---

[103] Key, *Politics, Parties, and Pressure Groups*, 307–15.

[104] Earl Fry, "The United States of America," in *Federalism and International Relations:
The Role of Subnational Units*, ed. Hans J. Michelmann and Panayotis Soldatos (Oxford:
Clarendon Press, 1990), 289.

the executive and legislature and the possibility for bridging this institutional divide. It may also alter the character and size of the opposition bloc the president might confront on particular policy questions, thus altering the possibility of constraints on the use of military force.

In the U.S. political system we find a complex mix of federal symmetry and asymmetry that affected the ability of political parties to bridge the institutional gap between the executive and legislature, between the House and Senate, and among individual legislators. Overall, the experience of political parties in the United States is riven by perpetual tension between the demands of national-level competition to win elections and to pass legislation, which fosters unity, and internal party pluralism that exerts a centrifugal pull on party cohesiveness.[105] According to James Gimpel, the nineteenth century provides "ample evidence" that "voting allegiances emanated from local orientations rather than from the rhetoric of national political leaders."[106]

Federal Democratic Peace

The preceding discussion points to five basic features of American federal democracy that describe how this distinctive institutional arrangement divides and distributes political power and how the system of electoral accountability and incentives is organized. These features include:

1. A separation of executive and legislative authority.
2. A federal distribution of political power within the legislature.
3. Strong electoral incentives that reward senators and representatives for supporting regional interests.
4. A federally organized electoral system that forces the president to be mindful of regional perspectives on policy questions.
5. A federally organized political party system that lacks the coherence to consistently bridge the institutional divisions between the president and Congress, between the two houses of Congress, and among individual members within Congress

[105] This is in contrast to the experience of many political parties in parliamentary democracies that must remain cohesive to sustain a government in power. Katz, "The United States," 203.

[106] James Gimpel, *National Elections and the Autonomy of American State Party Systems* (Pittsburgh: University of Pittsburgh Press, 1996), 4.

Together, these features provide the institutional mechanisms that facilitate political competition over policy decisions, circumscribe the ability of political leaders to make policy decisions unfettered by domestic opposition, and accentuate the electoral impact of geographically defined constituencies. The likelihood of actual competition over questions of war and peace will increase as federal asymmetry on particular issues increases.[107] No single perspective on the use of military force, whether realist, normative, commercial, or political, must be dominant in the state to produce constraints on state violence. In fact, it is the proliferation of different perspectives on military force that increases the likelihood of constraints on decision-making that push toward peace. In other words, asymmetry in the social, economic, geographic, or political characteristics of territorial communities produces divergent regional perspectives on how the state's interests are defined, how the relative distribution of power is calculated in conflict situations, how the costs and benefits of using military force are calculated for particular conflicts, and on the normative implications of using force against particular states. Strong federal asymmetry on particular policy questions decreases the likelihood that political consensus will emerge within Congress in support of crisis escalation, the mobilization or deployment of military forces, actual armed conflict, or to sanction particular gains that can be made through the use of force. The politics of federalism may push toward peace not because of any general, nationwide reluctance to use violence in foreign policy; neither generalized normative proscriptions on using force nor Kantian assumptions that the citizens' natural interests are best served by avoiding the costs and miseries of war are necessary to explain the monadic effects of federalism. Federalism will push most vigorously toward peace when domestic perspectives on the use of military force are most divergent, when these views are concentrated in particular

[107] This is not to imply that territorial interests are not influential in more centralized democracies. However, we would expect diverse territorial interests to have a greater and more consistent role in the politics of a federal democracy because the institutional arrangement of federalism provides a direct conduit into national decision-making and executive elections. For a general discussion of how the nature of different issues will affect the degree to which they become contentious in domestic politics, see Bayless Manning, "The Congress, the Executive, and Intermestic Affairs: Three Proposals," *Foreign Affairs* 55 (1977), 306–24.

geographic regions, and when elected officials are most sensitive to the demands and interests of their territorial constituents and less sensitive to a national-level orientation.

In concrete terms, Congress may play a constraining role in several ways (see Table 2.1 for a summary). Congress may actively vote down requests for legislation that would authorize or support crisis escalation or the mobilization or use of military force. Congressional constraints may also come in the form of the Senate rejecting a treaty negotiated by the president that sanctions the use of force under certain conditions or that sanctions certain gains that were made through the use of force. Congress may also vote to deny the president the financial resources necessary to pursue foreign policy initiatives that might include, or might lead to, military conflict. Congress may actually ignore requests from the president, members of the legislature, or individual states, to authorize certain foreign policy initiatives. Without taking a vote, the absence of congressional approval for a specific initiative might be sufficient to prevent it.

Federal asymmetry will also increase the likelihood of presidential self-restraint (see Table 2.1). First, the president may choose to avoid the use of force if he anticipates that Congress will withhold its approval for his preferred policy options. Second, the president may avoid the use of force or the pursuit of certain objectives if he believes that opposition to these policies within certain regions of the federal republic will produce electoral penalties that undermine his ability to attract a winning electoral coalition from across the national political

TABLE 2.1
Typology of Institutional Constraints on the Use of Military Force

Imposed by Congress	Presidential Self-Restraint
1) Rejects crisis escalation, mobilization, or deployment of forces; use of force, declaration of war; or territorial acquisition through force	1) Anticipates absence of congressional approval
2) Denies financial appropriation to support use of military force	2) Anticipates electoral penalties: a. Personal b. Political party
3) Ignores/takes no action on request for congressional authorization to use military force	3) To avoid fracturing and damaging political party solidarity

system.[108] The president might exercise self-restraint even if the expected electoral penalties would undermine his political party, and not necessarily his own tenure in office. The president might choose to avoid the kinds of issues or actions that would penalize loyal members of his party in particular regions and thus undermine the party's aggregate national strength. Finally, the president might exercise self-restraint to avoid splitting the party along territorial lines. The president has a strong interest in party unity, which will have a direct impact on his ability to influence legislative outcomes. Yet the latent internal party tension caused by federal asymmetry on particular issues may come to the surface if the president initiates policies that party members from particular regions find objectionable. To avoid the repercussions of dividing the party this way, the president might choose to avoid the types of policies that would have this effect.[109]

Federal Democracy and the Empirical Record

The specific objective of the remainder of this book is to evaluate whether the logic of federal democratic peace provides a convincing explanation of U.S. behavior in conflict situations. Much of the institutional logic discussed above comes directly from *The Federalist Papers*. It is important to note, however, that the *Federalist* is simply a theoretical treatment of federal union and foreign policy; because the United States was the first modern federation there was little the *Federalist*

---

[108] Much of the "electoral accountability" literature assumes that executives will be punished for foreign policy failures. For example, see Dan Reiter and Allan C. Stam, *Democracies at War* (Princeton: Princeton University Press, 2002), 6, 12, 19–20, 145; Rousseau et al., "Assessing the Dyadic Nature of the Democratic Peace." Yet in the American system, a president may be punished by regions that strongly oppose his policy whether he fails or succeeds. Even if the president expects the use of force to be successful in a particular conflict, certain regions may oppose the use of force whatever the outcome. As a result, the president has an incentive to avoid antagonizing important regions with his foreign policy if the policy itself has the potential to cripple his personal or party's electoral prospects.

[109] Despite the stability of the national two-party system for much of the early nineteenth century, political questions that involved territorial expansion and the use of military force were the kinds of questions that most frequently generated asymmetric perspectives among the various regions of the United States. Thomas B. Alexander, *Sectional Stress and Party Strength: A Study of Roll-Call Voting Patterns in the United States House of Representatives, 1836–1860* (Nashville, Tenn.: Vanderbilt University Press, 1967); Joel H. Silbey, *The Shrine of Party: Congressional Voting Behavior, 1841–1852* (Pittsburgh, Pa.: University of Pittsburgh Press, 1967).

could say about the actual practice of federal government. The American founders did not have an empirical record to examine in order to evaluate how closely the actual behavior of federal states matched their theoretical expectations. This is a task we can now assume with the passage of time: how well does the actual behavior of the United States conform to the theoretical expectations found in *The Federalist Papers*? Does the historical record support the Framers' contention that federal institutions and federal asymmetry tend to restrain the aggressive impulses of regional actors against external adversaries? What does history say about the ability of the president or legislators to mobilize political and material resources in an asymmetric federal system in order to use force in foreign policy? How did federal institutions and political parties interact? Did this system constrain the ability of the United States to respond to external threats with force or pursue territorial expansion through military initiatives?

Chapters 3 through 6 examine four different periods in the first sixty years of the nineteenth century. This time frame obviously includes the War of 1812 and the Mexican-American War. The very fact that the United States *initiated* armed conflict in each case demonstrates that federalism did not paralyze America's ability to mobilize the political resources necessary to fight. This time frame also includes the Monroe Doctrine of 1823, in which the United States declared that it would oppose, with military force if necessary, any effort by European states to impose a balance of power system in the Western Hemisphere.[110] While these are clearly major events in early U.S. foreign policy, they by no means provide a complete picture of the United States and international conflict. The following chapters isolate fourteen separate cases between 1807 and 1860 in which the United States was either: (1) engaged in an international dispute that could have, or did, end in armed conflict; or (2) faced an external threat or opportunity that generated domestic debate over whether, and to what extent, armed force should be used in response. Overall, this case set, which includes all of the significant disputes that may have involved the

---

[110] While a signal event in U.S. foreign policy, in practical terms the Monroe Doctrine played a small role in U.S. foreign policy in the nineteenth century. After this doctrine was proclaimed, it did not appear in U.S. foreign policy again for over twenty years. In 1844 it was used to justify vigorous American diplomatic and military action to block British efforts to convince the Republic of Texas to reject annexation to the United States. David M. Pletcher, *The Diplomacy of Annexation: Texas, Oregon, and the Mexican War* (Columbia: University of Missouri Press, 1973).

TABLE 2.2
Crisis Outcome and Institutional Explanations

Crisis	Outcome	Type of Institutional Constraint
1807 Chesapeake Crisis	C	Presidential (1, 3)
1809 Anglo-U.S. War Crisis	C	Congressional (1)
1812 Anglo-U.S. War Crisis	NC	
1812–1815 Invasion of Canada	C	Congressional (1, 2)
1811–1813 Occupation of East Florida	C	Congressional (1)
1845–1846 Anglo-U.S. Oregon Crisis	C	Congressional (1)
1845–1846 Deployment of Troops to Rio Grande	NC	
1846 Mexican War Crisis	NC	
1848 Annexation of "All Mexico"	C	Congressional (1)/ Presidential (1, 2b, 3)
1853 Mesilla Valley Crisis	C	Presidential (1, 2a, 2b, 3)
1853–1855 Cuba Crisis	C	Presidential (1, 3)
1859 Mexican Protectorate Request by President	C	Congressional (1)
1859 Intervention in Mexican Civil War	C	Congressional (3)
1860 Mexican Protectorate Treaty	C	Congressional (1)

Total: 14 Cases: 11 Constraints, 3 No Constraints
C = Constraint on use of military force or gains from force
NC = No constraint on use of military force or gains from force

United States in interstate armed conflict between 1800 and 1860, presents a clear pattern of constraints on the use of military force by the United States. The United States demonstrated restraint in eleven of the fourteen cases. Table 2.2 lists these cases in chronological order (the numbers in parentheses correspond to the type of institutional constraint listed in table 2.1).

The dependent variable in these cases, generally referred to so far as "constraints on the use of force," must be specified with greater precision. The prevailing method of defining the dependent variable in the democratic peace literature is simply in terms of war versus no war as an outcome of an international dispute.[111] Among the cases in this book, U.S. decision-makers made a purposeful decision *not to initiate war* against an adversary in five crises: against Great Britain in 1807 and 1809, against Great Britain during the Oregon Crisis of 1846, against Mexico during the Mesilla Valley crisis of 1853, and against Spain during the Cuba crisis of 1853–1855. The avoidance of war, how-

---

[111] For a discussion of the common definition of war in the democratic peace literature, see Russett, *Grasping the Democratic Peace*, 12–14.

ever, is not the only way to measure the constraining effects of democratic institutions. As Chan and Rousseau et. al. remind us, war is only one form of state violence, and political institutions may affect aggressive state behavior in important ways that will not be captured if we examine the war/no war dichotomy alone.[112] In this book, constraints on the use of force will include two other categories. The first category includes cases in which the United States chose *not to intervene militarily in a civil conflict* within a neighboring state. On three separate occasions between 1858 and 1860, President Buchanan requested authority to use military force in Mexico to either protect Americans along the border or within Mexico itself, or to determine the outcome of the Mexican civil war. The effort to use military force in each case was not an attempt to initiate a war against Mexico, but a more limited use of force to control the effects of political upheaval in a neighboring state. The final dependent variable category includes examples of constraint in cases in which some degree of military force had already been initiated. The constraint involves *limits on territorial expansion made possible by the use of force*. We find this type of constraint in three more cases: (1) the failure of U.S. efforts to seize and possibly annex British North America, at least Upper Canada, during the War of 1812; (2) the restriction of U.S. efforts to seize Spain's colony of East Florida in 1811–1813; and (3) the failure to annex "All Mexico" following the Mexican-American War in 1848. These types of cases would not ordinarily be included in any analysis of democratic peace, simply because military force had been used to some degree. Yet they are all puzzling because of the failure of the United States to realize its immense potential for territorial expansion in each case, despite its military advantages relative to its adversaries and prominent domestic political actors who championed these expansionist goals. Table 2.3 lists the cases according to the three dependent variable categories used in this book that match the circumstances of the cases being examined.

The claim that each of the cases described above is an example of constraints on the use of military force by the United States should be noncontroversial. The most important question, however, is how can we explain this pattern of constraints? Given the time period of these cases, it is important to consider whether domestic restraints on using

---

[112] Steve Chan, "Democracy and War: Some Thoughts on Future Research Agenda," *International Interactions* 18 (1993), 207; Rousseau et al., "Assessing the Dyadic Nature of the Democratic Peace."

TABLE 2.3
Constraints on the Use of Military Force by Dependent Variable.

War Avoidance	Limits on Territorial Expansion	No Military Intervention in Mexico
War Crisis of 1807 (Britain)	Upper Canada (1812–1814)	Protectorate Request (1858)
War Crisis of 1809 (Britain)	East Florida (1811–1813)	Military Intervention
Oregon Crisis (Britain)	All Mexico (1848)	Request (1859)
Mesilla Valley Crisis		Mexican Protectorate
(Mexico)		Treaty (1860)
Cuba Crisis (Spain)		

military force were merely a product of sectional tensions between the North and South rooted in differences over slavery and fears about provoking civil war rather than the result of the broader effects of federal union. Several key features of U.S. politics in this time period demonstrate that this pattern in U.S. behavior cannot be explained by merely referring to the domestic divisions that eventually produced the Civil War. First, regional divisions within the United States before the early 1850s were not simply along North-South lines. Frederick Jackson Turner was the first to point out that the most persistent geographic divisions in U.S. politics were defined by the states of the Northeast, the Old Northwest, and the South.[113] Even the South divided occasionally between the Atlantic states and the interior southern states in a way that had a serious impact on congressional alignments over a range of foreign policy problems. Among the cases examined in this book, slavery does not appear as a defining regional issue until the debate over expansion at the end of the Mexican War in 1848. Before this crisis, other regional differences rooted in economic structure, political culture, geography, and proximity or relative vulnerability to external threats were at work producing the differences over policy that had a direct impact on using force. This is true of the crises with Great Britain in 1807, 1809, and 1812; with Spain in 1811–1813; and with Britain over the Oregon territory in 1846. The continuity of regional competition over foreign policy

[113] Frederick Jackson Turner, *The Significance of Sections in American History* (New York: Henry Holt, 1932).

within the federally organized U.S. system, and the constraining effects it produced, holds both before and after the Mexican War and shows that this pattern in U.S. behavior is not simply the result of slavery or North-South antagonism. Even in the 1850s we find lingering support in the Old Northwest for southward territorial expansion, so the coalitions for and against expansion into Cuba and Mexico in this period did not reflect a pure North-South split. Additionally, the political strife over expansion into Mexican territory in the late 1840s included a split within the South itself over whether Mexico was actually suited for slave-based agriculture. A number of the political leaders of Atlantic slave states opposed extensive expansion because they believed it would inevitably produce free states, and they used their institutional positions within Congress to join the effort to limit U.S. gains here, in opposition to leaders of interior southern states who worked to maximize U.S. gains. These points will be developed in more detail in later chapters.

Chapters 3 through 6 examine both realist and federal democratic peace propositions to determine which approach offers a better explanation for U.S. behavior in each case. To evaluate realist propositions it is necessary to determine the degree to which decision-making was dominated by key political actors who converged on a common conception of the interests at stake, the relative distribution of power between the United States and its potential adversaries, and the expected costs and benefits of using military force. Realist explanations will be most convincing if there is evidence to suggest that U.S. political leaders avoided the use of military force, or limited the territorial gains made by the use of force, because of pessimistic strategic calculations about the ability of the United States to achieve its objectives at an acceptable cost.[114] Federal democratic peace explanations will be most convincing if the evidence shows that regional opinion was decisively split on the issues at stake in the crisis, on the assessment of the relative distribution of power between the United States and its potential adversaries, on the expected costs and benefits of using military force, or on the normative implications of using force in that particular dis-

[114] For examples of this realist approach in the democratic peace literature, see Christopher Layne, "Kant or Cant: the Myth of the Democratic Peace," *International Security* 19 (fall 1994), 5–49; and Stephen R. Rock, "Anglo-U.S. Relations, 1845–1930: Did Shared Liberal Values and Democratic Institutions Keep the Peace?" in *Paths to Peace.*

pute. A federal democratic peace explanation must show one of two things: (1) that federal asymmetry on these elements of the crisis is reflected in Congress and acts as an impediment to a winning coalition in favor of using military force; or (2) the president calculates a higher likelihood of future electoral penalties imposed in certain regions or dangerous intraparty tensions should the United States use military force, and avoids military force because of these political calculations. The next chapter begins this empirical analysis with the confrontation between the United States and Britain and Spain in the first two decades of the nineteenth century.

3

THE UNITED STATES CONFRONTS GREAT BRITAIN AND SPAIN, 1807–1815

We begin our empirical analysis of American federal union and conflict decision-making by focusing on the years 1807 to 1815, a period when the international context for U.S. foreign relations was most profoundly shaped by the epic struggle between Great Britain and Napoleonic France. The United States was drawn into this roiling conflict most directly in 1812 with its declaration of war on Great Britain. The importance of the War of 1812 for the study of U.S. conflict decision-making is clear: not only was it the first time the United States formally declared war against a foreign adversary, it is one of just a handful of cases throughout its history in which the United States actually declared war before engaging in armed conflict.[1] The apparent

---

[1] Realist critics of the democratic peace argue that the War of 1812 is an example of armed conflict between two democracies and therefore must be regarded as a disconfirming case for dyadic democratic peace theory. Kenneth N. Waltz, "The Emerging Structure of International Politics," *International Security* 18 (fall 1993), 78. Democratic peace theorists brush off this challenge by rightly pointing out that Great Britain cannot be considered a democracy until after the Reform Act of 1832 expanded the franchise. John M. Owen IV, *Liberal Peace, Liberal War: American Politics and International Security* (Ithaca: Cornell University Press, 1997); Spencer R. Weart, *Never at War: Why Democracies Will Not Fight One Another* (New Haven: Yale University Press, 1998), 186; Bruce Russett, *Grasping the Democratic Peace: Principles for a Post-Cold War World* (Princeton: Princeton University Press, 1993), 16; James Lee Ray, *Democracy and International Conflict: An Evaluation of the Democratic Peace Proposition* (Columbia: University of South Carolina Press, 1995), 106–7.

absence of domestic constraints in this case, and its implications for the logic of federal democratic peace, is an important subject for this chapter. Just as important, however, is that this event does not exhaust the discrete cases in which the United States faced a similar decision over the use of force to confront British pressure. In the *Chesapeake* crisis of 1807 and the war crisis of 1809 U.S. leaders openly considered a military challenge to Britain under conditions that made war seem even more necessary or likely than it was in 1812. Each crisis passed, however, as the United States backed away from the use of force. Here we have two cases that have been completely ignored by other students of American democracy and conflict decision-making in which the United States was constrained by the domestic political impact of federal union. This chapter also shows how the federal structure of the U.S. system and regional differences over the question of war imposed a severe challenge to advocates of war in 1812 and very nearly impeded a declaration of war in this case too. Moving beyond the decision for war in 1812, this chapter investigates whether the domestic politics of federal union affected the ability of the United States to achieve particular war aims through the use of force. Specifically, can the logic of federal democratic peace account for the failure of the United States to secure territorial expansion in Upper and Lower Canada? Finally, this chapter examines another case involving a decision over the use of force that has been ignored in the literature on democracy and U.S. conflict behavior: President Madison's efforts between 1811 and 1813 to conquer Spanish East Florida with military force. Despite the strategic reasons advanced for annexing East Florida and the superiority of U.S. forces deployed to seize it from a small Spanish garrison in the colonial capital, President Madison withdrew this force before his expansionist goals were achieved. Like the constraints involved in the earlier crises of 1807 and 1809, it is impossible to explain constraints on U.S. military force in the Canada and East Florida cases without the logic of federal democratic peace.

To War? Federal Politics and Confrontation with Great Britain

In the first decades of the American federal republic, no single external factor had more influence on foreign and domestic affairs than the French Revolution and the European wars that followed. The military conflict between France and Great Britain, which began in 1793 and was fought almost continuously for twenty-two years, quickly came to impinge on U.S. interests in a way that eventually led to war with Great Britain. During the entire period of the Napoleonic Wars the United States dominated the neutral shipping trade. In fact, the conflict produced a boom in the shipping industry as U.S. merchants gained access to markets in Britain and on the Continent that were normally closed, while scarcity allowed neutral traders to charge exorbitant prices for their products.[2] During the first decade of the nineteenth century, however, both Britain and France imposed increasingly strict measures to prevent neutral trade from reaching the other's ports.[3] As a result, between 1803 and 1812 the British captured 917 American ships attempting to trade with areas under Napoleon's control.[4] To help make up for a huge shortfall in manpower the Royal Navy routinely stopped U.S. ships to search for and seize deserters, and often ended up taking away U.S. sailors by mistake or by design. From 1801 to 1812 between six thousand and ten thousand Americans were forcibly impressed into service with the British Navy.[5] These insults to U.S. maritime interests finally ended on June 16, 1812, when British foreign minister Lord Castlereagh announced that the Orders in Council authorizing these seizures would be suspended. Unfortunately, news of this dramatic policy change did not reach Washington in time to prevent a congressional declaration of war just two days later.

The rich historical literature on the War of 1812 has, understandably, focused mainly on the various purported causes of this conflict. The arguments that have formed the core of this debate range from the need of the United States to defend its national honor and sovereignty from the bullying maritime policies of England to economic depression or the hunger of western settlers for the rich agricultural lands of

[2] Thomas A. Bailey, *A Diplomatic History of the American People* (Englewood Cliffs: Prentice-Hall, 1980), 116, 126.

[3] Daniel Lang, *Foreign Policy in the Early Republic: The Law of Nations and the Balance of Power* (Baton Rouge: Louisiana State University, 1985); Peter Onuf and Nicholas Onuf, *Federal Union, Modern World: The Law of Nations in an Age of Revolutions, 1776–1814* (Madison, Wis.: Madison House, 1993); Alexander DeConde, *The Quasi-War: The Politics and Diplomacy of the Undeclared War with France, 1797–1801* (New York: Charles Scribner, 1966), 9; A. L. Burt, "The Nature of the Maritime Issues," in *The Causes of the War of 1812: National Honor or National Interest?* ed. Bradford Perkins (New York: Holt, Rinehart, and Winston, 1962), 18–21.

[4] Bradford Perkins, *Prologue to War: England and the United States, 1805–1812* (Berkeley: University of California Press, 1961), 72.

[5] James F. Zimmerman, *Impressment of American Seamen* (New York, 1925), 259–75. According to Lord Nelson, the British navy lost forty-two thousand sailors to desertion in just the first eight years of the revolutionary wars. Bailey, *Diplomatic History,* 120.

Upper Canada. Yet often overlooked in the historical debate over war in 1812 is a related puzzle that is most relevant to this book on the relationship between federal union and U.S. conflict behavior. In Bradford Perkins's words, "Why did America *not go to war* earlier than they did?"[6] Reginald Horsman notes that it is "easier to show why America *should have* gone to war in 1807 or 1809 rather than in 1812."[7] British maritime policy in 1807 and 1808, particularly the impressment of U.S. sailors, was a much greater burden on the United States than it was in 1812. The unprovoked attack on the U.S. frigate *Chesapeake* in June 1807 was a much more compelling affront to national honor than anything that occurred in 1812. The main question then is why did the United States not go to war with Great Britain in the crises of 1807 and 1809, yet it did declare war in 1812? The explanation suggested by realist theory is that the different outcomes of these crises should be linked to changes in the relative distribution of military capabilities between the United States and Great Britain. In other words, the United States might have been in a better relative military position to defend itself and advance its interests through military force in the latter crisis than it was in the previous years. In 1807 and 1809 U.S. decision-makers may have calculated that Britain had the capability to inflict severe costs—a devastating blow to the U.S. merchant fleet, attacks on coastal cities, an invasion of U.S. territory, or perhaps even the total defeat of the United States and its resubjugation as part of the British Empire—if the U.S. chose forceful means to address its grievances. In 1812 the United States was obviously not deterred by such calculations. The realist explanation might be that Great Britain's ability to inflict this punishment on the United States had changed for some reason. Perhaps in 1812 Britain's struggle with Napoleon had intensified to the point that its ability to project power against the United States was significantly diminished compared to 1807 and 1809. Perhaps the United States had improved its naval or land forces to the point that U.S. decision-makers were confident they could now defend the country more effectively than before.

Changes in the relative power of the United States and Great Britain do not explain these outcomes, however. The United States was no better prepared to defend itself or inflict a blow against British power

---

[6] Perkins, *Causes of the War of 1812*, 2; emphasis added.
[7] Reginald Horsman, *The Causes of the War of 1812* (Philadelphia: University of Pennsylvania Press, 1962), 14; emphasis added.

in 1812 than it was in 1807 or 1809.[8] Nor had Britain's level of commitment in Europe intensified by 1812 to reduce its ability to project
power in North America. In 1806 and 1807, Britain's continental allies
were suffering successive defeats by Napoleon, who was stronger
than ever before on the Continent. Napoleon had defeated the combined armies of Austria and Russia at Austerlitz and the Prussian
army at Jena in 1806, and the Russian army again at Friedland in 1807.
With the Treaty of Tilset in November 1807, Napoleon brought Russia
into his Continental System. In 1807 and 1809, Britain was alone in the
struggle against France.[9] In 1812, Napoleon was on the move again, invading Russia itself. As in previous years, Britain was not in a position
to deploy a large number of naval or land forces away from Europe,
against the United States. Through the entire period of 1807 to 1812,
Britain's military commitment to Europe did not change. Another realist explanation might be that the level of pain inflicted on the United
States by Britain's maritime policy had reached an intolerable point.
Even though the United States was no better prepared to use military
force in 1812, the rising costs to U.S. interests may have justified the
risks of going to war. Yet this explanation also fails to account for
the different outcomes in these cases. The number of ship seizures and
the impressment of U.S. sailors, the reasons cited by U.S. decision-
makers for going to war, had actually been declining between 1807
and 1812. In the spring of 1812, the British Admiralty ordered its ships
to avoid any clash with the U.S. navy and to keep away from the U.S.
coast. Therefore, the burden imposed on the United States by Great
Britain was much less in 1812 than in 1807 or 1809.[10] If there was no
change in U.S. military capabilities relative to Great Britain between
1807 and 1812, nor an increase in the costs imposed by foreign pressure on U.S. maritime interests, external factors cannot explain the differences between these cases.

Alternatively, the explanation for the different outcomes in these
crises may be traced to domestic factors. According to the model of
federal constraints described in chapter 2, we must examine several
questions linking the U.S. political system with the crises themselves.

    [8] J. C. A. Stagg, *Mr. Madison's War: Politics, Diplomacy, and Warfare in the Early Ameri-
can Republic, 1783–1830* (Princeton: Princeton University Press, 1983), 3.
    [9] Curtis Cate, *The War of the Two Emperors: The Duel Between Napoleon and Alexander*
(New York: Random House, 1985); H. Ragsdale, *Detente in the Napoleonic Era: Bonaparte
and the Russians* (Lawrence: Regents Press of Kansas, 1980).
    [10] Donald R. Hickey, *The War of 1812* (Chicago: University of Illinois Press, 1995), 13.

First, did the question of war with Great Britain in 1807, 1809, and 1812 generate domestic opposition? If so, were the reasons for domestic opposition to war associated with the interests or political orientations of particular regions of the federal union? Second, what was the institutional point of constraint on a decision for war in 1807 and 1809? Was this constraint the result of distinctive features of the federal structure of the U.S. government? Third, what role did Republican party dominance of the national government play in decision-making in each crisis? Did federal asymmetry on the question of war divide the party into rival regional blocs in 1807 and 1809? Did Republican party unity bridge the institutional divisions in this system to provide a majority vote for war in 1812 that was missing in the earlier crises?

The Crises of 1807 and 1809: War Fever, But No War

In the summer of 1807, the United States and Great Britain were on the brink of war following a British attack on the USS *Chesapeake*. This was the most egregious case of British interference with U.S. maritime rights throughout the Napoleonic wars, and it was a dramatic symbol of the increasing number of sailors from U.S. ships who were being forcibly impressed into service with the Royal Navy. The crisis had its origins in the desertion of four sailors from a British warship during a port visit to Norfolk, Virginia, in February of that year. These same men enlisted in the U.S. navy and were assigned to serve on the *Chesapeake*. On orders from Vice Admiral Berkeley, commander of British naval forces in North America, to retrieve such deserters, the British frigate *Leopard* hailed the *Chesapeake* just ten miles off Norfolk on June 22. When the captain of the *Chesapeake* refused to allow the *Leopard*'s crew to search for their sailors, the *Leopard* fired three point-blank broadsides into the U.S. ship, killing three and wounding nineteen. The *Chesapeake* was boarded and the British crew retrieved the deserters (three of whom were actually Americans who had enlisted in the Royal Navy).[11] As news of the *Chesapeake* incident spread, popular demand for some form of satisfaction from Great Britain was on the rise, even if this meant war. According to

---

[11] For a detailed account of the incident see Spencer C. Tucker and Frank T. Reuter, *Injured Honor: The Chesapeake-Leopard Affair* (Annapolis, Md.: Naval Institute Press, 1996).

Horsman, "There seems little doubt that Jefferson could have carried America into war in 1807."[12]

Jefferson not only prepared for war through the summer and fall, he repeatedly expressed the belief that war was likely, if not inevitable, as a consequence of the *Leopard*'s attack. In the first week of July the president issued a proclamation ordering all armed British ships out of U.S. waters and denying them the right to resupply in U.S. ports. As British ships blockaded Norfolk, Jefferson notified state governors to be ready to contribute to a national militia force of 100,000, and he ordered gunboats deployed to vulnerable sections of the coast. He sent Secretary of War Henry Dearborn to New York to oversee defense preparations and maintained close contact with Virginia governor William Cabell to coordinate a defense of Norfolk and the Chesapeake Bay approaches.[13] As Jefferson explained to Senator Nicholas of Maryland, "Considering war as one of the alternatives which Congress may adopt on the failure of proper satisfaction for the outrages committed on us by Great Britain, I have thought it my duty to put into train every preparation for that which the executive powers . . . will admit of."[14] In September the president proposed marching a militia force to northern points in preparation for an invasion of Canada, and in return Madison acknowledged the "absolute necessity of a radical cure for the evil inflicted by British ships of war."[15] With adequate defense preparations along the coast, a superior U.S. military force for offensive operations in Canada, and a large privateer maritime force, Jefferson actually believed that America could engage Great Britain in armed conflict at relatively little cost.[16] In a report to Congress in October, Treasury Secretary Albert Gallatin argued that if the United States was to pursue war it should do so now, as it could

[12] Horsman, *Causes of the War of 1812*, 141. See also Perkins, *Prologue to War*, 149.

[13] Thomas Jefferson to William Cabell, July 8, 1807; Jefferson to General John Armstrong, July 17, 1807; Jefferson to Secretary of War Henry Dearborn, July 17, 1807, Jefferson to Secretary of State James Madison, August 9, 1807 in *The Writings of Thomas Jefferson* (Washington, D.C.: The Thomas Jefferson Memorial Association, 1905), 262–63, 283–85, 311–12. See also Henry Adams, *History of the United States During the Administrations of Thomas Jefferson* (New York: Literary Classics of the United States, 1986), 947–49.

[14] Jefferson to John Nicholas, August 18, 1807, *Writings*, 332–33.

[15] Jefferson to James Madison, September 20, 1807; Madison to Jefferson, September 20, 1807, in *The Republic of Letters: The Correspondence Between Thomas Jefferson and James Madison, 1776–1826*, vol. 3, ed. James Morton Smith (New York: W. W. Norton, 1995), 1498–1500.

[16] Henry S. Randall, *The Life of Thomas Jefferson*, vol. 3 (New York: Derby and Jackson, 1858), 226–27.

fund a full year of war without raising taxes or incurring debt.[17] As
the United States waited for the British response to its demands for a
public disavowal of the attack, a recall of Vice Admiral Berkeley, restitution for the ship and its crew, as well as a declaration ending the
impressment policy, President Jefferson professed to many correspon-
dents a belief that war was more likely than peace.[18]

Two characteristics of this case pose a severe challenge to the logic
of federal union as a potential constraint on the ability of the United
States to use military force. First, the attack was such a gross violation
of America's rights and accepted maritime practice that it produced a
rally around the flag effect to an extent rarely seen in U.S. history. According to Henry Adams, "For the first time in their history the people
of the United States learned . . the feeling of a true national emotion."[19] President Jefferson agreed. He wrote, "Never since the battle
of Lexington have I seen this country in such a state of exasperation as
at present, and even that did not produce such unanimity."[20] Britain
has "often enough, God knows, given us cause for war before; but it
has been on points which would not have united the nation. But now
they have touched a cord that vibrates in every heart."[21] At first blush,
regional differences over U.S. foreign policy do not seem relevant as a
possible source of contention and constraint on the use of force should
the president and Congress have decided to pursue this option.

The second challenge to the logic of federal union and constraints is
the political strength of President Jefferson and the Republican party
in this time period. Until 1800 the Federalists were the dominant
party; not only did the Federalists hold the presidency, they also maintained a two-thirds majority in the Senate and by 1798 increased their
majority in the House to hold 64 seats to the Republicans' 42. Thomas
Jefferson's election to the presidency in 1800 brought a rapid and radical shift in the electoral strength of the two parties. In the first two
years of his presidency, Jefferson's popularity soared with the U.S.
public. He saw this as an opportunity to improve the Republicans'

---

[17] Adams, *History of the United States*, 1034.
[18] Jefferson to William Duane, July 20, 1807; Jefferson to Colonel John Taylor, August
1, 1807; Jefferson to Madison, September 1, 1807; Jefferson to Attorney General Robert
Smith, October 8, 1807; Jefferson to James Maury, November 21, 1807, *Writings*, 290–91,
304, 350, 377, 397.
[19] Adams, *History of the United States*, 946–47. Horsman, *Causes of the War of 1812*, 103.
[20] Jefferson to Dupont De Nemours, July 14, 1807; Jefferson to James Bowdoin, July 10,
1807, *Writings*, 274, 269.
[21] Jefferson to William Duane, July 20, 1807, *Writings*, 291.

electoral strength in the Northeast, the region in which Federalists were traditionally dominant and where the Republicans were weakest. In the elections of 1802, his personal popularity and his active party leadership paid off; the Republicans turned their minority status in the House into an overwhelming majority of 102 representatives to the Federalists' 39. In the Senate the Republicans went from holding just one-third of the seats to gaining a majority of 25 to 9. In the elections of 1804 the Republicans won 80 percent of the House seats and 79 percent of the Senate seats. In the Tenth Congress, elected in 1806, Republican senators from the Northeast represented New Hampshire, Vermont, Rhode Island, New York, New Jersey, and Pennsylvania. Republicans won 11 of the 17 House seats from Massachusetts, a bastion of Federalism. The party won 15 of the 17 seats from New York, one half of the seats from Rhode Island and Vermont, 8 of the 11 seats from Pennsylvania, and all the seats from New Hampshire and New Jersey. In the summer of 1807 the Republican party held 82 percent of the seats in both the Senate and the House of Representatives.[22] According to one prominent historian, "In the country and in Congress, not only was Jefferson supreme, but his enemies were prostrate."[23] Should the president's popularity allow him to sustain public support for war across regions, and party unity carry it through Congress, Jefferson's belief in the inevitability of war in 1807 could become reality for the federal union.

Despite the various political forces that seemed ripe for generating a move toward war in 1807, this was not the outcome of the crisis. Instead, Congress passed the Embargo Act in December, decisively backing away from a military response to British pressure. The explanation has two components: a short-term military dimension that made it sensible to wait until fall to initiate hostilities, and a domestic political component that not only delayed firm action until late in the fall of 1807 but ultimately produced a decisive rejection of war as well. For military purposes Jefferson believed that a delay of several months would allow the United States to recover ships and sailors currently abroad, assets that would be essential for outfitting warships and privateers. As he explained to Governor Cabell of Virginia, a delay will "give us time to get in our ships, our property, and our seamen, now

---

[22] Keith Polakoff, *Political Parties in American History* (New York: John Wiley and Sons, 1981), 34–35, 54, 69–73.
[23] Adams, *History of the United States*, 1026–29; for a critique of this view see Dumas Malone, *Jefferson the President* (Boston: Little, Brown, 1974), 472 n. 7.

under the grasp of our adversary; probably not less than 20,000 of the latter are now exposed on the ocean, whose loss would cripple us in the outset more than the loss of several battles."[24] This was a reason for delay in hostilities, not the foreclosure of this option, however.

The domestic political dimensions provide the best explanation for the passing of the crisis without war, and the logic of regional diversity and federal institutions play a crucial role. The first point is that Jefferson was committed to the principle that Congress alone was authorized to declare war, and he stated frequently that he would take no action that would undermine Congress's freedom of choice in the matter.[25] Despite his fealty to the separation of constitutional war powers, Jefferson could have called Congress into early session to deal with the crisis. In fact, several advisors in July urged him to take this very step immediately.[26] Jefferson rejected this advice, opting instead to request Congress reconvene at the end of October, just a few weeks earlier than its planned session. The reason for this decision is impossible to separate from the politics of federal union. In short, the president believed that despite national outrage over the *Chesapeake* attack, regional divisions over *how* to respond demanded that the president pursue a diplomatic path that would take months to resolve, before war was politically viable in Congress.

While Jefferson had successfully marginalized the Federalist party and gathered strong public support since his first election in 1800, by the midpoint of his second term regional disputes and factionalism increasingly fractured the Republican party, which severely undermined his ability to use the party as a vehicle to exercise national leadership. He sustained the loyalty of southern and western states across issues, yet the mid Atlantic and northeastern states were wracked by internal party disputes and regional pressures that undermined the loyalty of members of Congress from these areas.[27] Henry Adams notes that a "strong chasm" had opened between northeastern and southern states over defense issues in 1806: "Whatever the North and East wanted the South and West refused."[28] For example, southern Republicans would

---

[24] Jefferson to William Cabell, July 16, 1807; Jefferson to John Page, July 17, 1807, *Writings*, 281, 287.

[25] Jefferson to Vice President Dallas, July 6, 1807, *Writings*, 258.

[26] Adams, *History of the United States*, 948–49.

[27] Ronald L. Hatzenbuehler and Robert L. Ivie, *Congress Declares War: Rhetoric, Leadership, and Partisanship in the Early Republic* (Kent, Ohio: Kent State University Press, 1983), 82–83.

[28] Adams, *History of the United States*, 844–47.

not vote to fortify New York on the theory that it was better to abandon coastal regions to destruction in case of attack than to defend them.

With this in mind, Jefferson determined that the only way to generate national support for confrontation with Great Britain was to seek restitution through diplomacy first. Only if Britain refused to make amends peacefully, he believed, would there be sufficient support in the Northeast for taking the country to war. As a result, Jefferson sent a message to his envoy in Britain with a set of demands to negotiate. The West remained solidly behind war, yet Treasury Secretary Gallatin reported that the people of New York were not. The British consul general in New York, who watched opinion in the United States closely, reported that the people of New York and New England did not favor war for commercial reasons, yet as one moved southward enthusiasm for armed conflict increased.[29] Opposition to war in the Northeast for commercial reasons may seem odd. New Englanders owned the bulk of the U.S. merchant fleet, which carried U.S. and foreign goods alike.[30] Massachusetts alone accounted for over one-third of the nation's shipping tonnage.[31] This was the very fleet that had been repeatedly plundered by Great Britain over the previous several years. The livelihood of most other New Englanders was tied in some way to U.S. maritime commerce, so it was truly a regional interest. We might expect then that this region would be the most aggressive in response to Britain's maritime policy. Yet the Northeast actually thrived economically because of British restrictions. There was ample opportunity for neutral trade during the Napoleonic Wars and ship owners were willing to tolerate British inspections and licenses for plying certain trade routes. The increased risk that came with British restrictions actually increased the profits that ship owners enjoyed.[32]

The president made this same observation about federal asymmetry on the question of war to the governor of Virginia. Virginia had been most vigorous in its preparations for war since the *Chesapeake*

[29] Horsman, *Causes of the War of 1812*, 105–6, 168.
[30] Ibid., 175.
[31] Donald R. Hickey, *The War of 1812: A Forgotten Conflict* (Urbana: University of Illinois Press, 1989), 230–31.
[32] Samuel Eliot Morison and Henry Steele Commager, *The Growth of the American Republic*, vol. 1 (New York: Oxford University Press, 1962), 394. Despite the Orders in Council, Americans could maintain trading connections with India, the East Indies, South America, and the Mediterranean. Paul A. Varg, *New England and Foreign Relations, 1798–1850* (Hanover: University Press of New England, 1983), 59.

incident, due to the geography of the clash and lingering British threat, and Governor Cabell was anxious to know when the United States was actually going to move toward war. Negotiations, Jefferson explained, were "requisite . . . to produce unanimity among ourselves; for however those *nearest the scenes of aggression* and irritation may have been kindled into a desire for war at short hand, the *more distant parts of the Union* have generally rallied to the point of previous demand of satisfaction" first. They would support war only if satisfaction were denied.[33] A week later he made the point that Congress would only declare war after the United States had given Britain time to make amends peacefully.[34] To Vice President Dallas, Jefferson observed that he would avoid any acts likely to produce war because he anticipated many in Congress would support "non-intercourse over war."[35]

At this stage of the crisis the institutional point of constraint remains with the president, who chose not to call an early session of Congress and advocate war based on anticipated opposition from the Northeast. The effect of this delay was decisive, as Senator Nicholson of Maryland warned: "A parley will prove fatal" to firm action "for the merchants [of the Northeast] will begin to calculate. They rule us, and we should take them [for the cause of war] before their resentment is superceded by considerations of profit and loss."[36] Over time passion for a violent response cooled not only in the Northeast but in most of the country as well. When Congress reconvened in late October it was clear that a declaration of war was impossible to attain, even when news reached the United States that Britain would not meet all its demands.[37] As a compromise measure, Congress approved Jefferson's recommended economic coercion instead by passing the Embargo Act, which prohibited trade with European belligerents.

While the immediacy of the *Chesapeake* crisis faded with time and peace was maintained, by 1809 a movement within the Republican party once again raised the specter of war with Great Britain. This movement occurred at a time when consensus was forming across the country that the Embargo Act of 1807 had failed to alter Britain's mar-

---

[33] Jefferson to William Cabell, July 24, 1807, *Writings*, 295.
[34] Jefferson to General Samuel Smith, July 30, 1807, *Writings*, 301.
[35] Jefferson to Dallas, July 6, 1807, *Writings*, 258.
[36] Adams, *History of the United States*, 949.
[37] Perkins, *Prologue to War*, 149; Malone, *Jefferson the President*, 460–67; John Quincy Adams to John Adams, December 27, 1807, in *Writings of John Quincy Adams*, vol. 3, ed. Worthington Chauncey Ford (New York: Macmillan, 1914), 167–68.

itime policy on neutral trade and impressment and could therefore not remain U.S. policy. The question, however, was over which new direction U.S. policy should take. This was the question that revealed how bitterly divided the country was on a regional basis over policy toward Great Britain, even more divided than it had been in 1807. Republican congressmen from the Northwest and the South pressured President Jefferson to adopt tougher measures against Great Britain. In January 1809, the Republican Congress passed the Enforcement Act, which greatly enhanced the president's authority to enforce compliance with the embargo against European trade. These Republicans were not the only ones dismayed by the embargo or calling for its repeal. The embargo was also under fire from Northeasterners who were adamantly opposed to any more forceful measures meant to coerce Great Britain. The U.S. embargo was the catalyst for severe economic contraction in the Northeast, a surge in popular protest, and organized regional opposition. Despite the fact that smuggling across the border with Canada thrived under the embargo, the embargo was quite successful in shutting down shipping from U.S. ports. "By the summer of 1808 the bulk of American shipping lay idle . . . under the effective control of the government."[38] The economic effects of this were not limited to the seacoast or the ship owners, as economic depression quickly spread inland to those areas that had direct economic ties to the shipping industry.[39] As a result, the Massachusetts legislature passed resolutions decrying the extreme pressures imposed by this policy on its people and expressing fear for "our domestic peace, and the union of these States." Senators and representatives from Massachusetts were instructed to use their "most strenuous exertions" for a repeal of the embargo.[40]

An important indicator of opposition in the Northeast is the change in the electoral strength of the Federalist and Republican parties during the elections of 1808. Republican identification with the embargo and a war movement dealt an "almost fatal blow" to the Republican parties of New England as the Federalist party reestablished its control here and expanded its institutional base in other parts of the Northeast. In the presidential contest of 1808 the Republican party split between supporters of James Madison, Jefferson's appointed heir,

[38] Leonard D. White, "The Embargo," in *Causes of the War of 1812*, 35.
[39] Albert Z. Carr, *The Coming of War: An Account of the Remarkable Events Leading to the War of 1812* (Garden City, N.Y.: Doubleday, 1960), 252–53.
[40] White, "The Embargo," 35.

and the supporters of DeWitt Clinton of New York, Madison's primary Republican rival. Although Madison won the election, Clinton attracted wide support in the Northeast because he defended the commercial interests of his constituents by opposing the embargo.[41] In the elections for the Eleventh Congress, the effect of the embargo on the Republican party is most evident in the House. The Republicans' overall strength in this body dropped from 82 percent to 65 percent. The Republicans lost all the seats from New Hampshire, which had traditionally been a faithful Republican state, and the Republican majority in the Massachusetts delegation was reversed as the Federalists took ten of the seventeen seats. The party was not able to reorganize and win a statewide election again in Massachusetts until 1823.[42] In New York, the Republicans lost six seats, and they lost seats in Vermont and Rhode Island. While the Republicans maintained a majority in both the Senate and the House, the loyalty of northeastern members to the president's program was questionable; they could not stray too far from northeastern sentiment against war without paying an electoral price. Federalist John Quincy Adams actually paid the ultimate political price for supporting the embargo. Adams resigned his Senate seat in June 1808 after both houses of the Massachusetts legislature passed resolutions condemning his role in its passage.[43]

After the Enforcement Act was passed in January 1809, northeastern outrage became overwhelming. The Enforcement Act was condemned in town meetings across New England, the General Court of Massachusetts ordered its congressmen to work against it, and the legislature attacked the powers in the act as unconstitutional. Governor Trumbull and the legislature of Connecticut publicly supported these measures by Massachusetts.[44] If such opposition was generated by commercial policy alone, it was clear that any move toward war would be internally explosive. A leader of New England Republicans, Ezekiel Bacon, confronted his northwestern and southern colleagues with the argument that the rights of commerce could only be resurrected by dropping the embargo that had done so much damage to the northern economy.

[41] Roger H. Brown, *The Republic in Peril: 1812* (New York: Columbia University Press, 1964), 140–45; Hickey, *War of 1812: A Forgotten Conflict*, 101.

[42] Stagg, *Mr. Madison's War*, 485.

[43] Adams to the Honorable Senate and House of Representatives of the Commonwealth of Massachusetts, June 8, 1808 in *Writings of John Quincy Adams*, 237–38.

[44] Perkins, *Prologue to War*, 179.

> Our Southern friends . . . now tell us . . . that they are willing to support
> our commercial rights by the present System [embargo] or by War as we
> shall think best, but . . . I am satisfied that New England will not bear the
> Embargo . . . [or] War, the other parts of the Union will support their
> commercial rights in no other Way, because they say the Nation can do
> nothing short of it honorably. The Result, in my opinion, is that the
> rights of Commerce will be abandoned by the Nation.[45]

Jefferson himself declared, "I felt the foundations of the government shaken under my feet by the New England townships."[46] The Northeast's opposition to war with Great Britain was based on more than simple material interests. Many northeasterners, primarily in New England, also held a strong sense of ideological and cultural affinity with Great Britain, particularly when they considered Britain's great struggle with Napoleon. Most in the Northeast appreciated Britain's role in preserving a conservative social order against the chaos created by the French Revolution. This was the respect held for one conservative state by political conservatives in another. Napoleon, on the other hand, was widely derided in the Northeast as "the great destroyer," the "monster of human depravity," even the anti-Christ.[47] Federalist senator Thomas Pickering was hailed across the region for his well-known toast to Great Britain—"the world's last hope—Britain's fast-anchored Isle."[48] The idea of the United States implicitly aiding Napoleon by declaring war on Great Britain was repugnant.

In January 1809, as Madison prepared to assume the presidency in March, he let his intended policy be known to his party supporters. He wanted to maintain the embargo until June, call a new congressional session for May 22, and declare war unless Britain made concessions in its maritime policies.[49] But in the face of the rising tide of violent protest in New England and the election results from the previous fall, Republicans from the Northeast could not support either the administration's desire for a continuation of economic coercion or the call for war to force Britain's hand. The Enforcement Act was the catalyst for a split in the Republican party along regional lines and a solidifying coalition of northeastern Republicans and Federalists who were de-

---

45 Ibid., 227–28.
46 Carr, *Coming of War*, 259–60.
47 Hickey, *War of 1812: A Forgotten Conflict*, 256; Julius W. Pratt, *Expansionists of 1812* (New York: Macmillan, 1925), 131; Varg, *New England and Foreign Relations*, 8–10.
48 Pratt, *Expansionists of 1812*, 131.
49 Adams, *History of the United States*, 1224.

manding relief from the embargo by June. The initiative to declare war on Great Britain produced the same regional division, and on February 5, 1809, the House rejected a resolution supporting war by a vote of 76 to 40. More than half the Republicans, most from New England and Pennsylvania, joined the Federalists in this vote. A number of Republicans from outside the Northeast recognized regional divisions as the ultimate impediment: "Look at the sensation in New England and New York," exclaimed David Williams of South Carolina, "and talk about going to war when you cannot maintain an embargo!"[50] Jefferson too made this observation: "I thought Congress had taken their ground firmly for continuing their embargo till June, and then war. But a sudden and unaccountable revolution of opinion took place the last week, chiefly among the New England and New York members . . . they voted . . . for removing the embargo, and by such a majority as gave all reason to believe they would not agree either to war or non-intercourse."[51] A desperate Republican caucus failed to come up with a new policy that demonstrated real resolve to defend U.S. honor against British pressure. In March, just three days before the end of Jefferson's term, Congress passed the Non-Intercourse Act, a measure acceptable to the Northeast only because it could not be enforced.[52]

The Smoldering Crisis in 1812: A Divided Federal Republic Declares War

The institutional constraints that prevented the use of military force in the earlier crises of 1807 and 1809 failed to have this effect in 1812. It is important to note from the outset, however, that the United States did not march resolutely to war. The same regional and institutional divisions that defeated earlier war moves were part of this crisis too. In fact, when we review the course of domestic events leading up to this decision it is amazing that the vote for war took place at all. The key difference in 1812 was a dramatic increase in the intensity with which the proponents of war, all of whom represented the Northwest and the South, pushed this policy option. Their intensity in favor of war easily

[50] Ibid., 1217; Perkins, *Prologue to War*, 181–82, 228.
[51] Jefferson to Thomas Mann Randolph, February 7, 1809, *Writings*, 248.
[52] The Non-Intercourse Act required U.S. ships to avoid calls in British or French-controlled ports. Ship captains could declare their intentions to comply with the act before sailing, yet once clear from U.S. ports they could sail unhindered to any destination.

matched the determination of northeasterners to prevent it. In addition, the leaders of this movement, the so-called War Hawks of the Twelfth Congress, managed to assume important leadership positions, particularly in the House of Representatives, from which they were better equipped institutionally to push war legislation forward. Among the three major regions of the United States, the Northwest was the most insistent on a coercive policy against Great Britain and the most enthusiastic for war in 1807, 1809, and 1812.[53] A majority of the War Hawks, who took a decisive leadership role in moving the Republican party and President Madison toward war in 1812, hailed from the Northwest. What was it about this region that produced such bellicose attitudes and political leaders? Certainly, most northwesterners believed that Britain's maritime policy was a threat to genuinely national interests of the United States. In the grandest terms, northwesterners consistently argued that these maritime restrictions were an affront to national honor, and if left unanswered this affront would demote the United States to second-class status in the international system. Northwestern Republicans could also argue that they were mainly interested in upholding a key tenet of Republican philosophy, which was that neutral trading rights were essential to U.S. independence and security in the midst of a competitive international system.[54] But what really drove them to demand an increasingly forceful response was how British pressure impacted the particular economic and security interests of their regional constituents. According to Perkins, a number of northwesterners were actually embarrassed by appeals to "such naked self-interest" as a justification for war. As a result, northwesterners often combined multiple arguments in favor of war.[55] Like many of his Republican colleagues in the Northwest, Speaker of the House Henry Clay of Kentucky often discussed the

[53] The Northwest Territory was organized into three new states, Ohio, Tennessee, and Kentucky, and the region now included the Indiana and Michigan territories. While representing just a small percentage of the total population in the United States, these states of the Northwest constituted a distinct territorial community whose identity was shaped by geographic separation from the Atlantic coast and by agrarian life on the U.S. frontier. The Northwest constituted a section separate and distinct from the Northeast and the South. Frederick Jackson Turner, *The Significance of Sections in American History* (New York: Henry Holt, 1932). According to Horsman, "The debates leading to war with England marked the coming of age of western politicians on the national scene." Reginald Horsman, *The Frontier in the Formative Years, 1783–1815* (New York: Holt, Rinehart and Winston, 1970), 172.

[54] Onuf and Onuf, *Federal Union, Modern World*, 145–46.

[55] Perkins, *Prologue to War*, 287.

prospects of war in terms of national honor and national interests. Yet according to Carr, "it was the practical interest of the frontier, more than the sentiment of patriotism, that had determined his position."[56] And the practical interests of the frontier, northwesterners believed, demanded an increasingly aggressive U.S. reaction to Great Britain.

Northwesterners understood that the loss of European markets for agricultural products was potentially disastrous in practical economic terms. Or, if northwestern products could only be sent to British markets, the price for their commodities would plunge.[57] Losing export income meant that northwestern farmers lost the means to purchase land on which the entire process of economic growth and continued westward expansion depended. Export income was also essential for the purchase of manufactured items and luxuries for the home.[58] Northwesterners voted nearly unanimously for the original Embargo Act in 1807 and for its renewal in 1808, and they worked vigorously for continued economic sanctions in 1809 when the policy was rapidly losing support in other regions.[59] During this period the Northwest suffered through two severe economic depressions that were blamed in the region on British restrictions, not on the Republican party embargo.[60] In 1808, prices for cotton and tobacco fell 20 percent, the winter of 1809–1810 brought continued economic struggle and bitterness to the region, and in the depression of 1811–1812 wholesale prices for northwestern goods fell below 1808 prices.[61] Senator John Calhoun of South Carolina, in a sympathetic explanation of the outrage expressed by northwestern politicians, newspapers, and through citizen petitions noted that the "people of that section . . . see in the low prices of their produce, the hand of foreign injustice; they know well, without the market to the Continent, the deep and steady current of supply will glut that of Great Britain; they are not prepared for the colonial state to which again that Power is endeavoring to reduce us."[62] Samuel McKee, Republican congressman of Kentucky, posed the Northwest's economic dilemma in stark terms: "How long shall we live at this poor dying rate, before [economic sanctions] will effect the

[56] Carr, *Coming of War*, 297.

[57] George R. Taylor, "Depression Stirs Western War Spirit," in *Causes of the War of 1812*, 74.

[58] Horsman, *Causes of the War of 1812*, 176.

[59] Taylor, "Depression Stirs Western War Spirit," 73.

[60] Perkins, *Prologue to War*, 287.

[61] Taylor, "Depression Stirs Western War Spirit," 75–76.

[62] Ibid., 79.

repeal of the Orders in Council? . . . In the meantime our prosperity is gone; our resources are wasting."[63] By 1812 most northwesterners were demanding war as the only option that could break the suffocating effects of these commercial restrictions.

In addition to the economic pressures imposed on the Northwest by Great Britain, this region also faced what was perceived to be an increasingly threatening confederation of Native American tribes along the northwestern frontier. Moreover, this confederation had the apparent support of the British government in Upper Canada.[64] Prior to 1810, U.S. citizens in the Northwest and their representatives in Washington displayed little concern for frontier security. There was relative quiescence along the frontier in the years between the U.S. victory over northwestern tribes at the battle of Fallen Timbers in 1794 and the rise of Tecumseh's confederation in 1810. While tensions between the United States and Britain flared repeatedly from 1807 on, there was no public outcry or congressional action to indicate that northwesterners feared British intriguing with the Indians in this period.[65] In fact, before 1807 there was little interaction between British agents in Upper Canada and tribes in the Northwest, and British policy after 1795 was to minimize contacts with Indians and expenditures for Indian policy.[66]

By 1807, two features of frontier relations began to change that ultimately produced extreme anxiety over security among U.S. citizens in the Northwest and fueled demands for war and the expulsion of Great Britain from Canada. The first change was among the Native American tribes themselves. Under the leadership of Chief Tecumseh, they began to organize a confederation in an effort to coordinate resistance to the continual advance of U.S. settlers into Indian lands.[67] The second change was an effort by the British government in Canada to strengthen its ties with this confederation, driven by a growing sense that both the United States and France threatened Britain's position in North America. Whether an attack came from the United States or from France, Sir James Craig, the British governor-general of Canada,

[63] Ibid., 77.

[64] Upper Canada was that part of British North America west of Montreal and around the Great Lakes.

[65] Pratt, *Expansionists of 1812*, 23–38.

[66] Horsman, *Causes of the War of 1812*, 159; Morison and Commager, *Growth of the American Republic*, 347; J. Leitch Wright, Jr., *Britain and the American Frontier, 1783–1815* (Athens: University of Georgia Press, 1975), chap. 6.

[67] Stagg, *Mr. Madison's War*, 181; Morison and Commager, *Growth of the American Republic*, 404; Carr, *Coming of War*, 293; Horsman, *Causes of the War of 1812*, 165.

knew that the allegiance of northwestern Indians was essential for the
defense of Canada. In a letter to British foreign secretary Castlereagh,
Craig argued, "If we do not use them there cannot be a moment's doubt
that they will be employed against us."[68] Britain's Fort Amherstburg,
near the U.S. settlement at Detroit, became an active center for contacts
between Indians and British agents, who provided supplies and advice
and facilitated public councils among the various tribes. By the spring
of 1812 Fort Amherstburg and Fort Malden, south of Detroit, "had become focal points for hundreds of dissatisfied Indians seeking food,
weapons, and support against the United States."[69]

Even though the British saw these contacts in purely defensive
terms, U.S. settlers throughout the Northwest reacted with increasing
alarm to news of expanding British-Indian relations. And no matter
how often the British may have warned against provoking conflict
with the United States, Tecumseh ultimately chose to order attacks on
U.S. settlements in late 1809 and 1810.[70] By 1810 northwesterners and
their representatives in Congress were convinced that the Native
American threat along the frontier was serious, and that British support was the key to its intensity.[71] For the majority of northwesterners,
the answer to this growing threat in 1812 was not simply to fortify the
frontier, nor to conduct sporadic raids against the confederation. The
answer was to attack the problem at what was considered the source—
British possession of Upper Canada. For Senator Felix Grundy of Tennessee, "the War, if carried on successfully, will have its advantages.
We shall drive the British from our Continent—they will no longer
have an opportunity of intriguing with our Indian neighbors, and setting on the ruthless savage to tomahawk our women and children . . .
and by having no resting place in this country, her means of annoying
us will be diminished."[72] Considered together, it is easy to understand
how severe economic distress blamed on British maritime policy, and
the growing insecurity of the frontier inspired by Britain's relationship
with northwestern tribes, caused northwestern political leadership to
join the War Hawks of 1812.

[68] Carr, *Coming of War*, 292; Horsman, *Causes of the War of 1812*, 159–60; Perkins, *Prologue to War*, 285; Stagg, *Mr. Madison's War*, 181; Pratt, *Expansionists of 1812*, 19.

[69] Stagg, *Mr. Madison's War*, 190.

[70] Donald W. Meinig, *The Shaping of America: A Geographical Perspective on 500 Years of
History*, vol. 2 (New Haven: Yale University Press, 1993), 46; Horsman, *Causes of the War
of 1812*, 204–7; Brown, *Republic in Peril*, 118.

[71] Pratt, *Expansionists of 1812*, 42; Perkins, *Prologue to War*, 283.

[72] Brown, *Republic in Peril*, 121; Perkins, *Prologue to War*, 154.

A common economic interest in ending British restrictions was a powerful political link between the Northwest and the South in the years preceding the declaration of war.[73] In congressional debates, newspapers, letters, and in public meetings, southerners "repeated almost verbatim" the arguments made by their allies in the Northwest.[74] The South too was hit hard by the depression of 1811–1812. A boom in cotton production, which had doubled since 1801, intensified this depression. Forty percent of this crop was meant for export, and with England as the only outlet for surplus cotton and tobacco, prices were driven perilously low.[75] In turn, export earnings, which fueled much of the South's hopes for economic prosperity, languished. William Lowndes of South Carolina explained the South's special concern with U.S. commercial rights: "The interests of agriculture and commerce are inseparable. What is commerce but the exchange of the surplus produce of . . . one nation for those of another? . . . it is this commerce which makes agriculture valuable."[76] To many in the South, war seemed imperative as the only remaining measure that might relieve the region from this economic pressure. The particularly harsh effects of British policy on a state like South Carolina, which was so dependent on agricultural exports, also helps explain why this state, and not others, became a main source of political agitation and leadership for armed conflict.

As in the earlier crises of 1807 and 1809, the Northeast remained the focal point for resistance to any move toward war with Great Britain. Most northeasterners continued to view Britain in favorable normative terms, as the last bulwark against the radicalism of Napoleonic France. The Northeast also remained at odds with the Northwest and the South on the economic implications of British policy and the prospects of war. While the Northeast too suffered through economic depression in the years prior to the war, most northeasterners rightly blamed the U.S. embargo on trade with England and France for their difficulties. To these normative and commercial reasons for opposing war, Northeasterners added a geographic component. An antiwar statement signed by thirty-four House Federalists expressed the fear that "a war of invasion may invite a retort of invasion," particularly if

[73] Horsman, *Causes of the War of 1812*, 175.
[74] Ibid., 231.
[75] Margaret K. Latimer, "The South Also Feels the Depression," in *Causes of the War of 1812*, 82.
[76] Ibid., 80.

it involved an attack against Canada.[77] This fear was more salient for
coastal regions that were expected to suffer the brunt of a British naval
assault on U.S. territory. As the U.S. efforts to coerce Britain with economic and military measures evolved from 1807 on, there was a grad-
ual convergence between the widespread northeastern opposition
to this policy and the role of the Federalist party as the official voice
and hand of the opposition. Because coercion of Great Britain was
identified as a Republican party issue, the Federalists enjoyed dramatic electoral gains in the Northeast in 1808, 1812, 1813, and 1814. According to Samuel Morison, "The war slogan of the administration,
'Free Trade and Sailors' Rights,' seemed mere hokum to Federalists
and to the ship-owning community generally."[78] The Federalists, with
their core support in the Northeast, became the natural voice for opposition as the move toward war grew in 1812.

While northeastern opposition persuaded President Jefferson to
resist a military response to the crisis of 1807 and stalled a congressional initiative to declare war in 1809, congressional War Hawks of
1812 managed to surmount the institutional obstacles to war that
had maintained peace in previous years. In June 1812 Congress declared war on Great Britain by the wide margin of 79 to 49 votes in
the House, and more narrowly in the Senate by a vote of 19 to 13.
This case certainly demonstrates that federalism did not paralyze the
U.S. republic's ability to initiate armed conflict. However, when we
review the politics of conflict decision-making in 1812 and the events
that preceded the vote it seems remarkable that the war bill was even
introduced and voted on in the first place. For all the arguments
made in 1811 and 1812 (and since then among historians) that British
affronts to national honor, integrity, sovereignty, or interests demanded war from the United States, it is clear that this war was not
inevitable. The federally divided U.S. political system worked as intended in 1812 by throwing up repeated challenges to consensus on
bold action against Great Britain. The constraining effects of federal
union were not absent in this case, but posed an immense hurdle to
those in the United States who insisted on war, and at several key
points these institutional hurdles nearly derailed the War Hawks' efforts. In fact, it is fair to argue that at one point in the decision-mak-

---

[77] Hickey, *War of 1812: A Forgotten Conflict*, 54–55.
[78] Samuel Eliot Morison, "Dissent in the War of 1812," in *Dissent in Three American
Wars*, ed. Samuel E. Morison, Frederick Merk, and Frank Freidel (Cambridge: Harvard
University Press, 1970), 5.

ing process it was a historically contingent quirk that tipped the balance toward those favoring war.

In the midst of such institutional challenges to a more aggressive U.S. policy, without the leadership of the alliance of northwestern and southern congressmen, driven by the needs of their respective regions, it is doubtful that the United States ever would have overcome the federal obstacles to a declaration of war. First, the War Hawks had to pursue this goal in the absence of strong leadership from the executive branch. President Madison certainly did not oppose war. In the fall of 1811 he tried to nudge Congress in this direction with his report on the failure of diplomacy to move Britain to repeal its Orders in Council. Madison also believed that war would serve to unite his fractious Republican party and silence his critics.[79] Yet Madison found it impossible to openly support the War Hawks' call for the use of force,[80] he had no control over Republicans in Congress, he seldom maintained firm direction of his own cabinet, and his policy seemed to drift over time.[81] Second, there was no widespread popular consensus within the country on what was in the national interest or what the United States should do to protect those interests. The War Hawks, therefore, had no general popular sentiment to which they could appeal for support on a war policy.[82] Third, the War Hawks had to confront the continuing opposition of northeasterners, both Republicans and Federalists, at the state and national levels. This regional coalition could be counted on to resist any effort to take a more aggressive stance against Great Britain. As in earlier votes on U.S. policy toward England, the vote on war in 1812 showed that the opposition concentrated in the Northeast. The majority of senators and representatives from New York, New Jersey, Delaware, and Maryland voted against the war, while the vast majority of senators and representatives from New England joined them.[83]

What worked in the War Hawks' favor was that even if every senator and representative from the Northeast had cast a vote against the

[79] Stagg, *Mr. Madison's War*, 79.

[80] Madison believed that calling for war on Great Britain because of its predatory maritime behavior would also require a demand for war on France. Madison was aware that between 1807 and 1811 France had seized a far greater number of U.S. ships than the British had. This was a fact that he did not share with the public. Carr, *Coming of War*, 307–8.

[81] Bradford Perkins, "Madison Was a Failure," in *Causes of the War of 1812*, 113.

[82] Perkins, *Prologue to War*, 392.

[83] Morison and Commager, *Growth of the American Republic*, 402.

war, this region would not have had enough votes to prevent passage of the war bill over the affirmative votes from the rest of the Union. In other words, a purely regional vote in Congress by representatives concentrated in the Northeast would not have constrained the use of military force in this case. This outcome assumes that the members of the Republican party, dominant in the rest of the country, could actually agree on a set of policy measures that would move the country in a more violent direction. In the spring of 1812, however, this level of consensus was elusive. In fact, the opportunity to vote on war was nearly lost amid confusion within the Republican party over foreign policy. This was the fourth major obstacle the War Hawks had to overcome and it proved the most problematic. The decentralized nature of the party, which was a result of the state-based U.S. electoral system and the subsequent absence of any mechanisms for enforcing party discipline, provided space for a diverse range of views on foreign policy to flourish among a diverse group of legislators. This in turn promoted factionalism and prevented the Republicans from establishing a consistent policy. According to Perkins, Republican "congressmen divided into a kaleidoscope of shifting factions so intricate and febrile that classification baffled even the members."[84]

Republicans disagreed on and defeated tax bills needed to support war preparations and legislation to build up the navy in preparation for maritime conflict failed. They disagreed on whether the war should be primarily a naval or a land war, so measures to raise a provisional army were defeated.[85] The Republican party was so divided that the Federalists did not actually take the possibility of war seriously. As a result, the Federalists and northeastern Republican dissidents were slow to organize political resistance to War Hawk efforts.[86] In March it was apparent that "if the President put the question of war to Congress, the administration would not get a majority,"[87] and by April war spirit in the party was seriously flagging.[88] The prolonged and frustrating effort to come to consensus on war preparations reached a breaking point in April, when a series of events nearly defeated the entire move toward war. On April 10, the House approved

[84] Perkins, *Prologue to War*, 346.
[85] Ibid., 361; Stagg, *Mr. Madison's War*, 90–91, 147–49; Hatzenbuehler and Ivie, *Congress Declares War*, 31–33.
[86] Brown, *Republic in Peril*, 106; Perkins, *Prologue to War*, 396.
[87] Stagg, *Mr. Madison's War*, 100.
[88] Carr, *Coming of War*, 316.

in principle an early congressional recess by a vote of 72 to 40. While a recess would have allowed congressmen to escape the confusion of war politics in Washington and feel out their constituents on the issue, it would also have delayed the vote on war. Had the vote been delayed beyond June 20, when the *USS Hornet* arrived with news that Britain had canceled the Orders in Council, it is likely that the United States would never have declared war on Great Britain.[89] Even without the contingent arrival of the *Hornet*, an early summer recess may have given time for the war spirit to dampen, as in 1807. As many members of Congress prepared to return home during the pending recess, northwestern War Hawks stepped into the legislative morass to fight the delay on the war vote. This was the key move that kept the United States on track toward war. One week after the House had voted overwhelmingly for an early recess, the issue was again brought to a vote by the congressional leadership and a recess was defeated by eight votes. This reversal was only possible because a number of antiwar congressmen, believing that Congress would adjourn without further action, had already left Washington. Without these antiwar votes Congress remained in session, the possibility of war opened once again, and any check on war was further weakened by the reduced number of antiwar Republicans.

According to Perkins, "From early April until the end of May the War Hawks fought a defensive battle against fear, second thoughts, weakness, and pressure of public opinion."[90] As a number of historians note, the Northwest only contributed nine House votes out of seventy-nine for war. Compare this to the thirty-five votes that came from Virginia, Pennsylvania, and Maryland alone. Obviously, the weight of northwestern votes did not carry the United States into war. Republicans from the Northwest certainly relied on their allies from southern states. Yet there was no other source of pressure or leadership for moving the issue of war forward, not from the general public, not from the president, not from any other bloc within Congress—the War Hawks of the Northwest, and particularly Henry Clay, were indispensable. In the end, the War Hawks managed to stir a majority from the Northwest and the South, and even attract some party loyalists in the Northeast, to support the war bill, despite the regional divisions that would plague the United States during the war itself.

[89] Perkins, *Prologue to War*, 396–97.
[90] Ibid., 399.

Federal Politics and the Failure of Territorial Expansion

The previous sections on the crises of 1807, 1809, and 1812, pursue a common question in democratic peace literature: did democratic institutions prevent the initiation of armed conflict? The dependent variable in most of this research is simply the presence or absence of war. Yet as Chan has argued, this dependent variable is unnecessarily restrictive in a research agenda that could explore other questions such as the intensity or duration of war, or the goals that can be achieved through military force.[91] This next section looks specifically at the last of these alternative questions. In the case of the War of 1812, the official objective of the United States was to force Great Britain to end its repressive maritime policies. But for the purposes of evaluating other possible effects of democracy on the use of military force, the War of 1812 offers an opportunity to test whether features of the U.S. federal system explain the outcome of two ancillary objectives: namely, territorial expansion into British North America and Spanish East Florida. Territorial expansion to the north and the south was not a primary motive for this war. Yet once underway, the war became a vehicle for achieving expansion in these regions through military force. Despite the favorable external conditions for forcible U.S. growth and the confidence that U.S. decision-makers had in their ability to achieve these goals, the end result in each case was failure. The question then is to what degree can the failure of these war goals be explained by the logic of federal union and armed conflict?

Canada

Among Americans who supported the war with Great Britain there was early consensus that the invasion and occupation of Canada was a legitimate war aim. Proponents of this goal offered numerous reasons why this would be generally beneficial to the United States: it would secure the northwestern frontier from the depredations of Indian tribes and their British allies; it would allow the United States unrestricted use of the St. Lawrence River for commercial transportation; it would open up fisheries in the maritime regions of the east; it would

---

[91] Steve Chan, "Democracy and War: Some Thoughts on Future Research Agenda," *International Interactions* 18 (1993), 205–13.

permanently relieve the United States from British pressure in North America; and it would offer rich land for U.S. farmers and eliminate competition in the fur trade. Some argued that it would strengthen the North's political base in the Union, which had become a concern for many northerners after the Louisiana Purchase opened the possibility for rapid growth and the addition of new states in the South. Some Republicans even saw expansion into Canada as a way to solidify Republican party support in the Northeast.[92]

Among these various arguments for expansion into Canada, two were predominant. Many argued that the problem of northwestern security could only be solved if the United States occupied, then annexed, at least Upper Canada. This expansion, it was explained, was not for territorial aggrandizement but was driven by defensive needs in the face of a persistent threat.[93] The second argument for the occupation of Canada, the one most often provided by the Madison administration, was that it would serve mainly as a tactical war move. According to this argument, the United States would not seek to annex Canada, even for security purposes, but would hold it as a bargaining chip and return it to Great Britain in exchange for concessions on maritime issues. A number of eminent historians have argued persuasively that this was the Madison administration's purpose for the war fought along the northern frontier.[94] Madison held strong views on the commercial and military value of Canada to Great Britain. Along with his minister to Russia, John Quincy Adams, Madison believed that at some time in 1812 Napoleon would succeed in cutting off the Baltic to British commerce. Once this was accomplished, Britain would be nearly totally dependent on North America for natural resources, particularly timber, which was essential for maintaining British naval supremacy. The purpose of invading Canada then, Monroe explained, was "not as an object of the war but as a means to bring it to a satisfactory conclusion."[95] At this point one might reasonably ask, if the Madi-

[92] Brown, *Republic in Peril*, 120–21.

[93] Reginald C. Stuart, *United States Expansionism and British North America, 1775–1871* (Chapel Hill: University of North Carolina Press, 1988), 54–76. See Pratt, *Expansionists of 1812*, for the strongest and most widely cited argument that the desire for territorial expansion and frontier security fueled the demand for war in both the Northwest and the South. Also Pratt, "The Land Hunger Thesis Challenged," in *Causes of the War of 1812*, 53–70.

[94] For example, see Horsman, "The Conquest of Canada as a Tactical Objective," in *Causes of the War of 1812*, 96–107.

[95] Stagg, *Mr. Madison's War*, 38–47.

son administration did not intend a permanent annexation of Canada, does this case really constitute an example of failed territorial expansion because of federal politics?

Despite the avowed intentions of the Madison administration, the historic record also shows that the administration was highly elusive over what its ultimate goals really were. As the prospects of U.S. success in this effort waxed and waned over time, so did the alacrity with which the administration spoke of the conquest and permanent possession of Canada. At times, cabinet members and Republicans in Congress seemed to dismiss Madison's willingness to use Canada as a bargaining chip when it appeared that the United States might actually enjoy the many benefits that would come from retaining it.[96] Vice-President Elbridge Gerry and Secretary of State James Monroe expressed their desire to keep Canada, and Speaker of the House Henry Clay had argued "if Canada is conquered it ought never to be surrendered if it can possibly be retained."[97] Even those who made the tactical invasion argument acknowledged that once the United States possessed British territory it might be extremely difficult to relinquish this land. The Boston *Chronicle* explained in 1813, "It appears to be the universal opinion of the Republicans that the Canadas ought in no event to be surrendered . . . . Too much valuable blood has already been shed, and too much treasure expended, to permit us to indulge for a moment the idea of resigning this country."[98] Madison actually tried to convince the British that this was a serious U.S. sentiment in an effort to increase the pressure on Great Britain for concessions before a U.S. invasion was successful. Through his chargé d'affaires in London, the president wanted it made clear to the British government that unless it acted soon, it would be very "difficult to relinquish territory which had been conquered."[99]

One important indication of the administration's desire to retain Canada is the composition of a peace delegation sent to St. Petersburg, Russia, in the spring of 1813 for mediation talks sponsored by the czar. One key member of this peace delegation was Henry Clay, the War Hawk leader from Kentucky. Clay never hesitated to express his desire to expel Britain from North America, and the president nominated him for this mission specifically to fend off rumors spread by Secretary

---

[96] Stuart, *United States Expansionism and British North America*, 59–60, 63–64.
[97] Brown, *Republic in Peril*, 129.
[98] Hickey, *War of 1812: A Forgotten Conflict*, 74.
[99] Stagg, *Mr. Madison's War*, 4; Perkins, *Prologue to War*, 416.

of War Armstrong that Madison was preparing to trade Canada for peace. Northwestern Republicans would not stand for using Canada as a tactical concession and the pressure on the president to disavow this plan was intense. Madison also realized that Armstrong's dissent may have had merit—maybe the United States needed a more tangible goal for the war that would justify to the public the sacrifices and expense required. With Clay as a member of the delegation, Republicans felt confident that this group would not return with a peace treaty that abandoned an opportunity for the United States to gain territorial expansion to the north.[100] Secretary of State Monroe went one step further in the hopes of realizing this expansionist opportunity by instructing the peace delegation to seek a territorial cession from Great Britain of at least Upper Canada, and more if possible. Monroe argued that continued British possession of Canada would only "hereafter prove a fruitful source of controversy which its transfer to the United States would remove."[101]

A number of indicators suggest that the United States should have been able to invade and occupy Canada with little difficulty. Compared to Great Britain, the United States had a strong relative advantage in North America that many contemporaries expected would be translated into easy victory. The population of the United States was about 7.5 million, while the total population of Upper and Lower Canada was a mere 500,000.[102] Not only was this a small population for supporting a defense of Canada against U.S. incursions, their allegiance to the crown was dubious. In Lower Canada, two-thirds of the population was of French descent,[103] and in Upper Canada, around the Great Lakes, 80 percent of the population had been born in the United States.[104] According to the commander of British forces in Upper Canada, General Isaac Brock, the inhabitants of the province were "essentially bad" and were "so completely American as to rejoice in the prospects of a change of Governments."[105] The United States had nearly twelve thousand regular soldiers in the army, while in 1812

100 Stagg, *Mr. Madison's War*, 372–74.
101 Ibid., 301.
102 Ibid., 5.
103 Hickey, *War of 1812: A Forgotten Conflict*, 73.
104 Twenty percent of these Americans were Loyalists who had fled the American colonies during the War of Independence, the rest were recent immigrants from the United States. Meinig, *Shaping of America*, 45.
105 Hickey, *War of 1812: A Forgotten Conflict*, 73. Hickey notes that many Republicans shared this assessment, which is one reason they were willing to go to war without adequate preparation.

the British had no more than seven thousand in North America. With additional enlistments, volunteers, and militia, the United States could establish a large margin of superiority in the total number of troops available. The quality of British soldiers in North America was highly mixed. According to Benjamin Stickney, an American who had toured Lower Canada in early 1812 to report his findings to the president, while the soldiers between Montreal and Kingston were "pretty good men," the garrison at Quebec was "totally ineffective and trained in 'drunken frolics.'"[106] England's military shortcomings in North America were compounded by the war in Europe, which prevented the deployment of sufficient reinforcements for Canada.[107]

Jefferson's assessment, ten days after the war began, was that "upon the whole, I have known no war entered into under more favorable auspices. Our present enemy will have the sea to herself, while we shall be equally predominant on land, and shall strip her of all her possessions on this continent." Several weeks later he exclaimed, "The acquisition of Canada this year, as far as the neighborhood of Quebec, will be a mere matter of marching, and will give us experience for the attack at Halifax the next, and the final expulsion of England from the American continent."[108] In a letter dated June 13, 1812, Monroe considered the ease of taking Canada: "My candid opinion is that we shall succeed in obtaining what it is important to obtain, and that we shall experience little annoyance or embarrassment in the effort."[109] Senator John Calhoun believed that "in four weeks from the time that a declaration of war is heard on our frontier the whole of Upper Canada and a part of Lower Canada will be in our possession."[110] And in a show of frontier bravado Henry Clay claimed, "The militia of Kentucky are alone competent to place Montreal and Upper Canada at your feet."[111]

Despite the favorable conditions for a successful U.S. invasion and the confidence of its statesmen, this expansionist effort into Upper and Lower Canada was a miserable failure. What those who confidently predicted success for the United States in this endeavor did not account for was that the question of taking the war into Canada was still a political issue that was to be shaped in decisive ways by the federal

[106] Stagg, *Mr. Madison's War*, 228–29.
[107] Hickey, *War of 1812: A Forgotten Conflict*, 73; Morison and Commager, *Growth of the American Republic*, 407.
[108] Pratt, *Expansionists of 1812*, 153.
[109] Perkins, *Prologue to War*, 416.
[110] Ibid., 427.
[111] Pratt, *Expansionists of 1812*, 40.

distribution of authority in the U.S. political system. While U.S. military efforts were hampered by incompetent leadership and by disorganization in the War Department and in the field, the greatest impediment to U.S. expansion into Canada in this period was the political opposition of the Northeast to the entire endeavor, and the unwillingness of southern states to fully support it out of fear that there would be a shift in political power to the North if Canada were absorbed into the Union. No matter how confident many Americans may have been after comparing the relative strength of the United States to Great Britain in North America, to achieve this expansionist war aim the United States first had to mobilize the men and supplies necessary for the task. This effort was impeded at both the national level and the state level in ways that make federal institutions crucial for understanding the failure of U.S. expansionist goals for this war.

Before we examine the specific institutional points of constraint on resource mobilization, it is important to consider the federal asymmetry on the goal of taking the fight into Canada. In regional terms, political leaders and citizens in the Northwest were the strongest supporters of this goal, yet in the Northeast and the South expansion into Canada was viewed with suspicion, trepidation, or outright hostility. While southern Republicans had provided a large portion of the vote in favor of a declaration of war in June, by late 1812, as the administration was preparing for an assault across the Niagara River and against Montreal, many southern Republicans and Federalists were wary of giving the president the ability to add a vast territory to the northern section of the Union.[112] Hugh Nelson of Virginia expressed the widespread southern reluctance to aid "the New Yorkers and Vermonters [who] are very well inclined to have Upper Canada united with them, by way of increasing their Influence in the Union."[113] Federalist Senator Bayard of Delaware observed,

> Southern Gentlemen are alarmed at a point very seriously insisted upon by the Northern—that in case Canada is conquered it shall be divided into states and inalienably incorporated into the Union . . . . No proposition could have been more frightful to the southern men, and it seems that they had never thought of what to do with Canada before . . . but they prefer that Canada should remain a British Province rather than be-

112 Perkins, *Prologue to War*, 426.
113 Brown, *Republic in Peril*, 124.

come States of America. The consequence has been that they now begin
to talk of maritime war, and of the ocean being the only place where
Great Britain is tangible.[114]

While southern reluctance to support northern expansion was to
become crucial in congressional votes on war mobilization, the most
important regional perspective for the failure of this war aim was firm
opposition in the Northeast. Despite the fact that the United States
was now at war with Great Britain, northeasterners did not rally behind this national cause, nor were they drawn to the other parts of the
Union in a collective effort to defend the country. On the contrary,
northeasterners refused to treat Great Britain as the enemy, and overall, they refused to cooperate in the war effort. Many northeasterners
saw the plan to invade Canada as an objective driven by regional aggression. Josiah Quincy, a Federalist leader from New England, characterized northwestern Republicans as "backwoodsmen" bent on
"predatory invasion." His colleague, Elijah Brigham, claimed that the
United States was pursuing a "war of invasion . . . a war of Ambition,
a war of conquest."[115] Congressmen Miller of New York threatened
Republicans in 1813 that Federalists "will give you millions in defense;
but not a cent for the conquest of Canada."[116]

During the war the Northeast continued its robust cross-border
trade with Upper and Lower Canada, even with the British army. In
August 1814 the governor-general of Canada exclaimed, "Two-thirds
of the army in Canada are at this moment eating beef provided by
American contractors."[117] Trade with New England was so important
to Canada that while the British imposed a tight blockade of the U.S.
coast south of Narragansett Bay in Rhode Island, New England maintained free access to the sea. The British commander-in-chief in Canada
had ordered his subordinates "to avoid committing any act which may
even by a strained construction tend to unite the eastern and southern
states."[118] Another important indicator of regional sentiment was the
refusal of northeastern banks to subscribe to government loans to help
fight the war. According to Chester, "New England banks lent more

[114] Pratt, *Expansionists of 1812*, 147–48.
[115] Brown, *Republic in Peril*, 170.
[116] Hickey, *War of 1812: A Forgotten Conflict*, 256.
[117] Carr, *Coming of War*, 84; Meinig, *Shaping of America*, 47.
[118] Edward W. Chester, *Sectionalism, Politics, and American Diplomacy* (Metuchen, N.J.:
Scarecrow Press, 1975), 29–30; Hickey, *War of 1812: A Forgotten Conflict*, 152.

money to the British during the war than they did to the U.S. government."[119] Morison adds that there was a "good understanding between the financial powers of Philadelphia and Boston [which were all controlled by Federalists] to withhold subscriptions to government loans until assured of peace, hoping to force President Madison to abandon this strategy of conquering Canada. And they nearly succeeded in bankrupting their government at a very critical period."[120] Federalist bankers in Boston even put pressure on leading Republican banks in New York to prevent them from subscribing to loans.[121]

Another strong indicator of northeastern opposition is the continuing electoral penalties imposed on the Republican party by northeastern voters in the 1812 elections. In fact, a number of historians note that regional dissent over the war breathed new life into the Federalist party. This was to become particularly important when individual state governments were called on to support Madison's war effort with troops. In New York a split in the Republican party between Madisonian loyalists and antiwar dissidents helped Federalists gain a clear majority in the state assembly. Federalists now held eighteen of the twenty-seven U.S. House seats from New York and they took one of the Senate seats from the Republicans. In Massachusetts defections from the Republican party resulted in Republican governor Elbridge Gerry being replaced by Federalist Caleb Strong and continued control of the state legislature by Federalists.[122] Overall, Federalists gained control of six of the eighteen states (Massachusetts, Connecticut, Rhode Island, New Jersey, Delaware, and Maryland). In 1813 they lost New Jersey but picked up Vermont and New Hampshire, to dominate all of New England.[123] In the presidential election of 1812, Madison won the entire Pennsylvania delegation, which was crucial to his re-election victory. Yet his challenger, DeWitt Clinton, who had campaigned as an antiwar candidate, won four New England states, New York, New Jersey, and Delaware, and Madison and Clinton divided the Maryland vote.[124]

The question now is how did this asymmetry among the Northwest, the South, and the Northeast on the goal of expansion into

---

[119] Ibid., 29–30.
[120] Morison, "Dissent in the War of 1812," 9; Hickey, *War of 1812: A Forgotten Conflict*, 167.
[121] Stagg, *Mr. Madison's War*, 376.
[122] Perkins, *Prologue to War*, 394–95.
[123] Hickey, *War of 1812: A Forgotten Conflict*, 323.
[124] Stagg, *Mr. Madison's War*, 273; Hickey, *War of 1812: A Forgotten Conflict*, 105.

Canada impede President Madison's ability to mobilize a military force and prosecute the conflict? Specifically, what federal institutional points of constraint do we find in this case that might have contributed to the failure to achieve this goal? The first institutional point of constraint was at the national level, in the form of repeated congressional rejection of legislation that would have authorized the president to mobilize enough manpower to prosecute the land campaign in Canada. The federal character of each vote was reflected in the regional distribution of congressmen in favor of and against these provisions to support the president. The first major blow was the failure of a bill introduced in the House on February 18, 1812, by Republican Peter Porter of New York. Porter represented the frontier region of western New York near Buffalo, so he shared the sense of vulnerability to British machinations in the region with his Republican colleagues from the frontier regions of the Northwest. This bill would have authorized a provisional army of twenty thousand men under the direct command of the president and was intended to give him the capability to quickly overrun British troops in an early invasion. This bill was defeated in Congress, however, by a coalition of Federalists from the Northeast and a nearly solid block of Republicans from the South. Not a single state south of the Potomac River voted for the bill.[125]

The second legislative defeat came in late 1812. James Monroe, now both secretary of state and acting secretary of war, requested congressional authorization for an additional thirty-five thousand troops that he would use in an ambitious plan to seize all of British North America by the end of 1813. Yet by early 1813 Monroe's initiative was battered by Federalists in Congress who were relentlessly pressing their opposition to any initiative that would further the war effort. Federalists were quick to point out that with a U.S. peace delegation being planned for mediation talks in Russia, efforts to increase U.S. military capabilities were senseless and counterproductive. The Federalists introduced numerous resolutions calling for limits or an end to the war; with a 63 percent majority in the House and a 78 percent majority in the Senate, congressional Republicans had little difficulty voting down these Federalist initiatives. Yet this overwhelming majority in Congress had little meaning for passing war legislation because of the split in the Republican party in the Northeast between those who tended to support the Republican administration and those who felt

---

[125] Pratt, *Expansionists of 1812*, 145–47.

obliged to support northeastern dissent, and the trepidation of many southern Republicans over the administration's expansionist goals. The Republican party as a whole lacked the will and unity to confront aggressive Federalist opposition with resolutions of their own authorizing money or materiel to carry the war forward. Monroe's initiative for 1813 died in the midst of this partisan and regional tangle.[126]

The third major legislative defeat came late in the war in October 1814. With Napoleon defeated and exiled (for the first time) by the European allies, the British were now free to send reinforcements to North America. This allowed them to bring their strength at all points along the border above that of the United States for the first time in the war. In response, Monroe demanded that Congress pass a conscription bill to raise an additional seventy thousand soldiers, thus enabling the United States to continue the war against Canada into 1815. While Monroe argued passionately that the "conservation of the State is a duty paramount to all others," many Republican senators were more concerned about the open defiance from New England to the conscription bill. This bill produced such an outcry in New England that Republicans from across the country joined forces with Federalists to postpone it indefinitely.[127]

This lack of congressional support for a sizable national military force under the president's command meant that he could not independently pursue his war aims in Canada. Instead, he was dependent on state governments and their militias. The division between the states and the national government, and their respective capabilities and authority in military affairs, is the second institutional point of constraint in this case. Arguably, this classic institutional feature of federal democracy was the primary constraint on the effort to invade and occupy Canada, and it goes a long way toward explaining the failure of northern expansion at this time. To make matters worse for Madison, his task was complicated by dependence on state-level governments controlled by the opposition party in a region that was rabidly opposed to the war, and by the fact that geographically northeastern states were the most important for attacking the cities of Montreal and Quebec, key targets in the strategy of the United States. With this combination of geography and state authority over military forces

[126] Stagg, *Mr. Madison's War*, 278–79, 374.
[127] Hickey, *War of 1812: A Forgotten Conflict*, 241–43; Morison, "Dissent in the War of 1812," 17 n. 7.

it is not surprising that many historians agree with Stagg's blunt assessment: "Monroe's offensive plans for Canada depended for success
far more on the cooperation of state political leaders than it did on the
efforts of the War Department."[128] Unfortunately for the Madison administration, Federalist leaders at the state level did not hesitate to use
their privileged institutional positions in the Northeast to actually
stop the invasion of Canada and work toward a rapid peace with
Great Britain.[129] Federalists dominated New England to such an extent
that Republicans found it impossible to counter them politically or
even openly support administration policy without generating severe
local hostility.[130] The greatest difficulty presented by the New England
states was their refusal to provide militia forces for the purpose of invading Canada. The first of many requests came on June 22, 1812, from
the ranking army officer in New England, General Henry Dearborn.
While the Republican governors of New Hampshire and Vermont
complied with this initial request, Governor Strong of Massachusetts,
Governor Griswold of Connecticut, and Governor Jones of Rhode Island, flatly refused. As early as July 1812, General Dearborn had informed Secretary of War Eustis that it would be impossible to raise the
necessary troops in the Northeast for an assault on Montreal.[131] The resistance of these governors grew more intense through 1813 and 1814.
After the election of a Federalist governor in Vermont in the fall
of 1813, one of his first official acts was to withdraw the Vermont militia from service on the northern frontier.[132] Vermont Governor Chitten-
den then threatened to use force himself to resist any administration
effort to compel him to assist in the war effort.[133] In New York the Federalist lower house refused to help raise a force meant to retaliate
against British raids on New York border towns. The lack of support
from Federalists in New York was compounded by the split in the
Republican party between Madison's loyalists and the supporters of
the antiwar Republican DeWitt Clinton. The region north and west
of Albany was the heart of Clinton country, and Republicans in this region refused to cooperate in the administration's efforts.[134] Even

[128] Stagg, *Mr. Madison's War*, 468, 230–31, 253; Horsman, *Frontier in the Formative Years*,
122–23; Hickey, *War of 1812: A Forgotten Conflict*, 80, 259; Meinig, *Shaping of America*, 47;
Pratt, *Expansionists of 1812*, 163.
[129] Morison, "Dissent in the War of 1812," 6.
[130] Stagg, *Mr. Madison's War*, 231, 265; Morison, "Dissent in the War of 1812," 12.
[131] Ibid., 262.
[132] Ibid., 362.
[133] Chester, *Sectionalism, Politics, and American Diplomacy*, 29–30.
[134] Stagg, *Mr. Madison's War*, 232.

though it was imperative that the United States engage Great Britain from the Niagara frontier across Lake Champlain to the area north of New Hampshire and Maine, this strategy failed because of regional dissent and the political system that empowered it.[135]

After two and a half years of war, Madison himself realized that this well-orchestrated opposition from Federalists and Republicans in the Northeast, in the U.S. Congress, and the states themselves had been fatal to his efforts to take the war into Canada. By the fall of 1814 Madison was described by a friend as "miserably shattered and woe-begone . . . . His mind seems full of the New England revolt."[136] In this same period Madison wrote to another friend, "You are not mistaken in viewing the conduct of the [North]eastern states as the source of our greatest difficulties in carrying on the war."[137]

East Florida

The military adventurism of the United States in East Florida is a forgotten episode in U.S. history.[138] Yet it is an important case in which forceful territorial expansion was possible and military means were chosen to pursue the objective. Between 1811 and 1813 the Madison administration conducted a covert operation to undermine Spanish authority in East Florida and then assembled a large military force in preparation for an overt invasion to seize the province and demand its cession from Spain.[139] For nearly a year, U.S. army, navy, and militia forces occupied large sections of East Florida. These U.S. forces fought sporadically with Spanish troops, Seminole Indians, and free black militia, and they were busy preparing for a final assault on St. Augustine, the capital of the Spanish colony. This bold, forceful expansionist effort failed, however, but not because of flagging will, inadequate military force, or skilled Spanish resistance. This was an effort driven by the executive branch with considerable determination. The force

---

[135] Horsman, *Frontier in the Formative Years*, 172–73.

[136] Hickey, *War of 1812: A Forgotten Conflict*, 231.

[137] Ibid., 86.

[138] Virginia Peters notes that this is a part of U.S. history "seldom mentioned in text books except by a passing reference or an unobtrusive footnote." *The Florida Wars* (Hamden, CT: Archon Books, 1979), 18. See also Joseph Burkholder Smith, *The Plot to Steal Florida: James Madison's Phony War* (New York: Arbor House, 1983), 14.

[139] Spain divided its Florida colony into western and eastern sections. East Florida was that part of present day Florida east of the Apalachicola River.

deployed for the offensive, composed of regular army troops and militia from Georgia and Tennessee, was capable of overwhelming any adversary in the region. And Spain's pitiful forces at St. Augustine were expected to fall easily to the U.S. assault. Forceful expansion into East Florida failed because of domestic politics, specifically, because of a clash of contending regional interests within the federal democratic system. President Madison and his southern supporters simply could not overcome strong Republican and Federalist opposition from northerners in Congress who ultimately forced the administration to withdraw from the region. The United States came to possess East Florida several years later, but only because Spain agreed to sell this colony as part of its effort to recover from bankruptcy produced by the Napoleonic Wars.[140]

President Madison made no secret of his belief that East Florida must become a permanent part of the American Union. For Madison, there were three compelling reasons for pursuing this expansionist goal: strategic, political, and regional. Publicly, he most frequently advanced the strategic rationale for gaining possession of East Florida, and was not alone in his understanding of the strategic value of this territory to the United States. The Republican party's interest in obtaining East Florida from Spain predated 1812 by several decades. In 1793 Thomas Jefferson expressed his belief that in the hands of the decrepit Spanish monarchy East Florida posed no security problem for the United States. Yet should this province be occupied by Great Britain, this adversary would "thus completely encircle us with her colonies and fleets," and immediately become a grave threat.[141] As secretary of state in 1803 Madison argued that with the Louisiana Purchase, Florida lost its importance to Spain but became of great value to the United States. If Spain should refuse to sell East Florida, he predicted that it would be "a source of irritation and ill blood with the United States."[142] In 1811 Madison and Monroe were making the same arguments about the dangers of British occupation of East Florida. Not

---

[140] Herbert Bruce Fuller, *The Purchase of Florida: Its History and Diplomacy* (Cleveland: Burrows Brothers, 1906); Philip Coolidge Brooks, *Diplomacy and the Borderlands: The Adams-Onis Treaty of 1819* (New York: Octagon Books, 1970).

[141] Frank Lawrence Owsley, Jr., and Gene A. Smith, *Filibusters and Expansionists: Jeffersonian Manifest Destiny, 1800–1821* (Tuscaloosa: University of Alabama Press, 1997), 24. Fuller finds that the relationship between the security of U.S. independence and its possession of Florida was raised as early as 1777. Fuller, *Purchase of Florida*, 30.

[142] Smith, *Plot to Steal Florida*, 116.

only could Florida be used as a base of operations against the United States, Florida was essential for guarding the passage between the Atlantic Ocean and the Gulf of Mexico, through which passed all U.S. commerce from the Mississippi River.[143]

In 1811 and 1812 Madison also believed that his vigorous pursuit of expansion into Florida would serve to strengthen his political position within the country and the Republican party. As the Republicans looked ahead to the presidential elections of 1812, Madison faced a challenge to his renomination from supporters of James Monroe, who had just been elected governor of Virginia. Monroe's support came largely from expansionists in the party who were attracted to his repeated calls for the immediate seizure of West and East Florida. Expansionists in the United States saw additional opportunities in Texas, Mexico, and South America, as Spain's grip on its colonies in the Western Hemisphere appeared to be threatened by internal rebellion. These expansionists looked to Monroe as the champion of their broad vision. By January 1811, Madison recognized the danger to his political future if this movement in support of Monroe was allowed to build.

Among expansionist groups in the United States, Americans living in the border regions of the South, and particularly the political leaders of Georgia, were instrumental in carrying the Madison administration's expansionist policy forward. While southerners would certainly approve of the strategic national reasons for the occupation and annexation of East Florida, Georgians supported this goal because of particular regional interests and fears. Each of these interests and fears was intensified by the uncertainty that accompanied the prospects of war with Great Britain.[144] As Meinig points out, the

> real pressure against Florida for American annexation was generated and sustained not so much as a national response to British machinations, the possible disintegration of the Spanish Empire, or larger geopolitical considerations, as from those who wanted to control, crush, even utterly destroy some specific peoples of Florida who were considered to pose a danger to immediate regional interests. The real pressure . . . came directly out of the frontiers and plantations of Georgia and Tennessee.[145]

[143] Rembert W. Patrick, *Florida Fiasco: Rampant Rebels on the Georgia-Florida Border, 1810–1815* (Athens: University of Georgia Press, 1954), 31.

[144] Brown, *Republic in Peril*, 127; Pratt, *Expansionists of 1812*, 121–24.

[145] Meinig, *Shaping of America*, 31.

One group that caused great anxiety among southerners was the large population of free blacks, many of them runaway slaves from the United States, living in East Florida. Florida had long been a refuge for runaway slaves, and their proximity to Georgia plantations and farms meant that they could serve as an inspiration for others to follow. Worse yet was the nightmare of a slave rebellion in Georgia, where half the rural population was composed of slaves. Newspapers in Georgia and South Carolina continually warned their readers that the U.S. South could suffer the same fate that France had suffered in the 1790s, when a French colonial army was slaughtered in a slave revolt on the island of Santo Domingo. The only way to prevent this in the United States, the editors would argue, would be through U.S. control of the free black population in Florida that could incite such a rebellion.[146] Southerners were also outraged that Spain was arming this free black population to foster their assistance in resisting U.S. incursions into Spanish territory.[147]

Southerners in the border region were also perpetually concerned with the threat posed by the Seminoles and other Native American tribes living in Spanish Florida. Because of the absence of effective Spanish control over its own province, the Seminoles roamed freely in the interior of Florida and often conducted looting raids across the border into Georgia.[148] Efforts by the United States to seize East Florida and crush the Native Americans became more determined once the Spanish began using them, as they did the black population, to help resist U.S. encroachments. By 1812, the Seminoles had formed their own alliance with organized black militias in this effort. For southerners like Governor Mitchell of Georgia, the regional stakes in the acquisition of Florida were clear. In a letter to Monroe he declared, "The inconveniences which our fellow citizens of the South Eastern parts of the State suffer, from the desertion & employment of their negroes, by the Spaniards, as soldiers, & the inducements which they hold out to the blacks to desert, together with depredations of the Indians, are so great, that I should be willing to obtain possession of [East Florida] on any terms."[149]

With his political interests threatened, and under pressure from southerners to take action against regional threats, Madison knew that

---

[146] Smith, *Plot to Steal Florida*, 15–16, 43–44.
[147] Patrick, *Florida Fiasco*, 31; Smith, *Plot to Steal Florida*, 265.
[148] Patrick, *Florida Fiasco*, 31; Peters, *Florida Wars*, 29.
[149] Brown, *Republic in Peril*, 221 n. 29.

the time was right to act on the strategic justification for annexing East Florida. As Madison moved ahead with his political and military measures to gain possession, it was clear to both U.S. and Spanish authorities that in terms of relative military capabilities, "Spain's hold on Florida or any other borderland territory could not withstand a concerted American attack . . . . Spain had no reinforcements to spare for far-flung military outposts, least of all unimportant ones in North America."[150] Governor White of East Florida could never maintain the core troop strength he desired; much of the problem was due to desertion, which was common. Those troops he did have were "motley recruits" from Mexico, Spain, Cuba, Germany, and Italy.[151] His successor, Governor Kindelan, described his force as "408 men of all nations, races and colors . . . for the most part a miserable city militia totally ignorant of the use of a rifle."[152] The government in Madrid also had a bleak assessment of Spain's situation in East Florida, which was revealed in a letter from the foreign minister to Spain's minister in the United States: "Spain has for a long time had abundant motives for considering itself in a state of war with the United States, but in the critical situation in which she sees herself, having to sustain destructive wars in both hemispheres [against Napoleon and her own colonies] which absorb all her resources, she cannot count on the necessary forces to oppose the insults of the American government with probability of success.[153] With such a clear relative advantage here, it would seem that Madison would easily overwhelm Spanish resistance and achieve his expansionist objectives.

The first concrete step in this direction came on January 15, 1811, when Congress acted on the general fear that the festering crisis with Great Britain might lead this adversary to take possession of East Florida. Congress declared "that the United States, under the peculiar circumstances of the existing crisis, cannot, without serious inquietude, see any part of the said territory pass into the hands of any foreign power."[154] To give force to this declaration, Congress authorized the president to seize and occupy Florida east of the Perdido River under two conditions: (1) if it became apparent that a foreign power was about to take possession of the province from Spain; or (2) if the

[150] Owsley and Smith, *Filibusters and Expansionists*, 64.
[151] Smith, *Plot to Steal Florida*, 93.
[152] Pratt, *Expansionists of 1812*, 103–4.
[153] Brooks, *Diplomacy and Borderlands*, 21.
[154] Pratt, *Expansionists of 1812*, 68.

government of East Florida or any "local authority" should *voluntarily* "surrender" the province to the United States. The resolution further authorized the president to use the army and the navy if this became necessary, and it provided a special appropriation of $100,000 for the task. The vote on this resolution was split mainly on party lines; Republicans rallied behind the president and his concerns for the strategic value of East Florida to the United States, and thus overwhelmed Federalist opposition that was unanimously against any move toward the Spanish colony.[155]

While Madison now had the authority to take the province under certain circumstances, the actual situation in East Florida posed a dilemma for him. At no time could Madison produce evidence that Spain intended to hand the province over to Britain. There was no evidence to suggest that Britain was about to invade East Florida and take it by force, or that Britain even desired such a move. Nor was there ever a truly indigenous effort within East Florida to foment rebellion against Spanish authority. Much of the population in East Florida was actually made up of U.S. citizens who had taken advantage of Spain's liberal immigration policy to establish plantations and businesses. These U.S. settlers were quite content with Spanish rule and the autonomy with which they could live their lives.[156] Therefore, Madison had no legal pretext for seizing the region. The only solution was to engineer the conditions under which he was authorized to take possession of East Florida: by either convincing the government of East Florida to cede the province willingly, or if this failed, to mount a covert mission to organize and equip a local rebellion against Spain.

On the recommendation of Senator Crawford of Georgia, the president selected General George Mathews, a hero of the Revolutionary War and a former governor of Georgia, as his executive agent for this mission. After a meeting with the president in Washington, Mathews hurried to Pensacola, Florida, to meet with Spanish colonial authorities to discuss a voluntary cession of the territory. Mathews was soundly rebuffed by Governor Foch, colonial administrator for both West and East Florida, who had been given strict orders by the Spanish government to hold onto all of Florida. Mathews also knew that Governor Estrada of East Florida would never surrender the region

---

[155] Ibid., 133; Patrick, *Florida Fiasco*, 4; Smith, *Plot to Steal Florida*, 117–18.
[156] Pratt, *Expansionists of 1812*, 227; Smith, *Plot to Steal Florida*, 147–48; Patrick, *Florida Fiasco*, 49.

voluntarily, so this avenue for the cession of the province was closed.[157] But Mathews was not deterred. If the existing Spanish authorities were not willing to turn over East Florida to the United States, he had been instructed by Madison to "pursue the recruitment of suitable persons who could constitute the local authorities mentioned in the written instructions [in congressional legislation] and who would be willing to offer him the province." In other words, Mathews was to recruit his own indigenous "revolutionary" force that would seize power and turn East Florida over to the United States.[158]

A little more than a year after Congress had expressed its concerns about East Florida falling into foreign hands, Mathews had succeeded in creating the necessary conditions for the president to legally take possession of the province. In a ceremony on March 13, 1812, the force Mathews had recruited, organized, and funded declared its independence from Spain and immediately requested that the United States take possession of all territory between the St. Johns and St. Mary rivers. While Mathews insisted that this was a local revolutionary force, it only included nine actual residents of East Florida, the remainder of the seventy-odd-man force was made up of Georgians. Now "independent" from Spain, it was clear that the "Patriot" movement would require direct U.S. assistance for the final task of defeating the Spanish garrison at St. Augustine. Despite Madison's public disavowal of Mathews's actions, by April 9, 1812 Madison had decided to protect the Patriot movement and thereby maintain a U.S. presence in the region. The president appointed Governor Mitchell of Georgia to replace Mathews and ordered him to continue the occupation of East Florida with a force of regular army troops, navy ships, and Georgia militia.[159]

With U.S. forces in place and St. Augustine under siege, political resistance in Congress to U.S. occupation of East Florida began to take shape by the end of June and the beginning of July 1812. This was the beginning of the domestic struggle over the use of military force in

---

[157] Patrick, *Florida Fiasco*, 33–41.

[158] In order to deny official U.S. involvement if the operation were exposed, Madison never provided Mathews with written instructions explicitly ordering him to organize a rebellion in East Florida. Yet historians agree that Madison and Monroe were fully aware of Mathews's actions. Mathews sent numerous detailed reports of his plans and his progress, he had Senator Crawford brief the administration personally, and never once was he ordered to halt his activities. Monroe had even authorized a shipment of weapons to the "Patriot" movement Mathews had organized. Pratt, *Expansionists of 1812*, 108–12; Patrick, *Florida Fiasco*, 58–64; Smith, *Plot to Steal Florida*, 118–19, 233–60.

[159] Patrick, *Florida Fiasco*, 83–100, 128–30; Smith, *Plot to Steal Florida*, 176–83, 246.

East Florida that would eventually bring the operation to an end and compel the withdrawal of American forces. The institutional point of constraint was located with Congress, specifically, the Senate. It was in this body that two major votes on the issue denied President Madison the authority to continue occupying East Florida with military force. The Republican party had a Senate majority of thirty to six in the Twelfth Congress. Any legislative constraint on the Republican president's actions depended on the defection of nearly half of the Republican senators. The two major votes on East Florida reflected a clear division between northern and southern states overall, and a regional split in the Republican party.

The first major political defeat for the president came on July 3, when a bill that would allow the United States to occupy and establish a temporary government in East Florida, based on the Patriot's declaration of independence in March, was defeated in the Senate by a vote of 14 to 16. Senator Crawford of Georgia, who was following the lead of a colleague from Georgia in the U.S. House, Representative George Troup, sponsored the amendment authorizing this temporary U.S. government for East Florida. Troup had introduced a resolution on June 19 asking the Special Committee on Spanish-American colonies to evaluate whether the United States should take immediate possession of West and East Florida. On June 25, the Republican majority in the House authorized the president "to occupy and hold, the whole or any part of East Florida, including Amelia Island," and Madison was confident that the Republican majority in the Senate would follow suit. He was shocked, however, by the loss of key Republican votes from the northern states. The Republican delegations from Georgia, South Carolina, North Carolina, Tennessee, and Ohio unanimously supported the administration on occupation. The Republican delegations from New Hampshire, Rhode Island, New York, Pennsylvania, and Maryland joined the Federalist delegations from Connecticut and Delaware to vote unanimously against the occupation. One Republican senator from Vermont, New Jersey, Kentucky, and Virginia voted against the occupation. The Federalist senator from Massachusetts voted against the occupation, while the Republican senator from that state remained loyal to the president.[160] The defection of these northern Republican senators defeated the bill, thus denying Madison the legal grounds for continuing to hold much of East Florida with the

---

[160] Pratt, *Expansionists of 1812*, 150–52; Patrick, *Florida Fiasco*, 147–50.

forces now in the region. This Senate defeat also prevented him from mounting a final assault on St. Augustine.

On July 6, 1812, Monroe wrote to the governor of Georgia to inform him that "since the rejection of the bill in the Senate, the President thinks that it will be more advisable to withdraw the troops from East Florida."[161] Dismayed by the threat that the situation along the southern frontier posed, particularly when the United States had just declared war on Great Britain, Mitchell retorted,

> I feel that it is a duty that I owe to the United States, and Georgia in particular, to assure you that the situation of the garrison of St. Augustine will not admit of the troops being withdrawn. They have armed every able-bodied negro within their power, and they have also received from Havana a reinforcement of nearly two companies of black troops! . . . it is my settled opinion that if they are suffered to remain in the province; our southern country will soon be in a state of insurrection . . . . These may be considerations of little import in the opinion of those gentlemen of the Senate who voted against the bill, but they are of vital interest to every man in the southern states.[162]

Mitchell was supported in his argument by the Georgia legislature, which condemned the Senate vote and authorized the governor to deploy a volunteer cavalry to patrol the southern border and to assist the federal government in any way to bring East Florida under the complete control of the United States.[163] Monroe chose not to fight the strong sentiment in Georgia. Using the original congressional authorization of 1811 he argued that the threat of British occupation justified continued U.S. intervention in East Florida, despite the recent Senate disavowal of this policy and the absence of current legal authority for doing so.

In December 1812 Madison and Monroe determined that the time had come for an aggressive military operation to secure East Florida once and for all. To prepare for this, Governor Mitchell was relieved as commander of the U.S. operation so he could return to his duties in Georgia. Major General Thomas Pickney was given the command to ensure that a skilled military leader would achieve victory. Pickney was ordered to concentrate all U.S. forces south of Virginia at the military outpost of Point Petre, just north of the border with Spanish

---

[161] Patrick, *Florida Fiasco*, 151.
[162] Pratt, *Expansionists of 1812*, 194 n. 8.
[163] Ibid., 212–14; Patrick, *Florida Fiasco*, 215–17.

territory. These forces would be prepared to reinforce army troops currently in East Florida and to initiate offensive operations when ordered. In his instructions to Pickney, Monroe explained that the "force is ... to be embodied ... for offensive operations, preparation to the entire possession of the Province of East Florida."[164] To the west, Andrew Jackson had assembled a force of 2,070 volunteers from Tennessee and was moving south to New Orleans. He planned to then move east to combine forces with Pickney for the conquest of St. Augustine. An overwhelming American force was poised to make the final strike, and with little expected difficulty would sweep the Seminoles, free blacks, and Spain from the region.[165]

Moving in tandem with these military preparations was a drive by administration supporters in Congress to deliver the legal authority the president needed to pursue offensive operations. Both Madison and Monroe were confident that they would receive Senate approval this time.[166] The previous bill of July 1812 was defeated by only two votes. Since then Louisiana had become a state, adding two enthusiastic southern votes for the annexation of Florida. Additionally, they hoped that after a disappointing start to the land campaign against Great Britain the widespread national feeling that the United States needed a victory somewhere might convince some of the dissenting Republicans to back the administration's initiative.[167] To capitalize on what was considered changing opinion, Senator Anderson of Tennessee introduced a bill on January 19, 1813, that authorized the president "to take possession of a tract of country lying south of the Mississippi Territory and of Georgia." This included both West and East Florida. But on January 26 Republican senator Smith of Maryland introduced an amendment to the bill that would eliminate authority for the East Florida portion of the operation. On February 2, 1813, for the second and final time, the Senate voted to deny Madison the authority to seize East Florida from Spain by approving Smith's amendment 19 to 16.

The vote on the amendment reflected a clear regional division between North and South, splitting the Republican party on regional lines as many northern Republicans once again forged a coalition with northeastern Federalists to defeat Madison's use of military force. The only southern or northwestern votes against Madison came from two

---

[164] Patrick, *Florida Fiasco*, 223.
[165] Ibid., 220–23, 241–47; Pratt, *Expansionists of 1812*, 221–26.
[166] Patrick, *Florida Fiasco*, 248.
[167] Smith, *Plot to Steal Florida*, 273.

Republican political opponents, Giles of Virginia and Pope of Kentucky, who were declared enemies of the president that consistently opposed him whatever the issue. The only northern votes in support of Madison were from loyal Republicans in Massachusetts, New Hampshire, Vermont and Ohio. Aside from these exceptions, Connecticut, Rhode Island, Delaware, New York, New Jersey, Pennsylvania, and Maryland voted solidly to constrain Madison, while North and South Carolina, Georgia, Tennessee, and Louisiana voted solidly to support the adventure. In all, eleven of the sixteen Republicans from north of the Potomac and Ohio rivers voted against aggressive expansion.[168] In combination with Federalist opposition, Madison's expansionist drive was doomed in Congress. As a result, Madison and Monroe abandoned their plans, Secretary of War Armstrong notified Jackson to send his volunteers back to Tennessee, and he ordered Pickney to withdraw U.S. troops and naval units then in East Florida.

Conclusion

During the period under study in this chapter the United States faced a range of external pressures that jeopardized its economic prosperity, its territorial integrity and autonomy as a state, and the safety of its citizens. While geographically buffered from the direct effects of the Napoleonic Wars, the United States suffered economically through maritime restrictions on its ability to trade with the belligerents as a neutral nation. These restrictions, combined with the impressment of U.S. sailors by the Royal Navy, were an insult to the rights of the United States, its honor, and its reputation as a sovereign state. Other states have certainly gone to war over matters much less grave. Do these external pressures then explain the decision of the United States to use military force in 1812? Clearly they do not tell the whole story, particularly for our interest in the effects of democratic institutions on the use of military force. Any explanation that looks solely at external factors for this decision is unconvincing when we ask a question that many historians and social scientists neglect concerning this case: why did the United States not declare war on Great Britain during the crises of 1807 and 1809, when external pressures on the United States

---

[168] Pratt, *Expansionists of 1812*, 229; Patrick, *Florida Fiasco*, 250–54.

were greater? This chapter suggests that the key to explaining the different outcomes in 1807, 1809, and 1812, is found at the domestic level. External pressures are still an essential part of the explanation. Without the underlying tension between the United States and Great Britain over restrictions on neutral trade and Britain's support for the Native American confederation along the frontier of the Northwest there would have been no reason for this military conflict. The reaction of the United States to these external pressures, however, was not determined simply by the purportedly objective weight of these threats to the "national interests." Within the United States perceptions of these external pressures and their effects on domestic interests were shaped in fundamental ways by federal asymmetry among the three main regions of the United States. As Madison himself anticipated in *The Federalist Papers*, the different "circumstances" geographically distributed across the federal republic produced widely different perspectives on the wisdom, justice, or consequences of using force to confront Great Britain and to address security issues on the periphery. From these cases we can see that regional interests were the seedbed of both compelling and constraining influences on decisions over the use of military force. But these asymmetric regional interests are then situated within a specific institutional setting. The characteristics of this institutional setting provided political incentives for representing certain interests, they determined the number of veto players that had a role in policymaking, and they shaped the kinds of institutional leverage that various political actors had in the competitive policy process. Taken together, federal asymmetry on questions of foreign policy and the institutional framework within which policymaking takes place acted as potent intervening variables between the external factors that might stimulate state behavior and the kinds of state behavior that resulted.

In 1807, the institutional point of constraint on the use of force was presidential self-restraint. Regional divisions on the question of war would have impeded a quick resort to force in the absence of diplomatic efforts to obtain redress from Great Britain. As the war spirit cooled, Jefferson lost his broad potential base of support for war and he chose not to risk a legislative defeat on a request for war. In 1809, pressure from the Northwest and the South for a more aggressive policy toward Great Britain again raised the prospects of war. The institutional point of constraint on this war movement was in Congress. The territorially organized, state-based system of representation in Congress provided the opponents of replacing embargo with war, concentrated in the Northeast, with an institutional basis for pressing their regional demands at the national level. The Republican majority in Congress did not believe that British threats to the United States at that time justified splitting the party or the Union so severely, and as a result the majority withheld support from their more bellicose colleagues. Northeastern dissent, therefore, dominated the issue. The War Hawks of 1809 simply could not muster a legislative majority for their resolution.

By 1812, however, the intensity of regional preferences on the question of war with Great Britain had changed dramatically. By this time, the economic impact of British maritime policies had become severe for the Northwest and the South. Additionally, the security of the northwestern frontier was now perceived to be seriously jeopardized by British intriguing with the Indian confederation that, after 1810, was conducting raids against U.S. settlers. The Northeast remained strongly opposed to resorting to military force against Great Britain, yet the War Hawks of the other regions now had little concern for party unity in the face of the threats they blamed on Great Britain. Without leadership from the War Hawks, who were desperately seeking relief for regional interests, the institutional impediments to consensus within Congress would have constrained a declaration of war once again. However, the War Hawks were able to maintain enough Republican party loyalty in all regions to pass a declaration of war in the Senate and the House, despite the coalition of Federalists and dissident Republicans in the Northeast who voted against it.

Regional interests were also crucial for advancing the expansionist drives into Upper and Lower Canada and East Florida. The federal system that had constrained the use of military force in 1807 and 1809 now provided an institutional outlet at the national level for regional demands for territorial expansion at the expense of Great Britain and Spain. Each of these initiatives failed, however. Based on relative capabilities alone we would expect a much different result. But in 1812 and 1813, domestic dissent, organized territorially within the context of the federal system, mattered more. Regional opposition mattered as a constraint on northerly expansion only because southern Republicans and northeastern Republicans and Federalists could form a congressional bloc to deny the president a provisional army for taking the fight into Canada. Northeastern opposition also mattered because the Federalists could use the autonomous political base and institutions of state governments to deny the president access to militia forces. Regional opposition mattered as a constraint on southerly expansion only because northern Republicans and Federalists could form a congressional bloc to deny the president the legal authority he needed for an overwhelming assault on East Florida. In each instance it was the combination of federal asymmetry and the institutional authority provided to regional representatives at the national level and in the states that raised obstacles to these war goals.

4

THE OREGON CRISIS OF 1845–1846

In the early months of 1846, the United States and Great Britain stood on the brink of war over possession of the Oregon Territory. For nearly three decades the United States and Britain had managed to avoid such a conflict and to accommodate their mutual claims in the Pacific Northwest through a joint occupation agreement. During the 1840s, however, domestic pressure was building for the United States to firmly establish sovereign control over some portion of Oregon as American settlers poured into the Willamette Valley south of the Co-lumbia River. Extreme expansionists were demanding the "whole of Oregon," from 42 degrees north latitude up to the border with Russian Alaska, which would eliminate the British presence on the Pacific coast. From his first day in office, President Polk prodded the British government through diplomatic brinkmanship in an effort to force a settlement on U.S. terms. Yet Great Britain was determined not to back down in response to the confrontational approach of the United States and certainly would not relinquish the entire territory. Britain main-tained material interests in the region through the Hudson's Bay Com-pany, which continued to use the Columbia River to support the fur trade. But more important, national reputation was at stake in the emerging standoff. Even the dovish foreign secretary, Lord Aberdeen, realized that Britain could not relent in the face of U.S. pressure. Nei-ther side wanted a war to resolve the Oregon problem, yet at the height of the crisis both parties stood firm on irreconcilable claims that only war or capitulation could resolve. Indeed, war was thought to be a real possibility across the political spectrum in both the United States and Great Britain.

Despite the intensity of this crisis in early 1846 and the serious risk of war, war was not the outcome. On June 18, 1846, the United States ratified a treaty that divided the Oregon Territory at 49 degrees north latitude. While Great Britain took the initiative by proposing the treaty terms that the United States eventually accepted, it was the United States that backtracked from the extreme territorial demands that had produced the crisis in the first place. The main question for this case then is why did the United States accept a compromise resolution to the crisis after pushing the dispute to the brink of war?

Two previous studies have posed this same question regarding the Oregon case, yet advance opposing answers. John Owen proposes a liberal normative explanation for constraints on military force, arguing that the United States chose compromise rather than war because a peace coalition in Congress, motivated by a perception of Britain as a fellow liberal state, imposed restraints on a war-prone President Polk.[1] Stephen Rock challenges this normative argument when he finds no overriding liberal affinity between the United States and Great Britain during this period. Instead, he argues, realist calculations of the limited value of the disputed territory and the expected heavy costs of fighting for it made restraint and compromise the prudent strategic choice for President Polk. Rock bluntly concludes, "Democratic peace theory is of little value in explaining the pacific resolution of the Oregon crisis."[2] As we will see below, Rock is correct to dismiss Owen's claim that liberal affinity was the overriding motive that kept the United States and Great Britain from an armed clash over Oregon. Owen's evidence certainly captures the fact that some political actors within the American and British systems opposed war for normative reasons. Prominent liberals and liberal newspapers did speak out against war between these fellow liberal states. However, there is no evidence to suggest that normative affinity

---

[1] John M. Owen IV, *Liberal Peace, Liberal War: American Politics and International Security* (Ithaca: Cornell University Press, 1997).

[2] Stephen R. Rock, "Anglo-U.S. Relations, 1845–1930: Did Shared Liberal Values and Democratic Institutions Keep the Peace?" in *Paths to Peace: Is Democracy the Answer?* ed. Miriam Fendius Elman (Cambridge: MIT Press, 1997), 109.

was the only motivation for opposition to war, or even the dominant reason. In fact, opposition to war with Great Britain from different segments of the U.S. political system emerged from a complex combination of commercial, political, realist, and normative concerns. Owen misses these other reasons for opposing the war held by various political actors, he neglects how these other opinions were distributed territorially across the Union, and he glosses over how the distinctive institutions of the United States actually produced a political victory for the peace coalition. While Rock is correct to critique Owen's explanation, his own conclusion that peace was the result of a strategic choice made by President Polk based on cost-benefit calculations and the distribution of power is simply not supported by the evidence. Throughout this crisis Polk never took the initiative to deescalate. Moderation in the U.S. position came from Congress, in the face of a persistently defiant president.

Rock's general dismissal of a democratic peace explanation for the Oregon resolution is based on a narrow theoretical perspective. There is no reason to assert that liberal norms are necessary for democracy to have a constraining effect on interstate conflict. His analysis fails to consider how the democratic *institutional arrangement* of the U.S. political system may have contributed to this outcome, and in the process misses crucial evidence of domestic competition over the Oregon policy. What matters for an institutional democratic peace argument is that the multiple sources of opposition to war become relevant for policy outcomes because the state's democratic institutional arrangement provided an outlet for competition among advocates and opponents of war. To address this point within the framework of the American federal union, it is essential to evaluate several questions. First, did the Oregon problem stimulate an asymmetric response among the various regions of the United States? Furthermore, were members of Congress representing regional interests in the policy process and the debates on how to resolve this crisis? Second, to what degree did the main political parties, the Democrats and the Whigs, centralize decision-making on the issue, or facilitate consensus among members from different parts of the country? Or, did federal asymmetry have any role in weakening party cohesion on the issue, thus making institutional divisions in the system more salient as a constraint on executive action? Finally, if Oregon policy was subjected to domestic political competition, what institutional points of constraint had an impact on the decision by the United States to avoid war and compromise on the problem?

The Origins of the Oregon Question as an International Dispute

Control of the Oregon Territory first became a point of conflict in
Anglo-U.S. relations shortly after the War of 1812. As both British and
U.S. fur trappers moved west in the early nineteenth century, it became
apparent that the Columbia River was a valuable site for shipping
North American furs to the insatiable market in Asia. Two attempts to
set an international boundary, in 1818 and 1826–1827, ended in diplomatic stalemate, but the joint occupation agreement of 1818 gave fur
trappers and traders from each country equal access to the region's resources. While this agreement removed the immediate source of tension between the United States and Britain in the region, the issue of
sovereign title to the entire Oregon Territory remained unresolved. A
confusing set of treaties in the mid-1820s, and the political forces behind this diplomacy, demonstrated that the conflict between the
United States and Great Britain over final possession would only worsen
with time. In 1824 Russia signed a treaty with the United States that
set 54 degrees 40 minutes north latitude as the line separating their respective spheres of influence in North America. For the United States,
this reflected the intent of the Monroe Doctrine of 1823 to contain the
growth of European power in the Western Hemisphere. It was also a
useful way for President John Quincy Adams to deflect political pressure from the states of the Old Northwest.[3] Adams had been roundly
criticized by westerners in the presidential campaign for being soft on
Great Britain to win fishing concessions for his fellow New Englanders, and for needlessly giving up Texas when he negotiated the
Florida treaty of 1819 as secretary of state. As western influence in U.S.
politics grew in the 1820s, Adams could not ignore charges from politicians who claimed that he was prepared to forsake western interests in
Oregon too. In response to this challenge from the United States,
Britain also signed a treaty with Russia less than a year later designat-
ing the same boundary between Russian and British spheres of influence in the region. It was clear from these treaties that the United
States and Britain both recognized the northern limits of the Oregon

---

[3] This region now included the states of Ohio, Indiana, Illinois, and Michigan. As
frontier states in the early decades of U.S. independence, Kentucky and Tennessee were
classified as part of the Northwest, primarily because their geographic position relative
to the U.S. periphery at that time oriented their sense of identity and external threat to
the northwest. By the 1840s, the orientation of Kentucky and Tennessee was directed
southward. Joel H. Silbey, *The Shrine of Party: Congressional Voting Behavior 1841–1852*
(Pittsburgh: University of Pittsburgh Press, 1967), 19–21.

Territory. They also served as an unambiguous symbol of the unresolved dispute, a legal manifestation of a more serious set of political
developments in each country that threatened to bring the United
States and Great Britain to blows over the balance of power in North
America.[4] Not ready for a violent breach over the issue, however, they
again put Oregon aside for a future date by extending the joint occupation agreement indefinitely.[5]

Quiescent through the 1830s, the Oregon question was again a serious diplomatic issue by the early 1840s, driven by the domestic politics of U.S. settlement and a general resurgence within the United
States of expansionist enthusiasm.[6] There was wide consensus across
the spectrum of regional and party interests behind the claim that the
United States should possess territory on the Pacific coast. What did
create great political contests, however, were the rival claims within
the United States to how much of the Oregon Territory the United
States should pursue, and at what risk in its relations with Great
Britain. Should the United States demand complete British abdication
of its claims to any portion of Oregon, so the United States could assume control to the Russian border at 54 degrees 40 minutes north latitude? Should the United States pursue this goal even at the risk of
war with Great Britain? Or, should the United States settle the dispute
at 49 degrees north latitude, thereby acceding a large portion of the
territory to its rival, but gaining access to Puget Sound through peaceful means?

As with similar questions of territorial expansion and war raised
decades before, these questions on Oregon produced strong regional
divisions that shaped the politics of the issue in decisive ways. And as
in earlier efforts to confront Great Britain over its role in North America, the Old Northwest was the center of agitation for a hard-line
diplomatic position and the region's politicians, press, and citizens became the most persistent source of bellicose rhetoric and ambitions for

---

[4] George H. Classen, *Thrust and Counterthrust: The Genesis of the Canada-United States Boundary* (Chicago: Rand McNally, 1965), 164.

[5] Frederick Merk, *The Oregon Question* (Cambridge: Harvard University Press, 1967), 10–31, 123–78.

[6] Anders Stephanson, *Manifest Destiny: American Expansionism and the Empire of Right* (New York: Hill and Wang, 1995); Frederick Merk, *Manifest Destiny and Mission in American History: A Reinterpretation* (Cambridge: Harvard University Press, 1963); Thomas R. Hietala, *Manifest Design: Anxious Aggrandizement in Late Jacksonian America* (Ithaca: Cornell University Press, 1985); William Earl Weeks, *Building the Continental Empire* (Chicago: Ivan R. Dee, 1996).

All Oregon in the 1840s. Because northwestern Democrats consistently edged out northwestern Whigs in the popular vote, in terms of party identity the most prominent activists on Oregon at the national-level were Democrats.[7] Despite the close association between Democrats and the Oregon issue in the Old Northwest, political opponents in their home states never seriously undercut their activist role. Instead, Democrats were often able to attract substantial support from northwestern Whigs on this expansionist goal. This was a regional issue on which politicians from both parties could agree. For example, as the question of America's Oregon policy became a dominant issue in national-level political discourse, the leading Whig newspaper in Michigan firmly declared that the United States' title to All Oregon was "clear and unquestionable," parroting the words of the Democratic party platform and President Polk's inaugural address.[8] Similarly, at the height of the debate in Congress in 1846 the rhetoric of Michigan Senator Lewis Cass, who supported a confrontational stance against Great Britain, found a sympathetic audience in many northwestern Whigs who were subsequently drawn away from the national Whig party's opposition to this policy.[9]

A flood of U.S. settlers who for the first time established a well-developed U.S. presence in the region generated renewed interest in Oregon in the early 1840s.[10] On the far side of the continent, living in a region governed only by the Anglo-U.S. joint occupation agreement, these settlers lacked both the physical and legal protection of the

---

[7] Silbey, *Shrine of Party*, 20. With the collapse of the Federalist party after the War of 1812, the United States lacked a well-organized party system until Andrew Jackson founded the Democratic party. By the 1830s it had become the "first mass party in the Western world." John Gerring, *Party Ideologies in America, 1828–1996* (Cambridge: Cambridge University Press, 1998), 162. In response to the organizational success of the Democrats, Henry Clay, the former Republican War Hawk from Kentucky, organized the Whig party and a two-party system quickly stabilized on a national level and lasted until the late 1840s. Keith Polakoff, *Political Parties in American History* (New York: Alfred A. Knopf, 1981). Democrats dominated the northwestern delegation by nearly three to one from 1844 to 1846 and by two to one from 1846 to 1848. Whigs dominated the New England delegation in the House by a two to one margin, and before the elections of 1846 Democrats from the South Atlantic region had a three to one edge. Thomas B. Alexander, *Sectional Stress and Party Strength: A Study of Roll-Call Voting Patterns in the United States House of Representatives, 1836–1860* (Nashville, Tenn.: Vanderbilt University Press, 1967), 58, 63–64.

[8] Willard Carl Klunder, *Lewis Cass and the Politics of Moderation* (Kent, Ohio: Kent State University Press, 1996), 151.

[9] David M. Pletcher, *The Diplomacy of Annexation: Texas, Oregon, and the Mexican War* (Columbia: University of Missouri Press, 1973), 320.

[10] Merk, *Oregon Question*, 191.

United States. For Americans in the Old Northwest, the United States had an obligation to extend its protection over these settlers. Lingering anti-British sentiment among northwesterners was rooted in dark memories of British support for the depredations of Native American tribes along the U.S. frontier in past wars and disgust with Britain's imperial global reach. These sentiments generated fears in the Old Northwest for the fate of U.S. citizens in Oregon sharing an un-governed area with the "rabble" that served the fur trade of the Hud-son's Bay Company.[11] The region's extreme expansionism was also fed by the desire to deny the economic benefits of the fur trade, Pacific coast ports, timber, and other resources in Oregon to Great Britain.[12] Another interest they saw was the chance to acquire a vast agricultural region and the economic advantages this would offer to northwestern-ers.[13] In an effort to broaden the regional appeal of the extreme expansionist movement, a number of northwesterners made commercial arguments they hoped would attract northeastern support. They emphasized that if the United States settled at 49 degrees north it would lose the harbors, fisheries, sea lane position and forests for shipbuilding provided by Vancouver Island.[14]

A bill introduced in December 1842 by Senator Lewis Linn of Missouri stoked the domestic debate on the extent of the U.S. claim to Oregon. Linn's bill called for the construction of American forts along the route to Oregon, fortifications at the mouth of the Columbia River, and land grants to U.S. settlers in Oregon sanctioned by U.S. courts. While in flagrant violation of the joint occupation agreement, Linn's bill attracted strong support in the Old Northwest and Missouri.[15] To sustain political momentum on the Oregon issue, a large meeting of prominent northwestern Democrats was held in July 1843 in Cincinnati, Ohio. It was at this meeting that the "All Oregon" movement was hatched and became clearly identified as a northwestern goal. While

[11] Ibid., 371–72.
[12] Because Britain used the Oregon Territory almost exclusively for fur trapping and shipping, this was the only real benefit Britain derived from the region at that time. Fur trapping was in rapid decline in this period but the British recognized these other values for the region. Frederick Merk, "British Government Propaganda and the Oregon Treaty," *American Historical Review* 40 (October 1934), 38–62.
[13] Paul H. Bergeron, *The Presidency of James K. Polk* (Lawrence: University Press of Kansas, 1987), 113.
[14] Norman A. Graebner, *Empire on the Pacific: A Study in American Continental Expansion* (Santa Barbara, Calif.: ABC-Clio, 1983), 129.
[15] Eugene Irving McCormac, *James K. Polk: A Political Biography* (New York: Russell and Russell, 1922), 560; Pletcher, *Diplomacy of Annexation*, 109.

still the province of a small clique in the Democratic party, this movement provided the nucleus of an Oregon lobby that drove this issue for the next three years. An indication of the tenor of the Cincinnati meeting was a bold statement by Senator Cass of Michigan, who was a contender for the 1844 Democratic presidential nomination. In an early pledge of his position that All Oregon was worth a fight, Cass declared, "I would take and hold possession of the Territory upon the Pacific, come what might . . . [I] would not waste time in fruitless diplomatic discussions."[16] Democratic Congressman John McClernand of Illinois summed up the consensus among northwesterners by arguing that All Oregon was nothing less than vital for "border safety" and the "relative . . . influence, wealth, and power" of the United States. His colleague from Illinois, John Wentworth, declared that it was the duty of the United States "to . . . let England know she can never have an inch of Oregon."[17] Despite the enthusiasm of Linn's supporters and the conventioneers in Cincinnati, the defeat of Linn's bill in Congress by an overwhelming coalition of Democrats and Whigs from the Northeast and South was an early indication of the kinds of political divisions this issue would produce.

While northwestern Democrats championed the most aggressive position on expansion in Oregon, there was consensus across regions and political parties on the general assertion that the United States had a rightful claim to some portion of the Oregon Territory. The Whig party, primarily in New England, had strong interests in maintaining U.S. influence in the Pacific Northwest. In fact, New England churches had been the first to send permanent settlers to the Oregon Territory. Among commercially minded Whigs in the Northeast and along the Atlantic coast there was strong support for maintaining access to ports on the Pacific. New Englanders dominated international trade with Asia and the Pacific whaling industry, each of which benefited immensely from ports on the West Coast.[18] Yet these commercial interests set clear limits to what the Whigs and most northeasterners wanted from the Oregon Territory, limits that determined how far they were willing to push Great Britain in the struggle over the region. For most Whigs the potential agricultural value of the Oregon Territory was meaningless.[19] Representative Robert Winthrop of Massachusetts ex-

---

[16] Klunder, *Lewis Cass*, 132–33.
[17] Graebner, *Empire on the Pacific*, 36.
[18] Paul A. Varg, *New England and Foreign Relations, 1789–1850* (Hanover: University Press of New England, 1983), 168.
[19] Pletcher, *Diplomacy of Annexation*, 214.

plained, "We need ports on the Pacific. As to land, we have millions of acres of better land still unoccupied on this side of the mountains."[20] The warnings issued by northwesterners of the dangers inherent in the British presence on the U.S. frontiers had little impact. Unlike their northwestern colleagues, easterners simply did not share this sense of threat to U.S. security, and the vast majority of Whigs were perfectly comfortable sharing the continent with Great Britain. In fact, the maritime component of a war with Britain would inevitably impose high costs to coastal regions along the Atlantic seaboard. For most Whigs then, the U.S. claim to 49 degrees north, which would include the Strait of Juan de Fuca and Puget Sound, was sufficient to satisfy their commercial interests and could be successfully negotiated with Britain without the need for the risks of war.[21] While Vancouver Island did hold certain commercial benefits, as northwestern Democrats pointed out, these benefits were marginal compared to the costs of going to war to wrest it from British control.

While Whigs could be counted on to oppose the bellicose demands of northwestern Democrats, real leadership in opposition to Linn's bill and all subsequent efforts to provoke Great Britain on Oregon came from the southern wing of the Democratic party. The most prominent southern Democratic dissidents on this issue were senators John C. Calhoun and George McDuffie of South Carolina.[22] As in the Northeast, the commercial interests of the South, tied closely to British manufacturing through cotton exports, led key southern Democrats to conclude that a war with England over Oregon would offer nothing but devastation. Many southern Democrats did not share the Northwest's security concerns, nor did they have any interest in Oregon's agricultural prospects. Senator McDuffie argued that Oregon was not worth a "pinch of snuff." For Calhoun, a militaristic U.S. policy would provoke the British to reinforce Oregon by sea, and the United States risked losing the entire territory if Britain moved forces to the region more quickly than the United States, which was likely.[23] As demands

[20] Graebner, *Empire on the Pacific*, 126.

[21] Ibid., 39–41.

[22] Pletcher, *Diplomacy of Annexation*, 109; McCormac, *James K. Polk*, 561.

[23] McCormac, *James K. Polk*, 560. Southern Democratic opinion was not unanimous, however. Some Democratic congressmen from the region saw territorial expansion in any direction as a national issue, not one that should be hindered by sectional concerns. John Hope Franklin, "The Southern Expansionists of 1846," *Journal of Southern History* 25 (August 1959), 323–38. Despite some Democratic support in the South for All Oregon, the Democrats in the region were strongly divided on the issue, so there could be no united front with their northwestern colleagues.

for extreme expansionism and a hard-line policy toward Great Britain intensified over the next two years, the southern Democrats held the balance of power between the Whig party and the northwestern Democrats. The defeat of the Linn bill demonstrated how southern Democrats were to exercise their power on this question over the next several years, but the issue was to intensify before being resolved—intensify to the point of near breakdown and war.

Regional Tension, Party Politics, and the Presidential Campaign of 1844

While defeat of the Linn bill in early 1843 delayed the coming conflict between the United States and Great Britain over Oregon once again, the domestic politics of territorial expansion took a dramatic turn over the next year. This gave the Oregon issue new life and northwestern Democrats a great opportunity to advance their agenda. The catalyst for this change was another contentious expansionist initiative—Texas annexation—this one led by southern Democrats. By 1844, Texas had come to dominate the tumultuous politics of the period. While not seeing eye-to-eye on U.S. interests in Oregon and Texas, northwestern and southern Democrats shared a mutual interest in a general expansionist agenda. This provided enough common cause for these two wings of the party to rally around an expansionist presidential candidate, James K. Polk, during the party convention of 1844 in Baltimore and to support an expansionist party platform. Throughout his administration Polk felt deeply obligated to this expansionist agenda and the demands of his northwestern and southern benefactors, without whom his nomination would have been stillborn. While the Oregon question proved to be a relatively minor issue in the presidential contest between Polk and his Whig opponent Henry Clay, Polk's victory ensured that Oregon would reemerge as a dominant issue in U.S. politics. But once Oregon annexation had become an accepted Democratic party issue and a key goal of the new administration, seeing it through depended on holding a coalition of northwestern and southern Democrats together in order to give Polk enough party unity to back up the hard-line position he was to pursue.

In order to understand how Oregon came to assume such a prominent position on the Democratic party agenda it is necessary to probe the politics of Texas annexation, because it was this problem that provided a political opening for the All Oregon champions to push their cause. For southern Democrats, like Senator Robert J. Walker of Mississippi and Calhoun of South Carolina, Texas annexation was an issue of utmost importance. It meant nothing less than the political survival of the South within the Union. Without Texas annexation, southerners feared, the slavery system was in jeopardy,[24] the region was vulnerable to the abolitionist meddling of Great Britain, even vulnerable to physical attack by British forces that might use the Texas Republic as a base of operations in some future conflict.[25] Calhoun had agreed to become President Tyler's third secretary of state in order to pursue a treaty of annexation with the Texas Republic, and from this position he rallied southerners to the cause.[26] He believed that "with Texas, the slave states would form a territory large enough for a first-rate power and one that . . . would flourish beyond any on the Globe—immediately and forever."[27]

The challenge for southern expansionists like Walker and Calhoun, however, was to overcome the fierce regional divisions that had blocked Texas annexation since its independence from Mexico in 1836. Presidents Andrew Jackson and Martin Van Buren both recognized the explosive potential of northern sentiment against annexation in the 1830s. Some northerners refused to play a role in extending the slave system by supporting the addition of new slave territory. Other northerners saw the issue as part of a southern conspiracy to establish its dominance in the U.S. federal system and to thereby force the North to accept the southern position on other issues, like the tariff.[28] In addition to the domestic implications of Texas annexation, such a move would immediately generate a crisis with Mexico. War with Mexico over Texas would surely split the Democratic party along regional

[24] Frederick Merk, *Slavery and the Annexation of Texas* (New York: Alfred A. Knopf, 1972); Charles S. Sydnor, *The Development of Southern Sectionalism, 1819–1848* (Baton Rouge: Louisiana State University Press, 1948), 322; Hietala, *Manifest Design*, 18–23.

[25] Sam W. Haynes, "Anglophobia and the Annexation of Texas: The Quest for National Security," in *Manifest Destiny and Empire: American Antebellum Expansion*, ed. Sam W. Haynes and Christopher Morris (College Station: Texas A&M University Press, 1997), 115–45.

[26] Charles M. Wiltse, *John C. Calhoun: Sectionalist, 1840–1850* (Indianapolis: Bobbs-Merrill, 1951), 164; James C. N. Paul, *Rift in the Democracy* (Philadelphia: University of Pennsylvania Press, 1951), 107.

[27] Paul, *Rift in the Democracy*, 84.

[28] Pletcher, *Diplomacy of Annexation*, 74.

lines,[29] which would have jeopardized Van Buren's election as Jackson's successor, and a split in the country at large would put victory in a Mexican war in doubt. For these reasons both Jackson and Van Buren rebuffed all efforts to pursue southward expansion.[30]

Despite the refusal of his predecessors to pursue Texas annexation, President Tyler saw Texas as an issue that would secure his historical legacy and perhaps give him a fighting chance in the election of 1844 as an independent candidate. Early in his term Tyler had broached the subject with Daniel Webster, his first secretary of state: "Could the North be reconciled to it, would any thing throw so bright a lustre around us?"[31] As a northern Whig, Webster had his doubts, and Tyler too hesitated at that time. The Whig party had been unified against Texas annexation, southern Whigs to maintain party solidarity, northern Whigs to prevent a significant increase in the power of slaveholders and the Democratic party.[32] Tyler's break with the Whigs had freed him to pursue the issue, and by December 1843 he and his second secretary of state, Abel P. Upshur, were engaged in secret treaty negotiations with the Texas government.[33] According to the Texan minister to the United States, Tyler advanced this cause, with its attendant domestic and international risks, "believing it would render him omnipotent in the South and West" during the coming elections.[34]

John Calhoun, as Tyler's third secretary of state, and Senator Walker of Mississippi, both recognized that the key to Texas annexation was to link the interests of southern and northwestern Democrats. Calhoun had long believed that westerners held the balance of power between the North and South on a range of issues, and a permanent coalition would serve southern interests in slavery, territorial expansion, and the elimination of the protective tariff system. Even

[29] Weeks, *Building the Continental Empire*, 88. The role of slavery in national politics had been neutralized with the "gag rule" in the early 1820s; northern and southern leaders of both parties agreed not to raise slavery as an issue because it would quickly and decisively fracture the parties and pose a danger to national unity. Sydnor, *Development of Southern Sectionalism*, chap. 10.
[30] Paul Varg, *United States Foreign Relations, 1820–1860* (East Lansing: Michigan State University Press, 1979), 123; Pletcher, *Diplomacy of Annexation*, 73–75; Merk, *Slavery and the Annexation of Texas*, 44–45; Sydnor, *Development of Southern Sectionalism*, 321–22.
[31] Pletcher, *Diplomacy of Annexation*, 86.
[32] Kinley J. Brauer, "The Massachusetts State Texas Committee: A Last Stand Against the Annexation of Texas," *Journal of American History* 51 (1964), 214–15; Graebner, *Empire on the Pacific*, 18.
[33] Sydnor, *Development of Southern Sectionalism*, 322.
[34] Pletcher, *Diplomacy of Annexation*, 114.

though as a senator in 1843 Calhoun had led the opposition to the Linn bill on Oregon, as secretary of state in 1844 he now saw the long-range possibilities of using the issue to gain northwestern support on Texas.[35] This coalition could also serve as the springboard for Calhoun's ambitions to secure the Democratic presidential nomination for himself during the coming convention. As the Baltimore convention approached, with northwestern Democrats eager to advance an All Oregon candidate and southern Democrats eager to secure support beyond their region for Texas annexation, the ground was prepared for a broad expansionist coalition to emerge victorious in the Democratic party.

Unfortunately for Calhoun's presidential ambitions, the prospects of his nomination quickly faded as Senator Walker and his "Nocturnal Committee" of ardent southern expansionists looked elsewhere for a Democratic candidate to carry the annexationist banner. Calhoun was too strongly identified as a southern partisan to attract support in the Old Northwest or the Northeast, and he would certainly lose in a national contest. And unfortunately for Martin Van Buren, who had remained in firm control of the party since losing the presidency to Harrison in 1840, his seemingly secure renomination in 1844 quickly succumbed to the political maneuvering of Senator Walker. Walker emerged as the Democratic kingmaker during the convention by skillfully manipulating the various factions in the party to craft his desired South/Northwest coalition. Ironically, it was Van Buren's attempt to neutralize Texas as a campaign issue that gave Walker the opportunity to make it the decisive campaign issue.

As early as 1842 Van Buren had agreed in confidence with Henry Clay, leader of the Whig party, that neither would raise the Texas question in their political contest. Texas was just too divisive for the internal politics of each party for either leader to control, so it was in the best interests of Van Buren and Clay to remove the issue from party politics altogether.[36] As the campaign of 1844 approached, and with it the debate on the treaty of annexation that President Tyler had submitted to the Senate on April 22, Van Buren and Clay took further steps to ensure that the issue remained neutralized. In response to an inquiry from a New York abolitionist newspaper, Clay published the first in a series of letters on Texas. In it he declared, "I consider the annexation

---

[35] Wiltse, *John C. Calhoun,* 164–65.
[36] Pletcher, *Diplomacy of Annexation,* 139.

of Texas, at this time, without the assent of Mexico, as a measure com-
promising the national character, involving us certainly with war with
Mexico, probably with other foreign powers; dangerous to the integrity of the Union; inexpedient in the present financial condition of
the country; and not called for by a general expression of public opinion."[37] On that very same day, Van Buren also published a letter on
Texas, declaring his opposition to annexation "at this time," and like
Clay, citing conflict with Mexico as the main reason.[38]

While Van Buren was securing support for his nomination state-by-
state in early 1844, even in the South, his statement on Texas produced
chaos in the Democratic party on the eve of the nominating convention.[39] As Senate debate on Texas continued into May it became clear
that the annexation treaty would be defeated by a coalition of Whigs
and Van Buren (primarily northeastern) Democrats.[40] Calhoun used
this coming defeat to stir up his followers in the South who condemned Van Buren for his position. Senator Thomas Ritchie, leader of
the Virginia Democrats, was the first to formally withdraw his state's
pledge to support Van Buren at Baltimore. Once Virginia abandoned
Van Buren, other southern states followed suit, "cut[ting] those thin
ties which had bound politicians in that region to Van Buren."[41]
Going into the convention northwestern Democrats were determined
to exploit southern support for Texas annexation and the sudden uncertainty in the party to champion All Oregon and a candidate that
would support this cause.[42] While there may not have been a formal
bargain between the northwestern and the southern delegates to the
convention, representatives from each regional group made the political connection between Texas annexation and Oregon occupation

[37] George R. Poage, *Henry Clay and the Whig Party* (Chapel Hill: University of North
Carolina Press, 1936), 138.

[38] Pletcher, *Diplomacy of Annexation*, 144–45.

[39] Paul, *Rift in the Democracy*, 85–95.

[40] As the Senate vote on Tyler's treaty approached, Secretary of State Calhoun made a
fatal blunder that destroyed his chances of securing enough northern support for the
treaty to obtain the necessary two-thirds majority. In a letter to Richard Pakenham,
British minister to the United States, Calhoun defended the United States interests in
Texas as primarily motivated by the need to protect the slavery system. Calhoun's letter
produced strong protest in the North, dooming the treaty to regional divisions that split
wide open. Haynes, "Anglophobia and the Annexation of Texas," 130; Hietala, *Manifest
Design*, 37–40.

[41] Paul, *Rift in the Democracy*, 125–28.

[42] Varg, *United States Foreign Relations*, 144; Edwin A. Miles, "'Fifty-four Forty or
Fight'—An American Political Legend," *Mississippi Valley Historical Review* 44 (1957),
293–94; Graebner, *Empire on the Pacific*, 35–36; Pletcher, *Diplomacy of Annexation*, 222.

clear. Senator Walker, in a widely published letter issued prior to the convention, had explicitly suggested that the annexation of Oregon would be legitimate compensation for the North to balance the territorial gains that would be made by the South in Texas.[43] On the other side of the nascent coalition, northwestern delegates made their interest in a quid pro quo on Oregon unambiguous. Samuel Medary, editor of the *Ohio Statesman* and a leading northwestern spokesman at the convention, declared that "he was a friend of the annexation of Texas; and should [southern delegates] give Ohio a candidate in favor of . . . extending the protecting aegis of our flag over Oregon, he would pledge that the 'lone star' of Texas should be blazoned on the democratic standard in Ohio, and that under it they would lead on to certain victory."[44] Congressman Kennedy and Senator Hannegan of Indiana made it clear that their support for Texas depended on reciprocal support on Oregon.[45]

Walker and his colleagues were just as intent on securing a pro-Texas candidate as northwesterners were about a pro-Oregon candidate, but at the beginning of the convention Van Buren still had majority support among the delegates. To prevent Van Buren from securing the nomination on the first ballot and to ultimately stalemate his selection, Walker and his southern compatriots demanded that the Democratic nominee be selected by a two-thirds majority of the delegates. This rule had been used during previous conventions to emphasize the party's solidarity on its candidate, when previous candidates faced little or no opposition from within the party. Walker knew that Van Buren could not muster two-thirds support after his damning letter on Texas. But to institute this rule a majority of the delegates would have to approve it, which meant that southern annexationists had to attract every vote possible to secure the measure. Of course, Van Buren Democrats were outraged by Walker's parliamentary maneuvers and would vote against the two-thirds majority nomination rule. Southern Democrats alone could not carry the rule, so Walker was "desperate" for every vote from northwestern delegates.[46] After two days of bitter and often violent debate, Walker had attracted enough support from northwestern delegates to win on the rule change. Three days later

[43] Pletcher, *Diplomacy of Annexation*, 140.
[44] Miles, "Fifty-four Forty or Fight," 295.
[45] Paul, *Rift in the Democracy*, 147.
[46] Ibid., 147–48.

southern expansionists acquiesced to the Old Northwest's demand for the All Oregon plank in the party platform.[47]

Predictably, Van Buren Democrats could not secure their man's nomination, and with each successive ballot Van Buren lost ground to the Old Northwest's preferred candidate, Lewis Cass. Yet Cass's supporters could not generate enough enthusiasm to secure his nomination and a stalemate developed out of the impossible task of finding a majority for any of the available candidates.[48] Out of the impasse came a proposal for a compromise candidate—James K. Polk—a true dark horse who was never a contender until regional deadlock forced the convention delegates to abandon the favorites. Polk was a firm expansionist who would support Texas annexation and, as he stated in an open letter prior to the convention, the All Oregon claim. Polk had not been involved in the intrigue that defeated Van Buren, and he was welcome relief to weary delegates, even Van Buren allies. In Andrew Jackson's words, Polk was "the most available man," and a unanimous majority quickly formed to secure his nomination as the Democratic party's candidate for 1844.[49] In the general election that fall against Henry Clay, Polk won a narrow plurality in the popular vote.[50] Northwestern expansionists, the champions of All Oregon and confrontation with Great Britain, now had their man in the White House and the Democratic party on record in support of their agenda.

James Polk Confronts John Bull: The War Crisis Emerges

The main questions for Polk now were how to proceed with this task, how much of Oregon he should seek, and at what cost. According to Frederick Merk, Polk had a "choice of two programs for Manifest Destiny." He could support the northeastern version, "leisurely in time schedule, unaggressive in temper, allowing for the niceties of international conduct." Or he could opt for the northwestern version "as envisaged by the war hawks—immediate, realistic, aggressive."[51] In

---

[47] Ibid. The platform stated: "Our title to the whole of the territory of Oregon is clear and unquestionable; that no portion of the same ought to be ceded to England or any other power." Miles, "Fifty-four Forty or Fight," 295.

[48] Sam W. Haynes, *James K. Polk and the Expansionist Impulse* (New York: Longman, 1997), 58.

[49] Paul, *Rift in the Democracy*, 164–65.

[50] Pletcher, *Diplomacy of Annexation*, 168–70.

[51] Merk, *Manifest Destiny and Mission*, 66.

practical terms, would he ease the way toward peaceful resolution by accepting a boundary at 49 degrees; or would he support the aggressive ambitions of the 54-40 men? While Polk was determined to resolve the issue, it is also certain that he had no desire to needlessly provoke a war with Great Britain; he wanted a peaceful resolution if at all possible. Polk had admitted privately to his cabinet that he tended to share the commercial Whig view on the Oregon Territory: that a settlement at 49 degrees would satisfy the real interest of the United States in ports on the Pacific and that the territory north of 49 degrees was of little value for agriculture. According to Secretary of State James Buchanan, Polk worried over "whether the judgment of the civilized world would be in our favor in a war waged for a comparatively worthless territory north of 49 degrees, which his predecessors had over and over again offered to surrender to Great Britain."[52] Despite Polk's unwillingness to actually *precipitate* war, his policy throughout the crisis was so confrontational that he ran high risks of actually *provoking* war. Even if he never intended to initiate armed conflict, his brinkmanship on this issue produced widespread belief on both sides that war was most certainly possible.

During his first few months in office Polk struck a position that seemed to draw from both programs for Manifest Destiny. On one hand, Polk issued bold statements on U.S. rights in Oregon. In his inaugural address Polk proclaimed that he had the "duty to assert and maintain the right of the United States to that portion of our territory which lies beyond the Rocky Mountains. Our title to the country of Oregon is clear and unquestionable, and already are our people preparing to perfect that title by occupying it with their wives and children."[53] The inaugural address did not explicitly call for All Oregon. Yet in combination with the Democratic party platform and his campaign pledge "not to permit Great Britain or any other foreign power to plant a colony or hold dominion over any portion of the people or territory" of Oregon,[54] many in his domestic audience, and most important, in the British government and press, inferred that the inaugural was a call for the 54–40 claim of the United States.[55] On the other hand, Polk moderated this provocative public stance with his

52 From Buchanan's diary, quoted in Graebner, *Empire on the Pacific*, 105.
53 James K. Polk, "Inaugural Address," March 4, 1845, in *James K. Polk: Chronology-Documents-Bibliographical Aids*, ed. John J. Farrell (Dobbs Ferry, N.Y.: Oceana, 1970), 33.
54 Merk, *Oregon Question*, 218.
55 Ibid., 282–83; McCormac, *James K. Polk*, 563.

first official act on Oregon, which was to renew a previous U.S. offer to divide the Oregon Territory at 49 degrees.

But his effort to appear accommodating to the British position was half-hearted, short-lived, and rather cynical. He knew that rejecting negotiations outright and demanding All Oregon at this early stage in his administration would mean war, so some type of diplomatic initiative was necessary to avoid the appearance of blatant provocation. But Polk also knew that the British would most likely reject important terms in his offer, specifically, exclusive U.S. control of the Columbia River which would deny its use to British subjects.[56] Such a rejection would allow Polk to avoid an outcome that would compromise his pledge to support the Old Northwest's demand. Secretary of State Buchanan explained Polk's logic in a letter dated July 12, 1845, to Louis McLane, America's minister in London:

> Suppose the American position of the 49th degree of latitude should be again made by the United States and again rejected by Great Britain, and war then be the consequence, we might appeal to all mankind for the justice and moderation of our demand . . . and our own citizens would be enthusiastically united in sustaining such a war. Should the negotiation end in disappointment, the President, having done all that can be required of him for the preservation of peace, will feel himself perfectly free to insist upon our rights in their full extent up to the Russian line.[57]

Polk's initial foray into diplomacy did not reflect an honest step toward resolving the dispute peacefully; it was designed to put the onus of failed diplomacy on the British and to rally the American people behind an aggressive policy to secure the entire Oregon Territory for the United States.

While Polk had expected (in fact, hoped for) British rejection of his diplomatic overture, the insolence of the rejection shocked the administration.[58] The British minister to the United States, Richard Pakenham, rejected the offer without even relaying it to London for consideration. Polk angrily retracted the offer and cut off further negotiations. In dismay, British foreign secretary Aberdeen denounced Pakenham's action to the U.S. government, notifying Polk that this rejection did not reflect the British government's position on a diplomatic resolution. In an ef-

---

[56] Graebner, *Empire on the Pacific*, 104–5.

[57] James Buchanan, "The Historic American Interest in Oregon," in *Manifest Destiny*, ed. Norman A. Graebner (Indianapolis: Bobbs-Merrill, 1968), 88.

[58] McCormac, *James K. Polk*, 570–71; Merk, *Oregon Question*, 218.

fort to keep diplomacy alive, Aberdeen privately requested that the United States resubmit the offer. Polk not only refused, but also used the occasion to harden his position and to ratchet up the crisis. Buchanan was to inform Pakenham that the United States would now "assert and enforce our right to the whole of the Oregon Territory from 42 degrees to 54 degrees 40 minutes North Latitude . . . . Let the argument of our title to the whole country be full, let the proposition to compromise at latitude 49 degrees be withdrawn, and then let the matter rest."[59]

In the tense debate that followed between the president and his secretary of state in this late August cabinet meeting, Polk laid out the strategy he would follow throughout the crisis. Not only would the United States declare its legal title to the whole Oregon Territory, the president would never again offer terms for settling the dispute. He even refused to accept Buchanan's repeated requests to invite new propositions from the British.[60] Polk expected the British government to initiate proposals and make concessions that might lead to a settlement.[61] Polk believed that the only way to get Britain to take the initiative was to bring the problem to the point of true crisis, to actually generate fears of war that would force Britain to meet the basic U.S. demands. In a letter to his brother he explained that Great Britain "for the last two centuries never was known to do justice to any country with which she had a controversy when that country assumed a supplicatory attitude, or was on her knees before her. The only way to treat John Bull is to treat him firmly and look him straight in the eye."[62] In a meeting with his archrival Senator John Calhoun, Polk argued, "Until the question reached a crisis there would be no prospect of our obtaining justice."[63]

In December 1845, Polk made another decisive move creating an air of crisis within the United States and direct confrontation with Great Britain. The occasion was his first annual message to Congress. In this message Polk did three important things regarding Oregon. First, he for-

[59] James K. Polk, *The Diary of James K. Polk*, August 26, 1845 (Chicago: A. C. McClurg, 1910), 2. Polk reasserted the U.S. right to All Oregon on October 24, 1845. Ibid., 69.

[60] Ibid., August 26, 1845, 2–4; October 21, 1845, 62–64; October 27, 1845, 75–76; December 9, 1845, 119–20.

[61] See his conversation with Senator Calhoun of February 25, 1846. Ibid., 251–52.

[62] Merk, *Oregon Question*, 346. He used this same phrase to defend his policy with a member of Congress. See Polk, *Diary*, January 4, 1846, 155.

[63] Polk, *Diary*, January 9, 1846, 159.

mally announced to the nation and outside observers that while the
United States made a good faith offer to compromise on Oregon earlier
in the year, it was Great Britain that was responsible for the breakdown
of negotiations. He could thus proclaim, "The civilized world will see in
the proceedings a spirit of liberal concession on the part of the United
States, and this Government will be relieved from all responsibility
which may follow the failure to settle the controversy."[64] Should it come
to war, the United States would carry no blame. Second, he declared that
Britain's rejection of a boundary at 49 degrees meant that the United
States could reassert its claim to All Oregon: "Our title to the whole Oregon Territory [is] asserted, and . . . maintained by irrefragable facts and
arguments."[65] Third, he requested that Congress, respecting the provisions of the treaty with Great Britain on joint occupation, give notice that
the treaty would be terminated at the end of a one-year period. This notice of termination was necessary, he argued, so the United States could
take action to uphold the Monroe Doctrine. Polk declared that the United
States must not allow any European state to impose the balance of power
system in North America "to check our advancement." The British position on Oregon, he implied, was a violation of the Monroe Doctrine,
"and should any such interference be attempted [the United States] will
be ready to resist it at any and all hazards."[66] To give some muscle to this
policy, Polk ordered the Pacific naval squadron to move north from Mexican waters to Oregon and to provide U.S. settlers with weapons.[67]

Within the United States this message gave new hope to the champions of All Oregon because it created a sense of unity in the Democratic
party around Polk's position. For several weeks Polk's declaration on
Oregon had a patriotic resonance that few were willing to challenge.
Calhoun, now back in the Senate, felt that throughout December 1845
"it was dangerous to even whisper 'forty-nine.'"[68] Congressman
George Fries of Ohio held a view that appeared ascendant: "We pitched
our tents, and, if God willing, they shall never be struck till the stars
and stripes wave over Oregon, every inch of Oregon." For Senator
Hannegan of Indiana it was "Oregon—every foot or not an inch."[69]

---

[64] Polk, "First Annual Message," December 2, 1845, in *James K. Polk: Chronology-Docu-
ments- Bibliographical Aids*, 41.
[65] Ibid.
[66] Ibid., 42.
[67] Pletcher, *Diplomacy of Annexation*, 311.
[68] Graebner, *Empire on the Pacific*, 126.
[69] Ibid., 125.

For others, including Secretary of State Buchanan, Polk's message was hostile in tone and potentially disastrous in effect. Until late in the conflict, Buchanan regularly expressed his fear that Polk's approach was too provocative and risked war over an issue that neither Congress nor the general public would support.[70] In his diary entry from December 9, Polk recorded that "Mr. B[uchanan] repeated his anxiety to settle the question at 49 degrees and avoid war." In another entry, Polk criticizes Buchanan for being "too timid and too fearful of War on the Oregon question," and for being "most anxious to settle the question by yielding and making greater concessions than I am willing to make." In response to Buchanan's concerns Polk's diary states, "I told him that I did not desire war, but that at all hazards we must maintain our rights."[71]

On a number of occasions Polk stated that he did not believe Britain would actually fight for Oregon.[72] Yet when the crisis reached its most dangerous points, Polk acknowledged that war was clearly a possibility, and the United States needed adequate military preparations in case the dispute did end in war. During what Polk described as a "grave discussion" on December 23, the cabinet weighed the "contingency of War." Polk concurred that the "country should be put in a state of defence without delay . . . if war came such preparation would be indispensable." The secretaries of war and the navy were directed to coordinate with the appropriate congressional committees to introduce the necessary defense appropriation bills.[73] The next day Polk repeated the urgency of increasing the readiness of the United States for war "without delay" to the chairman of the House Committee on Military Affairs: "for though I did not apprehend immediate war if it came at all, yet as we knew large preparations of an extraordinary nature were making in England, it was the part of prudence that we should be prepared for any contingency."[74] According to Secretary of the Navy George Bancroft, whom Polk treated as a confidant, Polk

[70] Ibid., 106; Varg, *United States Foreign Relations*, 152–53.

[71] Polk, *Diary*, December 9, 1845, 120; November 29, 1845, 107–8.

[72] For example, see Polk's letters to Andrew Jackson of April and May 1845, in Charles Sellers, *James K. Polk, Continentalist, 1843–1846* (Princeton: Princeton University Press, 1966), 236–38.

[73] Polk, *Diary*, December 23, 1845, 133–34.

[74] Ibid., December 24, 1845, 143. See also his conversation with Senator Cass and Vice President Dallas on January 19, 1846, 181, and directions to the secretary of the navy on February 28, 1846, 257–58.

seemed to have a fatalistic attitude about the prospects of war. "Either Great Britain decides to live with us on friendlier terms or is animated by a disposition which ere long will lead to acts of hostility which would certainly lead to war. If we must have war with Great Britain we may as well have it now as leave it to our successor."[75]

While Polk's rationale for pursuing a provocative approach to the Oregon problem had this international dimension, the domestic dimensions were crucial too. Polk knew that northwestern Democrats had been indispensable in his nomination for the Democratic ticket and his presidential victory, and they had pledged to support him on other key issues like tariff reduction and the creation of an independent treasury.[76] He simply could not desert this active wing of his party by giving in on Oregon.[77] Polk actually believed that the greatest threat to his administration and his leadership of the Democratic party would come from abandoning All Oregon. His strongest statement of this belief came during one of his policy debates with Buchanan, which Polk recorded in his diary. Buchanan argued, Polk noted, that the "greatest danger would be that I would be attacked for holding a warlike tone" when nothing could justify a war for territory north of 49 degrees. Polk replied,

> My greatest danger was that I would be attacked for having . . . agreed to offer the compromise of 49 degrees. I told him that if that proposition had been accepted by the British Minister my course would have met with great opposition, and in my opinion would have gone far to overthrow the administration; that, had it been accepted, as we came in on Texas the probability was we would have gone out on Oregon. I told him we had done our duty by offering 49 degrees, and that I did not regret that it had been rejected by the British Minister.[78]

Because of Polk's conviction that he would face unacceptable domestic penalties for personally abandoning 54–40, Buchanan observed in a letter that the "President . . . himself would not accept anything short of British surrender of All Oregon."[79]

[75] Sellers, *James K. Polk*, 244.
[76] Graebner, *Empire on the Pacific*, 143; Wiltse, *John C. Calhoun*, 217.
[77] Graebner, *Empire on the Pacific*, x; Merk, *Oregon Question*, 231.
[78] Polk, *Diary*, November 29, 1845, 107.
[79] To Louis McLane, U.S. Minister in London, January 29, 1846. Merk, *Oregon Question*, 343–44.

The British Reaction: Preparing for War

The Polk administration's efforts to force a resolution to the Oregon question put the British government in a difficult position. On the one hand, there was an implicit sense in the Tory cabinet, in the opposition Whig party, and in the press, that the limited value of Oregon hardly justified a fight with the United States. Foreign Secretary Aberdeen, the leading figure on Oregon in Great Britain over the course of the crisis, worked vigorously to make this assessment of Oregon's limited value explicit and the basis for compromise.[80] Aberdeen was most notable for his "dread of war" in Britain's foreign relations, and he "considered his ministership as an opportunity to clear away controversies, old and new, that threatened armed collision."[81] This was particularly true of the Oregon dispute, and Aberdeen was persistent in his international and domestic efforts to defuse the crisis and resolve the border issue through peaceful means.

Yet Aberdeen's pacific inclinations were constrained by the international and domestic implications of yielding to the U.S. position. At the international level, Polk's public statements, his coercive diplomatic posturing, and his efforts to generate domestic support for All Oregon were an affront to Britain's national honor. Yielding to U.S. demands for the entire territory right up to the boundary with Russian Alaska would be a humiliation to Britain's international prestige, which most political and opinion leaders felt was worth fighting to prevent. On the domestic level, if the Tory government yielded to U.S. demands, Prime Minister Peel and Aberdeen both feared the consequences of Whig opposition, particularly from Lord Palmerston. Palmerston had been the foreign minister in previous Whig governments between 1830 and 1841, and his role in the opposition was to persistently attack what he considered Aberdeen's feckless and timid management of Britain's foreign policy. The Tory leadership knew that yielding to the United States could generate tremendous criticism from Whigs in Parliament that might threaten the Tory hold on government.[82] These international and domestic dimensions of the issue meant that if the United States persisted in its claim to 54-40, as Polk appeared to be doing, war was the only recourse for resolving the dispute. Excitement over the possibility of war for Oregon first appeared

---

[80] Merk, "British Government Propaganda and the Oregon Treaty."
[81] Merk, *Oregon Question*, 263.
[82] Ibid., 255–84; Merk, "British Government Propaganda and the Oregon Treaty," 40.

in Great Britain following Polk's inaugural address. In response to
Polk, the Tories and Whigs formed a united front in Parliament to
demonstrate British resolve on the issue. Whig leader Lord John Russell declared in an aggressive speech to the House of Commons that
his party was dedicated to defending Britain's claim to Oregon. Prime
Minister Peel, mirroring Polk's inaugural language, asserted that
Britain's rights in Oregon were "clear and unquestionable" and his
government was prepared to defend these rights.[83]

In Oregon itself, the tense relations between U.S. settlers south of
the Columbia River in the Willamette Valley and members of the Hudson's Bay Company north of the Columbia presented the possibility of
a local clash. Combined with the bellicose attitudes of the U.S. and
British governments, this held the danger of escalation into a general
Anglo-American war. American settlers were threatening to cross the
Columbia to seize British territory and to pillage and burn British
homes and stores. The Hudson's Bay Company in turn strengthened
its settlements and demanded naval protection from the government.[84] In February 1845, Prime Minister Peel had expressed little confidence in Aberdeen's view that "we have the upper hand on the
banks of the Columbia—that the settlers connected with the Hudson's
Bay Company are actually stronger than the settlers, the subjects of the
United States are at present." Peel asked pointedly, "Have you carefully ascertained this fact?"[85] In anticipation of a potential clash following Polk's inauguration, Peel directed Aberdeen to write a report
on British preparedness should this clash occur, and in the meantime
to move a frigate to the Columbia River and put artillery ashore.

In the course of his investigation Sir John Pelly, governor of the
Hudson's Bay Company, informed Aberdeen that the Americans, not
the British, dominated the Columbia River valley. Of the three thousand inhabitants of the region, only one-third were British subjects.
Fearing a general conflict, Lord Metcalf, governor-general of Canada,
asked the government to put the North American colonies in a full
state of military readiness and to reinforce the Oregon Territory with
troops from Europe and troops from India.[86] Two army officers sent to

[83] Merk, "British Government Propaganda and the Oregon Treaty," 39; Merk, *Oregon Question*, 283.
[84] Merk, *Oregon Question*, 219.
[85] Classen, *Thrust and Counterthrust*, 181.
[86] Ibid., 182–84.

reconnoiter the balance of forces west of the Great Lakes reported that the United States had established a series of posts that could be used to cut off Oregon from Canada.[87]

As British confidence in its preparedness waned with this information, Aberdeen provided Pakenham, his minister in Washington, with an assessment in a letter of April 3, 1845: "Judging from the language of Mr. Polk . . . unless the question be speedily settled, a local collision will be liable to take place, which may involve the countries in serious difficulty, and not improbably lead to war itself. At all events, whatever may be the course of the United States Government, the time is come when we must be prepared for every contingency."[88] In September a fifty-gun frigate was ordered to the region to reinforce the British claim. It was followed by a sloop that sailed up the Columbia to Ft. Vancouver to serve as a military garrison. Later, a forty-two-gun frigate was added to the British naval force defending the Oregon Territory. In April 1846 the governor-general of Canada was informed that a force of 346 officers and men were being sent to Oregon and would sail in June.[89] In a letter to the secretary of the navy, Edward Everett, a former U.S. minister to Great Britain who had remained in London and in close contact with British government officials, argued that the British would not back away from war as the situation became more confrontational. Everett reviewed the political situation in Great Britain:

> The army and navy of course pant for service; no small portion of the People of England have got to think that a war with the United States affords the best hope of putting an end to Slavery, an object paramount with them to all others; the Whig party, who ought to be our friends, are led by political position to taunt the Ministers for their alleged want of spirit in their relations with America; and many of all parties think that after a generation of peace a foreign war would be no bad purge for the domestic maladies of the body politic.[90]

As the crisis intensified with Polk's message to Congress in December, Aberdeen himself confirmed that Britain was ready to wage war over Oregon if necessary. While he had worked throughout the crisis to bring it to a peaceful end, by January 1846 he admitted to U.S. minister

[87] Pletcher, *Diplomacy of Annexation*, 251.
[88] Classen, *Thrust and Counterthrust*, 179–80.
[89] Ibid., 190–99.
[90] Varg, *United States Foreign Relations*, 159–160.

McLane that the U.S. position made his continued opposition in the cabinet to war preparations untenable. Thirty ships of the line were being prepared for possible deployment to North America, along with steamships, other war vessels, and military armaments.[91]

Congress and Compromise: The War Crisis Resolved

In January 1846 the crisis reached its most dangerous point. Neither party seemed willing to back down from their overlapping claims, yet one party would have to relent in order to maintain peace. While it was Great Britain that renewed the offer to split Oregon at 49 degrees, it was Polk's willingness to submit this treaty to the Senate that brought the crisis to an end. It is now time to return to the question posed at the beginning of the chapter. How can we explain Polk's decision to back down in this standoff with Great Britain and relinquish the claims to All Oregon that he had been aggressively pressing since his inauguration?

Realist critics of democratic peace theory traditionally challenge its relevance to particular crises by advancing explanations for peaceful conflict resolution that focus on calculations of power and the expected costs of resorting to force relative to the expected gains. These variables must be considered in any case under study, including the peaceful resolution of the Oregon crisis. At least one prominent historian of this period asserts that Polk relented on Oregon in response to the clear threat posed by British power.[92] Stephen Rock, in his critique of the proposition that shared liberal norms may have kept the peace, provides a similar assessment to explain Polk's decision. He argues that there was a growing sense in the United States that the value of the Oregon Territory north of 49 degrees did not justify the costs of war, particularly as war with Mexico loomed on the southern frontier.[93] The assertion that Polk was deterred by British power does not hold up when we examine the president's behavior during this crisis,

---

[91] Pletcher, *Diplomacy of Annexation*, 324–26; Merk, *Oregon Question*, 345; Classen, *Thrust and Counterthrust*, 190; Varg, *United States Foreign Relations*, 160; Sellers, *James K. Polk*, 379–80.

[92] Julius Pratt, *A History of United States Foreign Policy* (Englewood Cliffs, N.J.: Prentice-Hall, 1972).

[93] Rock, "Anglo-U.S. Relations," 110.

even at its darkest moments. Rock's explanation for Polk's decision fails to account for the complexity of this case and thereby misses the essential relationship between the domestic structure in the United States and the outcome of this crisis.

At no time did President Polk himself decide that the *external* dimensions of the dispute made it prudent for him to back down. Polk never flinched in his All Oregon claim, even though the British government unambiguously stated its willingness to resist this claim with military force. As discussed earlier, Polk had no desire to actually confront British power in a military contest, yet his behavior remained consistent with his often-repeated claim that the way to deal with Great Britain was through direct confrontation, even if this increased the risk of war. Polk simply took no action whatsoever to defuse the crisis on his own initiative, despite the risk of war that he recognized.

Polk did relent on a settlement at 49 degrees, but this was a decision made necessary by the *internal* dimensions of the crisis. It was the domestic politics of the dispute, not the international politics, which forced his hand. However, this does not mean that realist calculations of the costs and benefits of war were irrelevant to the resolution of the dispute. On the contrary, these calculations are an essential part of the explanation, but certainly not the only important factor. Commercial reasons for opposing the use of military force in this case are also a key part of the explanation. Each of these motives was relevant because the U.S. federal system, with its territorial system of representation at the national level, provided an institutional outlet for realist and commercial perspectives emerging from particular regions of the Union to challenge the president's policy.

What the Oregon dispute demonstrates is that different domestic groups within a state may use the same realist logic to evaluate a particular foreign policy problem, yet they can come to dramatically different conclusions on the relative distribution of power and the costs and benefits of using military force. There was no unitary set of key leaders making strategic calculations to determine the appropriate course of action for the United States, as many theories of state behavior assume. What we find in this case is a rival set of power calculations that competed for supremacy in the decision-making process within the institutional setting of the U.S. political system. In this case, these rival power calculations were shaped by asymmetric regional perspectives on the issue at hand, and the asymmetric geographic relationship of the Old Northwest, the Northeast, and the South to the military action that was expected from a war with Great Britain.

As we have seen, northwestern Democrats were the most persistent and well-organized source of political support for the All Oregon position. This had a direct impact on their view of how much
risk the United States should assume to attain Oregon. By January
1846 this had become the crucial question in congressional debates
on Polk's policy. Their determination to achieve the All Oregon objective even influenced their calculations of relative power and how
the country would fare in a war with Great Britain. According to Senator Hopkins of Tennessee, northwesterners were "almost mad on
the subject of Oregon."[94] They consequently tended to argue confidently that the United States had little to fear from war. Their arguments emphasized what they thought to be domestic weaknesses
within Great Britain, challenges Britain faced in its empire, and challenges from other states that seriously undercut Britain's ability to
project power against the United States. Britain's image as a global
colossus was merely a facade masking its precarious international
position. Senator Allen of Ohio, a leader in the All Oregon movement, "argued that Britain would not dare fight over Oregon. Sur-
rounded by bitter rivals, threatened by domestic convulsion, crip-
pled by an unstable parliamentary system, exhausted by efforts to
keep 128 million colonists in subjection, they were helpless."[95] Senator Lewis Cass of Michigan, a dominant figure among northwestern
Democrats, condemned the timidity of those who believed that the
United States would be defeated in war. The essence of Cass's argument was that the United States did not have to defeat Great Britain
in a general war, but simply defend itself from the military force that
Britain could project to North America alone. Like Allen, Cass
pointed out that Britain could barely manage its global empire in
peacetime, and it had to worry about millions of oppressed and agitated subjects both at home and abroad. Should Great Britain take up
the U.S. challenge on Oregon it faced an "abundant harvest of ruin
and disaster," not because of U.S. superiority but because of Britain's
internal weaknesses. The United States was able to defend itself in
two previous wars with Britain, he argued, which showed the
"error" of the "sad forebodings" of the inability of the United States
to defend itself again. While British naval power was indeed formidable, Cass asserted that the U.S. navy, with the assistance of priva-

[94] Pletcher, *Diplomacy of Annexation*, 327.
[95] Merk, *Oregon Question*, 380.

teers, still held the ability to "sweep the British flag from this part of the continent." He concluded that All Oregon was worth the risk of war, because "we can be neither overrun nor conquered. England might as well attempt to blow up Gibraltar with a squib [small firecracker], as to attempt to subdue us."[96]

Few outside the Old Northwest held such a confident view of the ability of the United States to confront Great Britain in a general war, even one confined to North America. The leading opponent of the northwestern view in the Democratic party was John Calhoun of South Carolina, who had returned to the Senate mainly to take a leadership role against the threat of war brought on by Polk's bellicose approach to the Oregon question.[97] In a letter to Secretary of State Buchanan, Calhoun suggested, "It is beyond the power of man to trace the consequences of war between the United States and England on the subject of Oregon. All that is certain is, that she can take it and hold it against us, so long as she has the supremacy on the oceans and retains her Eastern dominions. The rest is rapt in mystery."[98] In an "electrifying" speech to the Senate in March 1846, Calhoun was more blunt in his opinion on war with Great Britain. He argued that war would be an unmitigated disaster. According to Calhoun's biographer, he

> painted a picture of the horror and cost of conflict over Oregon that might well last for years only to end in so altering [the United States'] form of government that victory itself would be a defeat. The alternative was a picture of material progress through increased trade and current technologies in transportation and communication that would eventually put the United States in the dominant commercial position in both oceans.[99]

Calhoun's strongest support came from the Whigs of the Northeast and Democrats from the South who had nothing to gain from a war for territory north of 49 degrees, and who shared his perspective on the devastating costs.[100] Those along the Atlantic seaboard were particularly sensitive to the fact that Britain was likely to inflict the most devastating blows against port cities up and down the coast. Northeastern

[96] Klunder, Lewis Cass, 152–53.

[97] Wiltse, John C. Calhoun, 217. With Texas annexation secured, Calhoun abandoned his earlier efforts to sustain a general expansionist coalition with northwesterners.

[98] McCormac, James K. Polk, 574 n. 37.

[99] Ibid., 260.

[100] Graebner, Empire on the Pacific, 130–34; Merk, Oregon Question, 224.

Whigs were outraged that northwesterners could take the prospects of war so lightly when the coastal cities would suffer bombardment and severe economic disruption.[101] This view was expressed well by one New York merchant who complained that war with Great Britain "will all do famously for the valley of the Mississippi, where they have all to gain by a war and nothing to lose. But we on the seaboard must fight all, pay all, and suffer all."[102] To these realist calculations, northeastern and southern opponents of war added commercial concerns as a reason to restrain Polk's provocative policy. Any interruption in relations between the United States and Great Britain, even one far short of outright war, could be disastrous for the commercial interests of Whigs and Democrats along the Atlantic coast and for Cotton Democrats of the southern interior. Daniel Webster observed that the northwestern states, "being so circumscribed as to have nothing which could be put to hazard by war, seem to look upon war as a pleasant excitement or recreation. They have no cotton crops, and no ships; while war would create much employment among them, raise the price of their provisions, and scatter money."[103] While Cotton Democrats were committed expansionists, they had little interest in the "frozen latitudes" of the north, particularly when pursuing this territory would cost them markets in England. They comfortably aligned with the Whigs and Democrats from the Atlantic coast in their assessment of the costs of war with Great Britain.[104]

These rival perspectives on the expected costs and benefits of war over Oregon are only part of the explanation. They certainly suggest the motivation for political opposition to the president's policy and help characterize the competition in the policy process. To more completely explain the peaceful outcome of this crisis, however, we must consider how the structure of the U.S. federal political system shaped the incentives that political leaders from the various regions responded to, the role of the political parties, and the institutional leverage that Polk's opponents had over the decision process. Specifically,

---

[101] Varg, *New England and Foreign Relations*, 180. One interesting exception to the solid opposition to All Oregon among northeastern Whigs was John Quincy Adams. Motivated by a desire to politically overwhelm the power of slaveholding states, Adams was among the most outspoken proponents of an aggressive U.S. policy to secure All Oregon. Adams was severely castigated by his Massachusetts constituents who strongly opposed war. Merk, *Oregon Question*, 227–29.

[102] Graebner, *Empire on the Pacific*, 135.

[103] Sellers, *James K. Polk*, 359.

[104] Merk, *Oregon Question*, 372; Sellers, *James K. Polk*, 360.

we must identify the institutional points of constraint in this case that held Polk in check and induced him to accept the compromise treaty. For this issue, like many in federal political systems, the intersection of party politics and regional loyalties within the House and Senate was the key to the persistent political divisions within the system that prevented unified political action on a bold and risky foreign policy.

It was Congress that imposed restraints on Polk's diplomacy and held the drift toward war in check. This constraint, however, was not simply a result of the separation of powers between the executive and legislature. Polk actually expected a quick debate in Congress and approval of his request to terminate the joint occupation agreement.[105] After all, the Democratic party controlled the Senate with a majority of 30 to 24 and the House with a majority of over 60. Polk had been elected on a platform calling for All Oregon, and he believed that public opinion, since his message to Congress in December 1845, was largely behind this bold position. President Polk most certainly expected his party to rally around his hard-line, risky diplomatic strategy on Oregon, to bridge the institutional divide in the U.S. federal system, and to carry his program through Democratic majorities in Congress.

Before the debate began in earnest, it appeared that Democratic party loyalty in Congress might sustain the president in his confrontational policy. When Calhoun first returned to the Senate determined to take a stand against Polk he was warned by several allies, Isaac Holmes of South Carolina and Robert Hunter of Virginia, that he would isolate himself and become ineffective from the start. They argued that Democrats in both houses would support the president and that Calhoun should join this majority for the president's program. Had loyalty to the Democratic party and its president been sustained after December 1845, Polk may have avoided any effort by Congress as a body to impose restrictions on his foreign policy. The separation of powers between the executive and legislature may have been meaningless under these conditions as a source of democratic constraints on state behavior.

Yet the crucial institutional feature that prevented congressional Democrats from rallying behind the president was the distribution of legislative authority within Congress itself, among senators and representatives who faced electoral incentives to support local inter-

---

[105] Pletcher, *Diplomacy of Annexation*, 318.

ests on this particular issue. Party unity was short-lived. The loyalty of southern Democrats, with few exceptions, resided with their regional constituents, not with the party, despite the damage caused to party unity and the president. Furthermore, the decentralized character of the Democratic party within this state-based electoral system denied Polk the ability to discipline party dissidents and force them to follow his agenda. Polk frequently lamented the absence of "harmony" among Democrats that was needed to support his policy.[106] In coalition with congressional Whigs, this regional bloc stanched the drift toward war and ultimately ratified a treaty dividing the Oregon Territory at 49 degrees. Congressional debate on Polk's request to terminate the joint occupation agreement became the vehicle for opponents of his policy in the Northeast and South to do two things: (1) to reject legislation proposed by extreme expansionists from the Old Northwest that would increase the risk of war with Great Britain; and (2) to approve Polk's request, yet with conciliatory language that not only limited Polk's freedom of action on the issue, but that also convinced the British government that the forces of compromise had the upper hand in the United States. The debate also highlighted the dangerous regional split in the Democratic party that Polk's policy had created.

For John Calhoun, regional loyalty was much stronger than party loyalty, so he could not be deterred from opposing his party on Oregon. His Senate seat gave him a secure and independent institutional position from which to attack Polk's diplomacy. Calhoun soon persuaded Senators Holmes and Hunter, along with a number of other southern Democrats, that loyalty to the party in this situation would harm the regional interests they were sent to Washington to defend. Calhoun persuaded them to stand with him against Polk and to help him fracture the shaky solidarity among Democrats.[107] To secure a majority against the president, and to present a large bloc for compromise in the legislative battles to come, these southern Democrats needed to reach out to the Whig party. Southern Democrats traditionally were bitter political rivals of the Whigs, based on their disdain for Henry Clay and his American System of protectionist tariffs.[108] Yet on Oregon the bulk of the Whig party and southern Democrats readily

---

[106] Polk, *Diary*, 260, 263, 265, 269, 272–74, 276.
[107] Wiltse, *John C. Calhoun*, 251.
[108] Sydnor, *Development of Southern Sectionalism*, 317; Wiltse, *John C. Calhoun*, 257.

agreed.[109] Senator Hunter approached Senate Whig leaders and received a pledge that Whigs would follow Calhoun's lead in opposition to All Oregon and any provocative policy measures.[110] The future of U.S. policy on Oregon and the likelihood of war with Great Britain were decided during the debates and legislative maneuvering on the joint occupation question. This legislative clash consistently pitted northwestern Democrats against the peace bloc of southern Democrats and eastern Whigs. As the New York *Herald* put it, "The chivalry of the West goes hot and strong for 54-40, while the ardent South, and the calculating East, coalesce, for once, on this point, and quietly and temperately call for 49."[111]

On December 18, Senator Allen, chairman of the Senate Foreign Relations Committee, opened debate by introducing a bluntly worded resolution terminating the joint occupation agreement with no conciliatory language attached. The peace bloc quickly defeated this resolution. It was reintroduced to the full Senate on January 12, but action on the measure was blocked for a month. On December 29, Senator Hannegan of Indiana introduced two resolutions on Oregon. The first declared that all territory west of the Rocky Mountains, from 42 to 54-40 degrees north, was U.S. territory. The second declared that any attempt to relinquish this territory would be unconstitutional because the United States government did not have the power to transfer the property of U.S. citizens to another country. Calhoun managed to have both resolutions tabled without a vote. Allen followed up by introducing a resolution announcing that "any effort of the Powers of Europe to intermeddle in the social organization or political arrangements of the Independent nations of America . . . would justify the prompt resistance of the United States." Whigs and southern Democrats defeated this declaration by a vote of 28 to 23.

In the House, a resolution terminating the joint occupation agreement was stuck in committee for a full month by disagreement between members of the expansionist and conciliation blocs. A resolution that contained no conciliatory language was reported out when several

[109] While much more united that the Democrats, the Whigs were not immune from regional divisions on Oregon. Once the debate was underway and U.S. nationalists were cheering on the champions of All Oregon, a number of western Whigs moved toward Lewis Cass's Democratic bloc. Pletcher, *Diplomacy of Annexation*, 320.

[110] Wiltse, *John C. Calhoun*, 251; Merk, *Oregon Question*, 224; Graebner, *Empire on the Pacific*, 136.

[111] Graebner, *Empire on the Pacific*, 137.

congressmen of the peace bloc were absent, yet once introduced to the full House it was debated in this form for another five weeks. Moderates won an important victory on Oregon with the amended resolution that was finally passed. It was approved by a margin of 3 to 1 and sent to the Senate only after an amendment was added supporting a compromise with Great Britain on the Oregon boundary.[112] In February it was increasingly clear to the president that two-thirds of the Senate would support a compromise treaty on the Oregon boundary. To keep up the pressure for a resolution giving Polk the authority to conclude the dispute on his own terms, on February 7 the administration provided the Senate a dispatch from U.S. minister Louis McLane in London. The dispatch, which had been edited to give the appearance that Britain's position on Oregon was hostile rather than pacific, had its intended effect. Fierce debate flared anew with northwesterners demanding swift approval of the termination notice in response to Britain's threatening views. Calhoun and his supporters held their ground during fourteen hours of fierce attacks from extreme expansionists. When the Senate resumed business after a weekend, the bellicose spirit had passed.[113] Polk was incensed that despite his party's control of both houses of Congress the debate on Oregon had lasted for months, with his partisans on the losing end of every resolution.[114] The administration's newspaper, the *Union*, began publishing attacks on dissident Democratic senators and demanded that Congress approve his request without delay or restrictions.[115]

The struggle in the Senate between the All Oregon enthusiasts and the peace bloc finally came to an end on April 16, with the peace bloc victorious. Setting aside a harshly worded form of the termination notice favored by Senator Allen, the Senate approved a moderate version by a vote of 40 to 14. On April 23, the House and Senate approved a joint resolution on Oregon that clearly asserted Congress's conciliatory position. The resolution urged "that the attention of the Governments of both countries may be the more earnestly and immediately directed to renewed efforts for the amicable settlement of all their differences and disputes in respect to said territory."[116] Bitter in defeat, northwestern Democrats turned their wrath on their southern col-

[112] Pletcher, *Diplomacy of Annexation*, 327–28, 332; Merk, *Oregon Question*, 378–79; Wiltse, *John C. Calhoun*, 252–53.

[113] Wiltse, *John C. Calhoun*, 357.

[114] Graebner, *Empire on the Pacific*, 145.

[115] Wiltse, *John C. Calhoun*, 261.

[116] Ibid., 261–62; Merk, *Oregon Question*, 229, 387; Pletcher, *Diplomacy of Annexation*, 350.

leagues, denouncing their defection from the Democratic platform and their pledge to support All Oregon in return for northwestern support on Texas.[117] The coalition that created the joint commitment to both Texas and Oregon during the Baltimore convention in 1844 could not survive the legislative process that decided the issue. Polk was now faced with a stinging rebuke of his diplomacy and no hope that his preferred approach to the Oregon problem would have sufficient legislative support. This was the crucial turning point in U.S. policy and the opportunity for a peaceful resolution.

To this point in the crisis, the U.S. federal system provided an institutional outlet for Calhoun and his peace bloc to challenge the Old Northwest's expansionist goals and to block President Polk's ability to continue with a policy that had the potential to provoke general war. In addition to the legislative constraint thrown up around Polk's foreign policy, the vigorous four-month debate on Oregon within Congress was instrumental in creating the domestic and international conditions necessary for compromise by the United States and Great Britain. This debate moved the issue beyond mere legislative blocking action to facilitate the actual resolution of the dispute. On the international level, the most important effect of the congressional debate was that it demonstrated to the British government that Polk's hard-line position did not represent a unified U.S. view on Oregon and war. In fact, Foreign Minister Aberdeen did not have to draw this conclusion on his own; he was informed on numerous occasions by active Democratic opponents of the All Oregon agenda that domestic divisions on Oregon would eventually force the United States to accept a boundary at 49 degrees, give Vancouver Island to the British, and grant temporary navigation rights on the Columbia River.[118] Edward Everett, the former U.S. minister to Great Britain and a close friend to Aberdeen, wrote to inform him that Calhoun's peace bloc was potent enough to "hold the balance of power in Congress and could prevent the passage of any bills for taking possession of the whole territory or compel acceptance of a reasonable British offer."[119]

In the absence of such a transparent and voluble debate within the United States and direct communication with Polk's opponents it is unlikely that Aberdeen would have been willing to take the politically

---

[117] Paul, *Rift in the Democracy*, 148 n. 8; Miles, "Fifty-four Forty or Fight," 300 n. 34; Pletcher, *Diplomacy of Annexation*, 333.

[118] Pletcher, *Diplomacy of Annexation*, 324.

[119] Ibid., 303.

risky step of submitting terms for a compromise treaty. Aberdeen was in a dangerous domestic position. Polk's behavior had convinced the British cabinet, the opposition Whig party, the press, and public that compromise over Oregon was really capitulation to the United States. Polk's unbending and seemingly extremist position and the warlike rhetoric from his northwestern allies had stiffened resistance within Great Britain to making concessions of any kind to resolve the conflict. Aberdeen, still committed to a peaceful resolution, was faced with the domestic task of convincing elite and popular opinion across the political spectrum that Oregon was not worth war and that compromise did not require capitulation. The debate in the United States helped him make this case,[120] and the conciliatory language of the termination notice passed by the congressional peace bloc was received in Great Britain as an invitation to resume negotiations. Aberdeen proposed a division of the territory at 49 degrees, then down the middle of Juan de Fuca Strait, reserving Vancouver Island for Great Britain. With these terms the British conceded their long-standing demand to divide the territory down the Columbia River, well south of 49 degrees, yet they reserved the large territory north to the 54–40 boundary with Russian Alaska.[121]

As Polk surveyed his position in the spring of 1846, he had to acknowledge how constrained he was. Congress demanded a spirit of conciliation with Great Britain. The debate in Congress had had a profound impact on the public image of the Oregon dispute. Two years earlier the public mood was enthusiastically expansionist. But four months of blistering debate "spread knowledge of Oregon . . . [it] revealed the intrinsic weakness of the American claim to the whole of Oregon, the likelihood of ruinous war if it were pressed to a showdown, and the irresponsibility and numerical inferiority of those pressing it."[122] The debate also revealed the glaring rift in the Democratic party that, according to Polk's diary, was an "irretrievable disaster."[123] It seemed to Polk as if the southern and northeastern Democrats were defecting from the party in droves to join the Whig camp.

Despite the seeming inevitability of compromise between the United States and Great Britain, Polk still would not take personal responsibility for abandoning his political obligations to his northwestern supporters and their demand for All Oregon. If the United States was going to

---

[120] Merk, "British Government Propaganda and the Oregon Treaty."
[121] Merk, *Oregon Question*, 230.
[122] Ibid., 394.
[123] Ibid., 391.

compromise on Oregon, he would not be blamed for taking a leading role in bringing the dispute to such an end. In essence, Polk wanted a way out of the war crisis, but was unwilling to be directly responsible for its resolution. The Senate, he determined, would help him out of this paradoxical situation.[124] Confident that a large majority in the Senate would quickly accept the British terms as the basis of a treaty, Polk decided to submit the British proposal directly to the Senate. While he did not provide a formal recommendation on the proposal, in his letter to the Senate Polk stated that he continued to stand by his December message to Congress, in other words, he still supported the All Oregon objectives.[125] With this tactic Polk hoped to use the Senate to extract the United States from the war crisis by ratifying an Oregon treaty, while at the same time using the Senate as political cover against the wrath of the 54–40 men. Despite the efforts of Hannegan and Allen to kill the treaty by bottling it up in the Foreign Relations committee, on June 18 the Senate ratified the text sent directly from Aberdeen by a vote of 41 to 14.

Conclusion

In an attempt to defend himself against charges of betrayal by his once-ardent supporters from the Old Northwest, Polk argued in a letter to the governor of Tennessee that "the executive arm was greatly paralyzed on the Oregon question, by the delegates and proceedings of Congress, especially in the Senate."[126] This claim is certainly true, as this chapter has demonstrated. The separation of powers between the executive and legislative branches allowed Congress to independently pass judgment on the Oregon question and the risks the United States should run in pursuit of its claims to this territory. Congress's conciliatory view on the problem, expressed through the amendment to the termination notice that urged compromise with Great Britain, and through the overwhelming support for a treaty setting the boundary at 49 degrees, denied Polk the legislative support necessary for pursuing a hard-line policy that held the clear risk of war.

But Polk's claim goes only a short distance toward our understanding of how the institutional arrangement of the U.S. political system

---

124 McCormac, *James K. Polk*, 584; Pletcher, *Diplomacy of Annexation*, 330–31.

125 Merk, *Oregon Question*, 231.

126 Hietala, *Manifest Design*, 82.

constrained the executive branch. To understand the source of opposition to Polk's risky diplomacy and to explain how such opposition
could come to dominate the proceedings of Congress it is necessary to
go beyond the president versus Congress view of the institutional
mechanisms at work. The most important feature of the political system for suggesting answers to these questions is its federal structure,
the division of authority within the legislature among territorial representatives whose electoral success depended on satisfying their territorial constituents' interests. Even though the Democratic party had
nominated an expansionist candidate and approved a platform that
was pledged to the All Oregon position, this position was merely that
of a temporary coalition formed during the Baltimore convention
among northwesterners led by Lewis Cass of Michigan, southerners
led by Robert Walker of Mississippi, and northeasterners who had rallied around Martin Van Buren of New York. Polk's message to Congress nine months into his presidency, which contained his claim to
the "whole of Oregon," had a short-term unifying effect on the party,
which rallied around the president as he stuck a blunt finger in John
Bull's eye. Had this level of party unity been maintained long enough,
the minority Whig party alone could not have prevented passage of
the provocative notice on joint occupation that Polk desired. Yet this
interregional coalition of Democrats that brought Polk in as a presidential candidate soon fell apart on the question of Oregon and war.
Because this issue produced such strong regional differences over U.S.
policy, party loyalty was overwhelmed by regional loyalty. Had the
U.S. political structure incorporated an electoral system that gave political parties a centralizing role on political issues, like many democracies do, the outcome of the Oregon crisis may have been quite different. Political unity among Democrats might have produced political
unity between President Polk and the majority in Congress, thus the
basis for democratic constraints rooted in the separation of powers between the executive and legislature would have been nullified in this
case. Yet in the U.S. system the federal division of authority provided
an irresistible incentive for most Democrats to stake a position in line
with constituents back home and to carry this position to the national
government. Under these conditions, an anti–All Oregon, procom-
promise coalition was formed that cut across party lines to unite legislators from two regions in a common cause derived from shared
regional perspectives.

5

THE MEXICAN WAR AND TERRITORIAL EXPANSION

By the mid-1840s the expansionist ideology of Manifest Destiny was flowering in the United States. With the expansionist Democratic party dominating both the executive and legislative branches of government, it is little surprise that the United States was embroiled in two territorial disputes simultaneously: with Great Britain over the Oregon Territory; and with Mexico over Texas annexation, the southern boundary of this new American state, and the future of Mexico's provinces of Upper California and New Mexico. The Mexican case provides an important contrast to the Oregon case. As we saw in chapter 4, while poised on the brink of war for several months, the United States and Great Britain resolved this dispute peacefully. Unlike the Oregon dispute, however, the building territorial conflict between the United States and Mexico produced a skirmish in April 1846 between U.S. and Mexican troops that led to a full-scale military conflict. The war ended with the U.S. occupation of Mexico City and the total defeat of Mexico's army. Along with America's military victory came a cession of territory from Mexico to the United States that Donald Meinig describes as "on a scale with those enormous transactions of previous centuries when European diplomats played geopolitical games with continents across the seas."[1]

---

[1] Donald W. Meinig, *The Shaping of America: A Geographical Perspective on 500 Years of History*, vol. 2 (New Haven: Yale University Press, 1993), 146.

In the context of democratic peace theory this case presents three important puzzles, the first two having to do with the origins of the war with Mexico. On the southern frontier, as with Oregon, President Polk demanded highly provocative territorial adjustments from a continental neighbor. But unlike Oregon, he backed up this demand with the deployment of a military force that greatly increased the chances of war, and he did so in the complete absence of a congressional reaction. In June 1845 Polk ordered U.S. troops under the command of General Zachary Taylor to cross the Nueces River in Texas and advance toward the Rio Grande. These American troops were thus occupying a disputed region that Mexico had repeatedly declared to be its sovereign territory and a vital interest it would fight for. Most historians agree that Polk did not intend to provoke a military conflict with this move, at least at the outset. This deployment was meant to intimidate Mexico into selling the territory Polk was determined to obtain.[2] Yet there is no doubt that the president realized this move would create an explosive situation as likely to result in violence as a peaceful resolution to the border dispute. The first puzzle then is why did Polk, in the same time period as the Oregon crisis, in the same highly divided political system, *not* face *ex ante* institutional constraints on his high-risk, confrontational approach in the dispute with Mexico? Why was there no domestic political opposition working through America's federal institutions to check Polk's force movements and thus reduce the likelihood of war?

The second puzzle raised by this case is why did Congress sanction Polk's war policy once the initial clash between U.S. and Mexican forces occurred? Two hours after the House of Representatives received Polk's notice of the border skirmish its members overwhelmingly approved a resolution that recognized a state of war between the United States and Mexico and provided reinforcements and supplies for General Taylor. While the Senate spent two days deliberating before its vote, this body also approved the resolution nearly unanimously. As with the earlier troop movements and confrontational diplomacy ordered by President Polk, the U.S. federal system failed to produce institutional opposition to Polk's war bill that could have prevented escalation of the conflict from an isolated border skirmish to

---

[2] For example, see Sam W. Haynes, *James K. Polk and the Expansionist Impulse* (New York: Longman, 1997), 129; and Paul A. Varg, *United States Foreign Relations, 1820–1860* (East Lansing: Michigan State University Press, 1979), 182.

full-scale warfare. This question is even more puzzling given the fact that there actually was widespread congressional sentiment against war with Mexico. This chapter presents these two phases in the origins of the war between the United States and Mexico as two separate cases that, along with the declaration of war against Great Britain in 1812, represent episodes in which the federal structure of U.S. society and political institutions did not act as a constraint on the use of force. Considered in the broader context of the many other crises in which the United States was constrained, these cases deepen our understanding of the conditions that either increase or decrease the likelihood that the domestic politics of federal union will actually produce constraints on the use of force.[3]

The third puzzle raised by the Mexican War concerns the gains that the United States was able to make through the use of force. As noted in earlier chapters, research on the constraining effects of democratic institutions should not be limited to cases involving either the presence or absence of war, but should also consider how democratic institutions limit what a state can achieve when war does result from an interstate dispute. In expansionist terms, the Mexican-American War is most noteworthy for the vast territory demanded and secured by the United States in the peace treaty, specifically, Upper California and New Mexico. Less well known, yet of great importance for the relationship between democracy and war gains, is how much more of Mexico the United States was in a position to annex. By early 1848 U.S. forces had shattered the Mexican government and its army. In the United States momentum was building behind a political movement calling for the annexation of *all* of Mexico, with support from two powerful members of Polk's cabinet, Secretary of State James Buchanan and Treasury Secretary Robert J. Walker. In the fall of 1847, frustrated by Mexico's unwillingness to negotiate over U.S. demands for California and New Mexico, Polk vowed to take a much larger bite as an indemnity against Mexican intransigence. With such a permissive international environment for the successful accession of an even greater parcel of Mexican territory, we must ask why the United States relinquished the gains demanded by the Polk administration to settle for just California and New Mexico. What role, if any, did America's

---

[3] Miriam Fendius Elman, "Introduction: The Need for a Qualitative Test of the Democratic Peace Theory," in *Paths to Peace: Is Democracy the Answer?* ed. Miriam Fendius Elman (Cambridge: MIT Press, 1997), 40–42.

federal democratic institutions have in facilitating political opposition to these larger U.S. claims, thus facilitating constraints on Polk's ability to secure them?

To resolve the first two puzzles presented in this chapter it is essential to determine what features of the dispute with Mexico may have negated or prevented domestic opposition, expressed through Congress, from constraining Polk's initiatives. From a realist theoretical perspective that looks to external incentives for state behavior, one explanation may be that Mexico was perceived to be a genuine threat to the Union's newest state. Mexico still claimed Texas, which had been annexed by the United States less than a year before the war. If the majority Democratic party remained unified across regions in the perception of a Mexican threat to Texas, or even if there were bipartisan support from the Whig party concerning the security of the southern border, then Polk may have had sufficient legislative support to pursue a high-risk policy and eventually war. Another realist explanation might be that the opportunity for territorial expansion in the Southwest and to the Pacific coast was enticing enough to generate support across the Union for Polk's coercive efforts to secure the continental potential of the United States. Each of these explanations, however, fails to account for the lack of *ex ante* constraints on Polk's Mexican policy. As with U.S. policy toward Oregon, there was no domestic consensus on either the threat posed by Mexico or the value of expansion into Mexican territory. Important factions within the Democratic party clearly broke with the administration on these questions and there was a great gap between the administration Democrats and the Whigs. Once Polk's war objectives became clear he faced fierce domestic opposition until the treaty ending the war with Mexico was concluded. This domestic opposition to war makes the absence of institutional constraints on Polk that much more puzzling. What this case does offer then is the opportunity to examine other domestic-level features that might have prevented this opposition from working within the U.S. federal structure to maintain peace.

The Move toward War

Sources of Friction in U.S.–Mexican Relations

Relations between the United States and Mexico during the 1820s were friendly; the United States had championed the cause of Mexican independence from Spain, and Mexico looked to the United States in its first years of independence as a model republic to be emulated. Beginning in 1830 this relationship went sour,[4] as three key areas of dispute set the stage for the clash of 1846. First, the most vexing issue for its southern neighbor was the United States' long-term efforts to separate Texas from Mexico. In the Adams-Onis Treaty of 1819, the United States had recognized Texas as part of New Spain—which in a few years was to become the independent Republic of Mexico. In the years that followed, however, the United States made repeated attempts to purchase Texas. The United States provided political and material support to the Texan independence movement and finally annexed the wayward Mexican province as a new state in 1845. Mexicans across the political spectrum saw annexation by the United States as outright theft of Mexico's sovereign territory. Even before annexation was approved by the U.S. Congress the Mexican government had repeatedly threatened the United States with war over the prospect of this move. Once annexation was approved, the moderate government of Mexican president Herrera had no choice but to treat this as such a serious affront to Mexican honor and sovereignty that it demanded the termination of diplomatic relations with the United States.[5]

The second source of friction was over the true southern boundary between Texas and Mexico. The Nueces River, with its mouth at Corpus Christi, had long been recognized by Spain, the United States, and Mexico as the boundary between the province of Texas and other Mexican provinces. During the war for independence in 1836, however, Texan leaders claimed that the boundary was actually 150 miles further south, at the Rio Grande. Mexico fervently held that the territory between the rivers was never part of Texas and would always remain Mexican, while as an independent republic Texas never stationed military forces or sent colonists or government officials south of the Nueces. Had the United States respected the traditional boundary at the Nueces there would have been no change in the status of this region or

[4] Varg, *United States Foreign Relations*, 170.
[5] General Mariano Paredes used the public uproar over Texas annexation to overthrow Herrera in a coup on the day President Polk admitted Texas to the Union. Seymour V. Connor and Odie B. Faulk, *North America Divided: the Mexican War 1846–1848* (New York: Oxford University Press, 1971), 27; John H. Schroeder, *Mr. Polk's War: American Opposition and Dissent, 1846–1848* (Madison: University of Wisconsin Press, 1973), 8; Norman A. Graebner, *Empire on the Pacific: A Study in American Continental Expansion* (Santa Barbara, Calif.: ABC-Clio, 1983), 108.

direct threat to Mexico's claim here.[6] This certainly would have made it easier for Mexico to accept Texas annexation as a *fait accompli*, thus diminishing the intensity of the initial source of friction. The U.S. Congress even left the boundary issue open to compromise and explicitly stated in a joint resolution that it consented to Texas annexation "subject to the adjustment by this government of all questions of boundary that may arise with other governments."[7]

President Polk never questioned the validity of the Rio Grande boundary. In a pledge to Texan leaders that he would defend the republic until annexation was complete, Polk established by fiat that the Rio Grande was the proper boundary and declared, "I would . . . not permit an invading army to occupy a foot of the soil East of the Rio Grande."[8] To give muscle to this pledge Polk ordered General Taylor to move across the Nueces in June 1845 to occupy the region near Corpus Christi, at the northern edge of the disputed territory. Polk instructed his envoy to Mexico, John Slidell, to inform the Mexican government that the U.S. claim to the Rio Grande was nonnegotiable. For the new Mexican government of General Paredes, Polk's behavior was nothing less than an act of war.[9]

In addition to settling the Texas boundary, Slidell's mission was to convince Mexico to sell Upper California and New Mexico and to demand that Mexico compensate a number of U.S. citizens for the loss of property and investments in Mexico during years of political instability. This became the third source of friction. Polk's desire to obtain California was driven by both security and commercial interests. Persistent rumors of Mexico's intention to sell California to either Great Britain or France revived long-standing U.S. fears of European states

---

[6] Frederick Merk convincingly shows that the Texas boundary was at the Nueces River and that U.S. claims to the Rio Grande cannot be confirmed historically. Prior to the war for Texan independence, all references in U.S., European, and Texan sources place the boundary at the Nueces. During the Texan war of independence, General Santa Anna, as a prisoner of war, signed an agreement under duress stating that the boundary was on the Rio Grande. The Mexican government immediately repudiated its terms, claiming it could only be valid if approved by the Mexican Congress. Frederick Merk, *The Monroe Doctrine and American Expansionism, 1843–1849* (New York: Alfred A. Knopf, 1966), chap. 6.

[7] Eugene Irving McCormac, *James K. Polk: A Political Biography* (New York: Russell and Russell, 1965), 373.

[8] David M. Pletcher, *The Diplomacy of Annexation: Texas, Oregon and the Mexican War* (Columbia: University of Missouri Press, 1973), 254.

[9] Schroeder, *Mr. Polk's War,* 8–9; Pletcher, *Diplomacy of Annexation,* 289; Connor and Faulk, *North America Divided,* 28.

expanding their influence in North America.[10] The commercial benefits of San Francisco Bay and San Diego Bay for supporting trade with
Asia were immense. Polk was determined to secure these benefits for
the United States rather than let California become a possession of its
commercial rivals. Obtaining New Mexico would allow the United
States to build a railroad south of the Rocky Mountains that would
connect the eastern half of the continent with Pacific ports.[11] While
Polk offered to compensate Mexico financially to settle each of these
issues, Mexico treated this overture as offensive and the government
refused to even grant Slidell an audience to present the U.S. offer.[12] To
Mexico this was no peaceful effort by continental neighbors to adjust
their borders, it was another example of the voracious territorial ap-
petite of the United States, a coercive attempt by the United States to
dismember Mexico in a time of vulnerability. The deployment of General Taylor's force into the disputed region while the United States
attempted to treat on the issue was further proof to the Mexican government of the aggressive U.S. intent.

Polk's Military Initiative against Mexico

Polk was furious over Mexico's unwillingness to settle these areas of
friction and he considered Slidell's rejection by the Mexican government a sufficient pretext for war.[13] In a message to Slidell in January
1846 Polk stated that if Mexico finally rebuffed his mission, "the cup
of forbearance will then have been exhausted. Nothing can remain
but to take the redress of the injuries to our citizens and the insults to
our Government into our own hands."[14] When the inevitable rebuff
came, General Taylor and more than thirty-seven hundred U.S. troops
were sent marching deeper into the disputed territory, and they arrived on the north bank of the Rio Grande on March 28. Taylor con-

[10] Graebner, *Empire on the Pacific*, 118; Pletcher, *Diplomacy of Annexation*, 265.

[11] Varg, *United States Foreign Relations*, 68–69.

[12] Polk offered to pay all Mexican debts to U.S. citizens and an additional $5 million
for the Rio Grande boundary and New Mexico. He raised the offer to $20 million if the
settlement included Northern California with San Francisco Bay, or $25 million for both
San Francisco and Monterey.

[13] James K. Polk, *The Diary of James K. Polk*, vol. 1, April 7, 1846, April 18, 1846
(Chicago: A. C. McClurg, 1910), 319, 337.

[14] Pletcher, *Diplomacy of Annexation*, 365.

structed a fort and positioned a battery of guns that could strike the Mexican town of Matamoros across the river. Polk had ordered the squadron of warships in the Gulf of Mexico to patrol the waters off Veracruz and to blockade the mouth of the Rio Grande. Whatever Polk's ultimate intent, two features of his military decision are clear. First, the president realized that ordering General Taylor to advance from the northern part of the disputed region to its southernmost section in January 1846 was a highly provocative act that greatly increased the risk of war. As Taylor advanced, Mexican army commanders "repeatedly informed him that his actions were considered an act of war and that he would be resisted with force."[15] Taylor kept Polk informed of these warnings and let the president know that he thought a clash was inevitable. While Taylor had informed the Mexicans at Matamoros that his intentions were peaceful, Mexican General Ampudia replied that Taylor had twenty-four hours to begin a move back to the Nueces or face a military reprisal. It was no real surprise then when on May 9 Polk received news that a Mexican force had ambushed a U.S. reconnaissance patrol fifteen miles from the U.S. encampment, resulting in sixteen U.S. casualties and the capture of the remaining soldiers in the patrol.[16] Polk fully anticipated a skirmish like this and actually expressed surprise on several occasions that a collision had not occurred earlier while Taylor's army sat on the Rio Grande.[17] A second feature of Polk's actions are also clear: as the possibility of war progressively increased over the course of a full year, throughout this long period there was absolutely no domestic effort to constrain Polk's confrontational policy toward Mexico or arrest this slide toward war. Polk was able to pursue his coercive diplomacy, move military forces, and create the conditions that made armed conflict seemingly inevitable with hardly a stir from potential legislative opponents. In a political system offering potent institutional outlets for opposition to such a high-risk foreign policy, the failure of these institutions to generate constraints is an important outcome that must be explained for a more sophisticated understanding of the relationship between democratic institutions and the use of military force.

---

[15] McCormac, *James K. Polk*, 410–14.
[16] Pletcher, *Diplomacy of Annexation*, 374–76.
[17] Polk, *Diary*, May 5, 1846, May 6, 1846, May 9, 1846, 379, 380, 384.

Why No *Ex Ante* Constraints on Polk's High-Risk Policy?

From a realist theoretical perspective there are several possible explanations for the absence of *ex ante* constraints on Polk's high-risk policy toward Mexico. The first such explanation concerns the threat posed by Mexico to U.S. security, particularly to the security of Texas and the new southern border of the United States. In the early summer of 1845 President Polk was alarmed by a report from the Prussian minister in Washington that a Mexican force was moving toward the Rio Grande.[18] This report seemed to confirm the concerns Polk had expressed that Mexico would follow through on its threats to use force to prevent the annexation of Texas, or at least to use force to maintain control of territory south of the Nueces River. Polk referred to this alleged Mexican threat in his war message to Congress in May 1846 to justify his earlier order that "an efficient military force . . . take a position between the Nueces and the Del Norte [Rio Grande]." "This had become necessary," he argued, "to meet a threatened invasion of Texas by the Mexican forces, for which extensive military preparations had been made."[19] In a July 1845 letter to a friend, Polk explained that this military deployment was meant to deter a possible Mexican attack. "I think she would have [attacked Texas]," he wrote, "but for the appearance of a strong naval force in the Gulf and our army moving in the direction of her frontier on land."[20]

The absence of domestic opposition to Polk's force movements on the southern border and in the Gulf of Mexico may simply have been the result of consensus on the threat posed by Mexico to U.S. security interests. If the majority of the general public and members of Congress shared Polk's view that a U.S. military response to this threat was necessary, then it is likely that Congress would step aside and let Polk take the lead as commander-in-chief to repel a sudden invasion. Even if the opposition Whig party chose to oppose Polk's deployment of U.S. forces, if the majority Democratic party remained unified behind Polk's perception of the threat and his actions, then congressional Democrats could prevent the Whigs from imposing legislative roadblocks to the president's actions. In either case, Democratic or bipartisan support for

18 Pletcher, *Diplomacy of Annexation*, 259.
19 James K. Polk, "Message to Congress on War with Mexico, May 11, 1846," in *James K. Polk, 1795–1849: Chronology-Documents-Bibliographical Aids*, ed. John J. Farrell (Dobbs Ferry, N.Y.: Oceana, 1970), 49.
20 McCormac, *James K. Polk*, 376.

the president would bridge the separation of powers between the executive and the legislature, making this institutional feature meaningless as a constraint on the use of military force. Widespread consensus on the national dimensions of the dispute with Mexico might push aside any particularistic regional interests involved, making the territorial system of representation within Congress less meaningful for legislators' behavior in response to the crisis.

According to many contemporary observers and several key indicators of national power, a U.S. perception of a significant Mexican threat might seem justified. The Spanish minister to the United States was often quoted on his belief that the Mexican army might be the strongest in the world. The British envoy to Mexico believed that the Mexican army could deploy and maneuver faster and could sustain the hardships of war longer than the U.S. army, while Britain's minister to the United States thought it impossible for the U.S. military to defeat a Mexican force. The Mexican army was in fact four times as large as the U.S. army, which had less that ten thousand troops in 1845, most of whom occupied scattered frontier posts and lacked the training or experience to be a cohesive fighting force. The Mexican army, on the other hand, numbered more than thirty-eight thousand and had been engaged in almost constant warfare since Mexican independence, as it was deployed to put down repeated internal insurrections.[21] Mexico had the advantage of short supply lines to support an aggressive move against Texas, while the United States had a great logistical challenge in moving and sustaining a sizable army over such long distances in desolate country.

Despite Polk's professed concerns about the Mexican threat and the many contemporary opinions that Mexico was in a superior military position compared to the United States, the alleged threat does not explain either Polk's long-term military initiatives on the southern border or the lack of institutional constraints on this high-risk policy. Instead of fearing Mexico, most Americans in the government, in the press, and among the public, from both political parties, in the executive branch and the legislative branch, had little but disdain for Mexican power. In fact, Americans denigrated Mexico to such an extent that it spilled over into routine arrogance directed at Mexican representatives in the

[21] John Edward Weems, *To Conquer a Peace: The War Between the United States and Mexico* (Garden City, N.Y.: Doubleday, 1974), 66–67; Connor and Faulk, *North America Divided*, 28–29; Haynes, *James K. Polk and the Expansionist Impulse*, 143.

United States. The respected Whig Waddy Thompson, a former U.S. minister to Mexico, summed up Americans' attitudes toward their southern neighbor when he said, "The truth is that I have never been able to elevate Mexico as to regard her as an adversary."[22] After all, Mexico suffered from crippling domestic political intrigue, insurrection, governmental decay and corruption, and the inability to maintain control over increasingly autonomous provinces and state governments.[23] The Mexican economy suffered from the lack of an even rudimentary industrial base and infrastructure. The Mexican army was not the well-armed and experienced force many Europeans described; Mexico's arsenal consisted mainly of Napoleonic-era weapons purchased from Great Britain and the army's greatest problem was recruitment and desertion. Most of the soldiers were Indians taken from their villages in chains, with little or no ability to understand their Spanish-speaking officers,[24] while leadership from the officer corps was hampered by incompetence and questionable loyalty to the government. The Mexican navy consisted solely of two new steam-powered warships and three new gunboats. The remaining ships were decrepit and all lacked trained crews.[25]

Initially, Polk took warnings about a Mexican force moving toward the Rio Grande at the end of July 1845 seriously. In the absence of a U.S. military presence in the region, Polk feared that despite the underlying economic and military weaknesses of the Mexican state Mexico could at least occupy and fortify the disputed region between the Rio Grande and Nueces to back up its territorial claims. Yet Polk's concern was short-lived. His subsequent orders to General Taylor in January 1846 to advance deep into the disputed region and to blockade the Rio Grande had nothing to do with a continuing sense of threat. By September 1845 the immediate fear of Mexican aggression faded and Polk remained convinced from this point on that Mexico would not take the military initiative.[26] His real purpose for ordering Taylor to take up a position right on the Rio Grande was not deterrence, but to coerce Mexico into settling the issues the Mexican government refused to discuss—the Rio Grande boundary, California and New Mexico, and the damage claims against Mexico raised by U.S. citizens. Mexico

---

[22] Varg, *United States Foreign Relations*, 170.
[23] Ibid., 171; Connor and Faulk, *North America Divided*, chap. 1.
[24] Haynes, *James K. Polk and the Expansionist Impulse*, 144.
[25] Pletcher, *Diplomacy of Annexation*, 257, 440–41.
[26] Polk, *Diary*, September 1, 1845, September 16, 1845, 12–13, 33.

wanted to let these issues drift, neither settling nor opting for war. For Polk this situation was too frustrating to let stand in limbo.[27]

This raises the possibility of an alternative realist explanation for the lack of political opposition and constraint. If Polk's intent was only to pressure Mexico into complying with his territorial demands and damage claims there may have been cross-regional consensus, or at least Democratic party support, behind this opportunity to enhance U.S. power in the international system. Mexican compliance with U.S. demands would provide the country with a territorial scope that spanned the continent, hospitable terrain for a transcontinental railroad to link the Atlantic Ocean and the Gulf of Mexico to the Pacific, some of the best harbors in the world from which to dominate the burgeoning Asian trade, and a fortune in mineral wealth estimated to lie in the soil of these lands. If there were sufficient consensus within the United States that these material benefits justified an aggressive policy toward Mexico, Polk may have been able to pursue this policy with the blessing, or at least without outright opposition, of potential political adversaries.

Yet there was no national consensus on using military coercion to secure the opportunity for territorial expansion presented by Mexico's weaknesses. In fact, this issue produced vigorous domestic opposition as Polk's objectives became clear. While U.S. possession of valuable ports on the Pacific coast was an objective shared by both Democrats and Whigs, the Whigs and key sections within the Democratic party were adamantly opposed to the use of force to attain them.[28] Polk knew that being frank about his intent to use threats of force or even a quick war to achieve his territorial objectives would produce enough domestic opposition to put his goals in jeopardy, so he kept his territo-

[27] Polk confirmed his belief in the value of military coercion after meetings with Colonel Alexander Atocha, a representative of the exiled former Mexican president Santa Anna, in February 1846. Polk recorded in his diary Atocha's argument that the United States "army should be marched at once from Corpus Christi to the Del Norte, and a strong naval force assembled at Vera Cruz . . . when [the Mexican government] sees a strong force ready to strike on their coasts and border, they would . . . feel their danger and agree to the boundary suggested." During a cabinet meeting the very next day Polk argued "that it would be necessary to take strong measures towards Mexico before our difficulties with that Government could be settled." Further, he argued, if Mexico refused to meet U.S. demands, "I would send a strong message to Congress . . . to confer authority on the Executive to take redress into our hands by aggressive measures." Polk, *Diary*, February 13, 1846, February 16, 1846, February 17, 1846, 222–23, 228–29, 233–34.
[28] Graebner, *Empire on the Pacific*, 171.

rial objectives a secret. He stated the objectives of his Mexico policy in such vague terms that members of Congress could only guess at what he intended to accomplish. Polk even lied to members of his own party to maintain Democratic unity. All of this was necessary, he confided, because "if [my plan was] made public it would probably defeat our object."[29]

The extent of domestic opposition to using force was most clearly evident immediately before and soon after the conflict erupted. By late April, Polk had resolved to seek a declaration of war from Congress before its current session ended.[30] To help him determine how Congress would treat this request, Polk assessed the weakest points in the ties holding the Democratic party together. Specifically, he canvassed the opinion of two powerful Senate Democrats, John Calhoun of South Carolina and Thomas Hart Benton of Missouri, who held influence over two mainly regional factions of the party. Calhoun held sway over a bloc of senators and representatives from Virginia, South Carolina, Georgia, and Florida. Benton was a leader of the Van Buren Democrats, most of whom represented large states in the North and Northeast, like New York, Pennsylvania and Ohio (even though Benton himself was from Missouri). If either of these factions broke with the administration over Mexico policy and worked with the opposition Whigs, the separation of powers could deal a fatal legislative blow to Polk's move toward war. While Calhoun and Benton both expressed an interest in Pacific ports, they refused to sanction war for this objective.[31] Senator John Dix, a leading Van Buren Democrat from New York, pressed Polk for a definitive answer on whether he intended to use force to take possession of any Mexican territory for the United States. Dix realized that northeastern Democrats could not defend their support for war with Mexico to constituents back home if the objectives included expansion into the Southwest. Without the institutional means to discipline northeastern Democrats who might break with the administration on this issue, Polk chose to misrepresent

---

[29] Ibid., 162. In both his war message to Congress and his annual message in December 1846, Polk refused to inform Congress that he intended to demand California and New Mexico because of the divisive domestic effect this would have. Ibid., 161, 169. In his annual message Polk would only say that he would seek an "ample indemnity for the expenses of the war, as well as to our much-injured citizens, who hold large pecuniary demands against Mexico." James K. Polk, "Second Annual Message, December 8, 1846," in *James K. Polk, 1795–1849*, 62.

[30] Polk, *Diary*, April 21, 1846, April 25, 1846, 343, 354.

[31] Ibid., April 18, 1846, May 3, 1846, 337–38, 375.

his goals in order to avoid the defection of Van Buren Democrats. Polk assured Senator Dix that his only interest was peace with Mexico and not territorial conquest.[32]

Despite the ambiguity of Polk's policy, Whigs like Joshua Giddings of Ohio were quick to assert that "the conquest of Mexico and California is the prize for which the game has been played."[33] Not a single Whig supported Polk's efforts to use coercion, then force, to make territorial gains at Mexico's expense. The Whigs were clearly motivated in their opposition by a normative perspective that infused the party's political philosophy, that put limits on what they considered to be legitimate circumstances justifying the use of force. As a party, the Whigs were traditionally less enthusiastic about territorial expansion, particularly if it came through violent means. Whigs consistently demonstrated a monadic liberal orientation toward U.S. foreign relations, that is, Whigs believed that military force was only justified as a response to serious security threats regardless of the regime-type of the potential adversary. The *National Intelligencer*, the leading Whig newspaper, summarized the party's view on Polk's Mexican policy in an August 1845 editorial:

> It is apparent that Texas [has] claimed, and we fear it is equally apparent that the Executive has granted, the occupation of everything up to the Rio Grande, which occupation is nothing short ... of an invasion of Mexico. It is *offensive war*, and *not* the necessary defense of Texas. And should it prove, as we think it will, that the President has gone this additional length, then the President will be MAKING WAR, in the full sense of the word, on his own authority, and beyond all plea of need, and even without any thought of asking legislative leave.[34]

After Polk's second annual message, which claimed the Rio Grande boundary for the United States, the Whigs assailed the president's assertion and in unity argued that at no time was the Rio Grande the rightful southern border of Texas, and thus not the rightful southern border of the United States.[35] For Whigs, Polk's military initiative was no less than raw aggression in support of a territorial claim that had

[32] Schroeder, *Mr. Polk's War*, 22; Graebner, *Empire on the Pacific*, 162.
[33] Graebner, *Empire on the Pacific*, 163.
[34] Weems, *To Conquer a Peace*, 71; emphasis in original.
[35] Frederick Merk, *Manifest Destiny and Mission in American History: A Reinterpretation* (Cambridge: Harvard University Press, 1963), 103.

no basis in history or law. This was a position the Whigs would maintain throughout the war.

It is clear from the outright hostility of Whigs, the reluctance of Van Buren and Calhoun Democrats to sanction territorial expansion through war, and Polk's efforts to keep his territorial objectives secret that the opportunity to make territorial gains through war was not embraced widely enough in the U.S. political system to ensure the absence of constraints on Polk's policy. Yet the fact remains that despite intense and widespread opposition to territorial aggrandizement, Polk did not exercise self-restraint in this policy, he did not appeal to Congress for support early in the building conflict, or give Congress an opportunity to share in decision-making as it entered its most explosive stage. This phase of the crisis ended as Polk had anticipated it might, with the armed clash on the Rio Grande, thus relieving Polk of having to send a war request to Congress in the absence of some act of violence by Mexico.

The most important point for this case, however, is that the border skirmish would not have occurred if Polk had not ordered the U.S. army to advance to the Rio Grande, thus creating a situation he knew could provoke violence. The most effective *ex ante* institutional constraints, in the form of legislation prohibiting this force movement, would have had to come *before* General Taylor reached a position that put him in close proximity to Mexican forces. The initiative for this congressional action could have come from the president or from members of Congress itself. Had Congress assumed a role in deciding whether the United States should move from its strictly diplomatic confrontation with Mexico to a volatile militarized dispute by marching forces to the Rio Grande, it is certain that the normative orientation of the Whig party would have produced partisan opposition in Congress. Because of the Democrats' majority in both houses of Congress, partisan opposition alone was insufficient to constrain Polk. However, it is also certain that a coercive force deployment would have split the Democrats into rough regional blocs, as federal electoral incentives prevailed over party loyalty. A core group of extreme expansionists from the North (primarily in the Old Northwest) and the southwestern states would have supported the administration. Yet Calhoun Democrats from southeastern states and Van Buren Democrats from the Northeast would have joined the Whigs to form a congressional majority that could vote down such a provocative policy. In the debate over the war bill Calhoun argued, "If it had been deliberately put to a vote whether it was right to order General Taylor to the del Norte, or for him to take a position opposite Matamoros and plant his cannon against it, or that Mr. Slidell should be sent to Mexico, when he was under the circumstances he was, or whether we should declare war on account of the claims against Mexico, most of which are without foundation, there would have been not a tenth of Congress in the affirmative . . . . I fear that what was done in a hurry will long have to be repented at leisure.[36] Senator Benton was furious when he read the war message from Polk because Congress had never approved of sending General Taylor to the Rio Grande. Benton argued that he would have voted men and money for legitimate defense, but never for "aggressive war on Mexico," which is how he characterized Polk's strategy. Benton notified Polk personally that he disapproved of both the Rio Grande boundary and marching the army to seize it.[37] Speaking for the Whig party, Senator Clayton of Delaware echoed these dissident Democrats' sentiments when he argued, "The whole conduct of the Executive in this case has been utterly unjustifiable." Polk had "sent an army to take up a post, where, as it must have been foreseen, the inevitable consequence would be war."[38]

Within a month of sending General Taylor across the Nueces, the president did consider calling Congress into session to discuss the possibility of war with Mexico, but he was advised by Senator Bagby of Alabama not to do so.[39] Independent executive action on Mexico was in full accordance with Polk's view on the role of the president in the U.S. political system. Unlike Congress, Polk argued, the president was elected by a national constituency. Individual members of Congress represented narrow regional constituencies that Polk believed had no business impeding the national interest. Polk actually recognized the constraining effects of federal asymmetry on foreign policy questions. In a country as diverse as the United States, Polk held that generating consensus on bold foreign policy initiatives was nearly impossible. Instead of allowing the logic of federal democratic peace to hold the United States in check, he was convinced that the president should pursue objectives he believed were in the best interest of the general public, even if there were no national unity on the issues at

---

[36] Ernest McPherson Lander, Jr., *Reluctant Imperialists: Calhoun, the South Carolinians, and the Mexican War* (Baton Rouge: Louisiana State University Press, 1980), 11.

[37] Polk, *Diary*, May 11, 1846, 390.

[38] Varg, *United States Foreign Relations*, 187.

[39] Polk, *Diary*, September 1, 1845, 12–13.

hand.[40] Taking such bold measures short of war to coerce Mexico, without congressional approval, was unproblematic for Polk. There was no legal requirement for him to seek congressional approval of his diplomacy or this military move that he claimed was defensive in nature and within his authority as commander-in-chief. Furthermore, Polk needed no special appropriations to support the deployment.

While Polk himself chose not to bring Congress into the decision process on Mexico, members of Congress could have assumed a role on their own initiative. Congress had the authority to impose legislation that would prohibit Polk from marching U.S. troops to the Rio Grande, or Congress could have demanded that he withdraw U.S. troops from the disputed region altogether. Yet not a single member of Congress took the initiative to put his Mexico policy to a vote. Until Polk actually introduced his war bill after the border skirmish, Congress did not even debate Polk's military initiatives over the course of the previous year. This was a major failure of the potential institutional constraints built into this federal system. But why was Congress not engaged in Mexico policy as it had been engaged in other critical foreign policy problems? The consensus among historians is that members of Congress, opinion leaders, newspapers, and the general public were simply distracted by the crisis over the Oregon Territory and the possibility of war with Great Britain in the fall of 1845 through the spring of 1846. While Polk pursued his increasingly aggressive military initiatives against Mexico, debate raged in Congress and in the press over U.S. policy in the Pacific Northwest, but members of both parties and the press were silent in this period over events on the southern border.[41] Moreover, when General Taylor's force was on the move to the Rio Grande, Polk's discussions with key members of Congress about Mexico only covered his desire to *purchase* Mexican territory. During the last week of March and first week of April the president conferred secretly with two members of the House and senators Allen, Benton, Calhoun, and Cass about his desire for a $1 million appropriation to support his effort to buy this territory. Each member of Congress he spoke to agreed with the proposal. However, he did not

[40] Thomas R. Hietala, *Manifest Design: Anxious Aggrandizement in Late Jacksonian America* (Ithaca: Cornell University Press, 1985), 208; Varg, *United States Foreign Relations*, 186.

[41] For example, see Charles Sellers, *James K. Polk, Continentalist 1843–1846* (Princeton: Princeton University Press, 1966), 409; Schroeder, *Mr. Polk's War*, 10; Pletcher, *Diplomacy of Annexation*, 363.

reveal his concurrent efforts to intimidate Mexico with the show of military force then underway, nor did he reveal that the United States was entering a period of dramatically higher risks of war with Mexico.[42] Polk never broached the prospects of war with Congress until he raised the subject cautiously with Calhoun and Benton, just days before the border skirmish.

When it was too late to turn back events, Calhoun could only lament that Polk's failure to seek congressional approval for his policy "divested Congress of its war making powers and transferred that to the president, and even to commanders on the frontier." Calhoun saw this as a "critical weakness in the system of checks and balances. The president had demonstrated his almost unrestrained power, independent of Congress, to involve the nation in war. American troops had been maneuvered into a position along the Rio Grande which virtually guaranteed Mexican reprisal."[43] In this case Congress simply did not have the kind of information necessary to foresee the potential consequences of American policy, which made it unlikely that Congress would have taken the initiative to interpose itself in the evolving dispute early enough to make a difference in the direction the dispute was taking. This provided the executive with tremendous latitude for engineering a volatile crisis and the armed clash that resulted.

Polk's War Bill Is Approved

While Polk avoided making his Mexico policy a public issue from July 1845 through May 1846, Congress was abruptly thrust into the decision-making process with Polk's war message of May 11, 1846. This war message provided the president's version of the events that led to the armed clash on the Rio Grande, and it asked Congress to recognize that a state of war existed by an act of Mexico and authorize money to support General Taylor with reinforcements and supplies. For the first time in this case Polk offered the legislature as a whole an opportunity to impose *ex ante* constraints on the president's desire to escalate the conflict from a border clash to full-scale warfare. Now the opponents

---

[42] Polk, *Diary*, March 25, 28, 29, 30, 31, 1846, April 3, 1846, 303, 306, 309–17.
[43] Schroeder, *Mr. Polk's War*, 24.

of Polk's policy, both Whigs and Democrats, had the opportunity to deny him the legal sanction for war and the money to prosecute it.

Considering the level of hostility toward Polk's policy among a majority of the members of the House and Senate, it is fair to expect that his war bill would have been defeated. Members of the Whig party from all regions were unanimous in their opposition to war. From the moment the war bill arrived on Capitol Hill, Whigs across the country ridiculed it as based on a patently false rendition of the events leading to the conflict; this was not a defensive war at all, Whigs maintained in unison, it was outright aggression and Polk was to blame.[44] The party's position was clearly characterized by a resolution passed in the Whig-dominated Massachusetts legislature that asserted this was a war of conquest "so hateful in its objects, so wanton, unjust and unconstitutional in its origin and character," which is being "waged by a powerful nation against a weaker neighbor."[45] Once Whigs gained a majority in the U.S. House after the elections of 1846, they were able to pass a resolution declaring that Polk had begun the war "unnecessarily and unconstitutionally."[46] A number of Whigs from the manufacturing and merchant class of the Northeast and the cotton growers in the South opposed war because of its potential to disrupt trade with Great Britain, which might come to the aid of Mexico in some way.[47] They also feared that if war resulted in territorial expansion it had the potential to divide northern from southern Whigs, which could be disastrous for their mutual political and economic interests.[48]

Among Democrats, the most vocal opponent of war with Mexico was John Calhoun, who Polk came to call the "most mischievous man in the Senate to my administration." Calhoun was so dangerous to Polk's foreign policy because the bloc he controlled in the Senate and the House, while small in overall numbers, could tip the vote balance

[44] Frederick Merk, "Dissent in the Mexican War," in *Dissent in Three American Wars*, ed. Samuel E. Morison, Frederick Merk, and Frank Freidel (Cambridge: Harvard University Press, 1970), 38; Varg, *United States Foreign Relations*, 190; Schroeder, *Mr. Polk's War*, 32; Pletcher, *Diplomacy of Annexation*, 392; Paul A. Varg, *New England and Foreign Relations, 1789–1850* (Hanover, N.H.: University Press of New England, 1983), 203.

[45] Merk, "Dissent in the Mexican War," 49.

[46] Weems, *To Conquer a Peace*, 441; Kinley J. Brauer, *Cotton versus Conscience: Massachusetts Whig Politics and Southwestern Expansion, 1843–1848* (Lexington: University of Kentucky Press, 1967).

[47] Varg, *New England and Foreign Relations*, 185–86.

[48] Pletcher, *Diplomacy of Annexation*, 458–59; Keith Polakoff, *Political Parties in American History* (New York: Alfred A. Knopf, 1981), chap. 5.

away from the administration if it aligned with the Whigs on any issue. Calhoun and his southeastern allies, strong states-rights advocates, opposed the war on constitutional grounds; it was the result, they argued, of an abuse of executive power.[49] They also opposed the war on economic grounds, fearing that the expenses of war would require an increase in tariffs, which the Calhoun Democrats saw as devastating for plantation agriculture.[50] Van Buren Democrats, concentrated in New York, Pennsylvania, and Ohio, saw the war as Polk's personal blunder, an explosive policy that would inevitably raise the thorny problems of territorial expansion and slavery, a politically deadly mix for Democratic party unity.[51] Van Buren Democrats also represented the core of antislavery sentiment in the party. Since Van Buren's defeat during the 1844 nominating convention, this faction believed that the party was increasingly under the influence of the South. A war with Mexico, they believed, would be fought for southern interests and to extend slavery. This put northeastern Democrats in the difficult position of either splitting with the party by withholding support for war, or in Van Buren's own words, committing "political suicide" by remaining loyal to the party and thus alienating their constituents.[52]

Despite such widespread and strongly held opposition to war, which clearly provided enough votes to reject Polk's war bill when it came to a vote in Congress, the bill passed by the overwhelming margin of 174 to 14 in the House and 40 to 2 in the Senate. With few exceptions, nearly every Whig and every Democrat voted with the president's supporters to approve the war bill.[53] How is it possible that with the legislative strength to constrain the president the opponents of war failed to realize this potential? What circumstances undermined the institutional incentives of the federal system and led these opponents of war to actually vote to carry the war forward?

The answer lies in how the president and his congressional allies manipulated the policy choice before Congress, and thus manipulated the political risk to the opponents of war if they failed to support the

---

[49] Charles M. Wiltse, *John C. Calhoun: Sectionalist, 1840–1850* (Indianapolis, Ind.: Bobbs-Merrill, 1951), 281.

[50] Graebner, *Empire on the Pacific*, 182.

[51] Ibid., 180; Varg, *United States Foreign Relations*, 191.

[52] Schroeder, *Mr. Polk's War*, 21.

[53] The only negative votes in the House and Senate came from northeastern abolitionists. In the Senate, Calhoun and two of his supporters refused to vote. Pletcher, *Diplomacy of Annexation*, 386–87; Merk, "Dissent in the Mexican War," 39–40.

president's program. First, Polk never asked Congress to declare war on Mexico. In other words, he never asked for legislative approval to take the United States from a state of peace to a state of armed conflict. Polk simply wanted Congress to recognize that the United States and Mexico *were already at war* "by the act of Mexico herself." With an indignant tone, Polk's message proclaimed, "Mexico has passed the boundary of the United States, has invaded our territory and shed American blood upon the American soil."[54] Despite the flagrant distortions in his account of the conflict, Polk was able to emphasize that as Congress considered the war bill, U.S. troops were already engaged in a violent struggle with Mexican forces along the Rio Grande. Second, the main purpose of the legislation was not to give Polk the authority to go to war, but to provide support for General Taylor's beleaguered army; an amendment to the war bill authorized fifty thousand volunteers and a $10 million appropriation.[55] This was the heart of what Congress was being asked to vote on. Despite strong and unanimous opposition to war, the vast majority of House and Senate Whigs were politically paralyzed by the fear that voting against Polk's war bill would not be seen by the public as a valiant act of conscience or wisdom to restrain an aggressive president's foreign policy. It would be seen, Whigs feared, as an act of disloyalty to U.S. soldiers engaged on a distant battlefield, and in turn, an unpatriotic stand against the United States itself.[56] According to Robert Winthrop of Massachusetts, Polk and his congressional allies "presented the most difficult case for an honest man to give a satisfactory vote upon, which I have ever met with."[57] Whig congressman Abraham Lincoln explained his vote for the bill, despite his strong opposition to war, this way: "When the war began, it was my opinion that all those who, because of knowing too little, or because of knowing too much, could not conscientiously approve the conduct of the President . . . nevertheless, as good citizens and patriots, remain silent on that point, at least till the war should be ended."[58]

This fear of being portrayed as disloyal to U.S. soldiers was heightened by Polk's success in portraying the conflict as unprovoked

---

[54] Polk, "Message to Congress on War with Mexico," 51–52.

[55] Schroeder, *Mr. Polk's War*, 13.

[56] Ibid., 13–15; Merk, *Manifest Destiny and Mission in American History*, 90–91; Brauer, *Cotton vs. Conscience*, 171.

[57] Schroeder, *Mr. Polk's War*, 15.

[58] Weems, *To Conquer a Peace*, 349.

Mexican aggression on U.S. soil. However inaccurate, Polk's characterization of the initial border skirmish was widely accepted among
the American people. As a result, the public initially rallied to Polk's
position.[59] Consequently, any asymmetric regional perspectives on
war with Mexico were initially swamped by Polk's ability to cast
this problem as a true national issue in which national identity and
interests were paramount. The Whigs' dilemma was compounded
by the memory of what happened to the Federalist party after the
War of 1812. At the end of that war the Madison administration and
the Republican party labeled the Federalists as traitors to the United
States for their political opposition throughout this conflict. This
was a charge that stuck and led to the complete demise of the
party.[60] Whig leader Henry Clay "ascribed the failure" of his party
"to resist more effectively . . . to the fear of repeating that traumatic
experience of the past." The Whigs of the 1840s were the political
and ideological successors to the Federalists of earlier decades, so
the historical parallel was unnerving. According to Merk, the Whigs
were "prisoners of the fear of what would happen to the party if
its actions impeded reinforcement of Taylor and disaster should
befall."[61]

Dissident Democrats faced the same fear of electoral retribution if
they failed to support U.S. troops.[62] Like the Whigs, the Van Buren
Democrats saw their vote on the war bill as a touchstone for their future relevance in U.S. politics. Since losing the presidential nomination in 1844, Van Buren Democrats believed that they could regain
control of the party in 1848. When elected, Polk had declared that he
would limit his tenure to one term in office and he reaffirmed this position regularly. There were few credible rivals to Van Buren in the
party for the next election, and this faction's hopes for 1848 were realistic. However, this meant that members of the faction could not risk a
position that was disloyal to the party, which a vote against war
would be. While a vote for war might threaten their political position
with constituents in their home states when the war rally faded, re-

[59] Meinig, *Shaping of America*, 145; Pletcher, *Diplomacy of Annexation*, 391–92. Merk
characterizes the public reaction in this case as "momentary hysteria." Merk, "Dissent in
the Mexican War," 43–44.

[60] Schroeder, *Mr. Polk's War*, 29; Merk, "Dissent in the Mexican War," 45.

[61] Merk, *Manifest Destiny and Mission*, 94–95.

[62] Lander, *Reluctant Imperialists*, 8–10.

maining faithful to the party was the only way to put their man in the White House.[63]

Polk knew the political risks his opponents from both parties faced if they defeated his war bill, and he counted on their unwillingness to assume these risks to hold the party together and even garner bipartisan support in the final vote. In his diary entry on the day he sent his war bill to Congress Polk expressed his concern that an alignment of Whigs and dissident Democrats opposed to the war was enough to defeat his policy. The bill could only be saved, he believed, by "the fear of the people by the few Democratic Senators who wish it defeated."[64] The fear of the people, combined with the legislative choice forced on Congress by the president and his congressional allies,[65] not only kept the Democratic party unified, it also forced the Whigs to choose the less risky political option of sanctioning the cause so many Americans were rallying around. When the voting was over, with Polk's bill approved, the United States was in the paradoxical situation of fighting a war that, as John Quincy Adams characterized it, was "now sustained by similar majorities [in both houses of Congress] professing to disapprove its existence and pronouncing it unnecessary and unjust."[66]

Federal Politics and Limits on Gains from War

U.S. Victory and Territorial Demands

An apparent anomaly in the outcome of the Mexican-American War is the mismatch between, on one side, the scale of the territorial indemnity desired by the president, his cabinet, certain congressional leaders, and a growing popular movement, all made possible by the United States' overwhelming military victory, and on the other side, the actual

[63] Schroeder, *Mr. Polk's War*, 21–22; Merk, "Dissent in the Mexican War," 45; Varg, *United States Foreign Relations*, 191.

[64] Polk, *Diary*, May 11, 1846, 393.

[65] Administration Democrats forced the bill to a vote within two hours of its arrival, thus preventing deliberate consideration of the issues and facts relevant to the legislation. The Speaker of the House refused to acknowledge all Whigs who rose to speak during the brief period allowed for debate, and he refused to allow examination of a large stack of documents provided by the administration. Weems, *To Conquer a Peace*, 123; Schroeder, *Mr. Polk's War*, 13. In the Senate, Calhoun was able to secure a two-day delay in the vote to build opposition and to remove the preamble authorizing the president to prosecute a war. However, Senator Allen, chairman of the Foreign Relations Committee, was able to block these efforts and force Polk's original war bill to a vote. Pletcher, *Diplomacy of Annexation*, 386–89; Merk, *Manifest Destiny and Mission*, 91–93.

[66] Merk, "Dissent in the Mexican War," 46.

territorial gains the United States achieved in the peace treaty. As Merk has observed, the "settlement did not reflect the military situation" that existed when the treaty was signed on February 2, 1848. The settlement "reflected what had been the military situation ten months earlier," before the United States completed its conquest of Mexico, before the United States had captured its capital city, decimated the Mexican military, and rendered the Mexican government impotent.[67] While the Polk administration secured Upper California and New Mexico in this treaty, the feeling among the president's supporters was that the territorial settlement did not fully compensate the United States for the cost in lives and resources that this victory required. The question then is why did the United States fail to extract more territory from Mexico when it was in a position to do so? Why did the United States fail to attain territory that would further reduce its vulnerability to European interference in North America, that would turn the Gulf of Mexico into a U.S. lake, and that would provide eagerly sought mineral wealth and easier overland access to the Pacific Ocean?[68] If external constraints did not limit America's territorial gains from this war, to what extent do domestic political opposition and the institutional structure of U.S. federal democracy account for this outcome?

From the beginning of the war, seizing territory from Mexico was Polk's main objective. In official explanations of his war goals Polk would simply say, "We go to war with Mexico solely for the purpose of conquering an honorable and permanent peace."[69] Such a peace required an indemnity from Mexico, but because the Mexican government was bankrupt Polk made it clear to his cabinet that he intended to exact a territorial cession to cover U.S. claims.[70] Polk's ambitions were

[67] Merk, *Manifest Destiny and Mission*, 184. For detailed accounts of the military experience and ultimate success of the United States in this war see Justin H. Smith, *War with Mexico* (New York: Macmillan, 1919); Robert Leckie, *From Sea to Shining Sea* (New York: Harper Collins, 1993); Roswell S. Ripley, *The War with Mexico* (New York: Harper, 1849); Robert S. Henry, *The Story of the Mexican War* (Indianapolis, Ind.: Bobbs-Merrill, 1950).

[68] Merk, *Manifest Destiny and Mission*, 120–29; Haynes, *James K. Polk and the Expansionist Impulse*, 169–71; Pletcher, *Diplomacy of Annexation*, 523.

[69] Pletcher, *Diplomacy of Annexation*, 397–98.

[70] Fearing that Great Britain and France would support Mexico and perhaps even intervene in the war if U.S. territorial ambitions were known, Buchanan suggested that Polk authorize a diplomatic note to all European capitals disavowing any territorial goals beyond the Rio Grande boundary. Polk exploded at the thought of forgoing this opportunity to make such valuable territorial gains for the sake of appeasing the British and French. In his diary Polk recounts, "I told him that before I would make the pledge which he proposed, I would meet the war which either England or France or all the Powers of Christendom might wage." Polk, *Diary*, May 13, 1846, 397–98.

not limited to California and New Mexico, however; in the early months of the war the debate in the cabinet on territorial expansion provides insight into how far Polk was willing to push his territorial demands. The two main antagonists in this debate were the most influential cabinet officers, Secretary of State James Buchanan and Treasury Secretary Robert J. Walker. While Buchanan was resigned to the fact that Polk would accept nothing less than California and New Mexico, he insisted that the United States seek nothing more. He argued that from El Paso west, the United States must accept a permanent border at 32 degrees North latitude and forgo territory south of this line. Buchanan, harboring presidential ambitions and hailing from the state of Pennsylvania, realized that U.S. expansion south of this line would be inflammatory in his home state and throughout the Northeast. Southward expansion would be interpreted in this region as a bold step by a southern-dominated Democratic administration to overwhelm the North with new southern states. In his diary Polk writes that Buchanan "spoke of the unwillingness of the North to acquire so large a Country that would probably become a slave-holding country if attached to the United States."[71] Walker, on the other hand, was a leader among "spread-eagle" U.S. expansionists. As a senator from Mississippi he had been a persistent advocate of any expansionist opportunity the United States could grab.[72] Walker had a much grander vision of the territorial gains to be made through this war with Mexico, and in Polk's words, he "warmly resisted Mr. Buchanan's views."[73] Walker proposed that the United States should demand a border with Mexico that began at the mouth of the Rio Grande, at 26 degrees North latitude, and extended due west from that point straight to the Pacific. This would include most of the states of Chihuahua, Sonora, and Lower California.

Polk is clearly on record as favoring the more expansive ambitions articulated by Secretary Walker. In his diary he expresses dismay that his secretary of state was "entertaining opinions so contracted and sectional." During a cabinet meeting on June 30, Polk agreed with Walker stating, "As to the boundary which we should establish by a Treaty of Peace, I remarked that I preferred the 26 degree boundary North of it."[74] In a letter written to his brother during this period, the president

[71] Ibid., June 29, 1846, 495–96.
[72] H. Donaldson Jordan, "A Politician of Expansion: Robert J. Walker," *Mississippi Valley Historical Review* 19 (1932–1933), 362–81.
[73] Polk, *Diary*, June 30, 1846, 497.
[74] Ibid.

affirms his insistence on California and New Mexico and foreshadows his commitment to even more territory if the war dragged on. "You may calculate I think that California and New Mexico—being now possessed by forces—will not be given up, but will be retained—to indemnify our claimants upon Mexico and to defray the expenses of the war. Indeed you need not be surprised if other Provinces also are secured in like manner. *The longer the war shall be protracted by the stubbornness of Mexico, the greater will be . . . the indemnity required.*"[75]

By the fall of 1847 Polk faced such a situation and was ready to follow through on his early pledge. Despite U.S. success in subjugating Mexico by this time, the Mexican government refused to negotiate a peace treaty. Frustration with this situation hardened Polk's resolve to extract a greater territorial indemnity. There certainly were no external impediments to any territorial goals the United States might establish. As Meinig points out, the "American military presence in Mexico . . . allowed the United States to consider imperial alternatives."[76] According to Senator Robert Hunter of Virginia, a Calhoun Democrat, by January 1848 "schemes of ambition, vast enough to have tasked even a Roman imagination to conceive, present themselves suddenly as practical questions."[77] The grandest of these schemes was embodied by the All Mexico movement, a political initiative to annex the entire country that was particularly popular in the Old Northwest, in the Southwest, and the urban centers of the Northeast. Only in New England and the Southeast was there resistance to this program.[78] Through the fall of 1847 and into January 1848 the All Mexico movement picked up momentum at the popular level and within the Democratic party, to the point where leading contenders for the Democratic presidential nomination endorsed the program, influential Democrats in Congress prominently supported the cause,[79] and members of

[75] Graebner, *Empire on the Pacific*, 158–59; emphasis added.

[76] Meinig, *Shaping of America*, 207.

[77] Graebner, *Empire on the Pacific*, 203.

[78] Edward G. Bourne, "The Proposed Absorption of Mexico in 1847–48," *Annual Report of the American Historical Association* 1 (1899); Chaplain W. Morrison, *Democratic Politics and Sectionalism: The Wilmot Proviso Controversy* (Chapel Hill: University of North Carolina Press, 1967), 86, 159; Haynes, *James K. Polk and the Expansionist Impulse*, 169–70; Schroeder, *Mr. Polk's War*, 127; Pletcher, *Diplomacy of Annexation*, 551–57; Merk, "Dissent in the Mexican War," 51; Lander, *Reluctant Imperialists*, 150.

[79] In January 1848 Senator Hannegan of Indiana introduced a resolution declaring "that it may be necessary and proper, as it is within the constitutional capacity of this Government, for the United States to hold Mexico as a territorial appendage." Bourne, "The Proposed Absorption of Mexico in 1847–48," 163. John D. P. Fuller, "The Slavery Question and the Movement to Acquire Mexico, 1846–1848," *The Mississippi Valley Historical Review* 21 (1934–1935), 38; Lander, *Reluctant Imperialists*, 157; Willard Carl Klunder, *Lewis Cass and the Politics of Moderation* (Kent, Ohio: Kent State University Press, 1996), 159.

Polk's own cabinet rallied to the vision of dramatic U.S. expansion. It is no surprise that Secretary Walker was an early booster of All Mexico,[80] and his influence on Polk gave the movement a tremendous advantage. What is surprising, considering his early position on territorial expansion and war, is that Secretary of State Buchanan was not only a convert to All Mexico, he became its greatest champion within the executive branch and the Democratic party as well.[81]

Despite the number of influential supporters putting pressure on the president, Polk was not ready to embrace the All Mexico program. In his third annual message to Congress of December 1847, he clearly stated, "It has never been contemplated by me, as an object of war, to make a permanent conquest of the Republic of Mexico or to annihilate her separate existence as an independent nation."[82] But his frustrations with the Mexican government and the duration of the war led him to regret the mild instructions he had issued to his envoy, Nicholas Trist, when he sent Trist to negotiate a peace agreement that previous April.[83] During a cabinet meeting in September 1847 Polk declared, "If Mexico continued obstinately to refuse to Treat, I was decidedly in favour of insisting on the acquisition of more territory than the provinces named."[84] During a cabinet meeting in November, with no progress in negotiations and the United States now occupying Mexico City, Polk repeated that "additional territory must be required as further indemnity." During this meeting Buchanan suggested that the United States acquire the "Province of Tamaulipas and the country East of the Sierra Madre mountains."[85]

---

[80] Walker was so insistent on All Mexico that he considered resigning if Polk submitted a more territorially modest treaty to the Senate for ratification. Jordan, "A Politician of Expansion," 374.

[81] Buchanan's conversion to All Mexico is linked to his presidential ambitions, for he believed that expansionism had become a winning issue in Democratic party politics, even in the Northeast. Frederick Moore Binder, *James Buchanan and the American Empire* (Selinsgrove, Pa.: Susquehanna University Press, 1994), 116.

[82] James K. Polk, "Third Annual Message, December 7, 1847," *James K. Polk, 1795–184*, 69.

[83] Louis Martin Sears, "Nicholas Trist, A Diplomat with Ideals," *The Mississippi Valley Historical Review* 11 (1924–1925), 95. While he was encouraged to secure Baja California, access to the Gulf of California and transit rights for a canal or railroad across the Isthmus at Tehauntepec, Trist's instructions allowed him to accept only California and New Mexico for the United States if Mexico refused to cede the additional territory. Eugene Keith Chamberlain, "Nicholas Trist and Baja California," *Pacific Historical Review* 32 (1963), 49–63.

[84] Polk, *Diary*, vol. 3, September 4, 1847, 161.

[85] Ibid., November 9, 1847, 216. The province of Tamaulipas runs south along the Gulf of Mexico nearly three hundred miles from the mouth of the Rio Grande.

Polk agreed with pursuing this objective "if it should be found prac-
ticable to do so," and also implied that he would still support
Walker's proposal to acquire all territory north of 26 degrees latitude.[86] While the specific territorial demands were still open to debate, it is clear that the Polk administration would insist on exacting
a higher price for peace from Mexico. To put additional pressure on
Mexico to meet these new territorial demands, Polk ordered Trist to
terminate negotiations and return home.

In an odd diplomatic turn, Trist refused to comply with Polk's order
to cut off negotiations. Believing that a peace agreement was in reach,
Trist decided to remain in Mexico and finish his mission. On February 2, 1848, Trist and his Mexican counterpart signed the Treaty of
Guadalupe Hidalgo that ended the war and ceded California and
New Mexico to the United States. However, the treaty completely neglected the new set of territorial demands the president intended to
pursue, and Polk was furious with Trist for his insubordination.
However, because Trist was not an authorized agent of the United
States when he completed the treaty Polk could have rejected it outright, thereby regaining the opportunity to press for a larger territorial indemnity. Surprisingly, Polk submitted the treaty to the Senate,
and it was ratified on March 10, 1848 with the necessary two-thirds
majority. In the process the advocates of larger gains from the war, including Polk himself, lost their opportunity. Why did Polk forego the
potential for greater territorial expansion produced by this decisive
military victory?

Regional Divisions and Limits on War Gains

Like the larger question of whether the United States should go to war
with Mexico, the question of whether it should expand territorially at
Mexico's expense, and how far, produced intense political disputes.
Yet there was an important difference between those two foreign policy questions, a difference that had a direct impact on the potency of
institutional constraints on the president and the range of policy options that could possibly emerge from the federal political system. The
difference was in the degree to which the policy options were per-

---

[86] Ibid., 217.

ceived as *national* in character, and the degree to which they were perceived as *regional*. From August 1846 until the end of the war the question of territorial gains was contested within a thoroughly regional
framework. Aside from a few extreme expansionists who thought of
vast war gains as a national interest, nearly every participant in the
struggle to shape U.S. policy considered the asymmetric effects that
expansion might have on the rival interests of the northern and southern
sections of the country. What gave expansion its regional dimension
was the question over whether new territory would be slaveholding
or free-soil. So compelling was this question for regional identities that
party solidarity for both the Democrats and Whigs collapsed. In turn,
the federal system facilitated intraregional, cross-party coalitions
within Congress on key legislation: first, over whether slavery should
be prohibited in the new territory, then later, over whether the United
States should expand at all. Northern and southern Whigs found the
issue so explosive for the party that they settled for a "no territory"
position, while the Democrats remained so hopelessly divided that
Polk feared the party would certainly lose the presidential election of
1848 and suffer serious damage in the process. Despite his efforts to
take advantage of the permissive external environment and the opportunity to secure an even greater territorial indemnity from Mexico,
Polk was actually relieved when the moderate Treaty of Guadalupe
Hidalgo provided him with an opportunity to escape the domestic divisions created by this problem.

The opening salvo in the regional struggle to put conditions on U.S.
expansion into Mexican territory came just months after the war
began. It took the form of a legislative initiative to prohibit slavery in
any territory annexed by the United States. In August 1846 President
Polk asked Congress for a special $2 million appropriation that he in-
tended to use to coax the Mexican government into a peace treaty. Like
the war bill, this request put the Whigs in a difficult position. They did
not want to give Polk free rein to negotiate the terms of a peace treaty,
particularly one that, as northern Whigs feared, might allow for the
expansion of slavery into new territory. Yet they did not want to vote
against the appropriation if Polk actually intended to use the money to
support a peace effort. Robert Winthrop, the Whig leader in the
House, summed up the position of many Whigs: "We believe that this
war ought never to have been commenced, and we do not wish to
have it made the pretext for plundering one foot of [Mexico's] lands.
But if the war is to be prosecuted, and if territories are to be conquered
and annexed, so far as we are concerned, these territories shall be the

abode of freemen."[87] The solution to this dilemma was to attach an amendment that, according to Whig Hugh White of New York, would "forever preclude the possibility of extending the limits of slavery."[88] The Democratic leadership in the House allowed debate on the measure, which for the first time linked slavery and war in Congress, but would not allow a vote on such an amendment to restrict the president's authority in any negotiations with Mexico.

Despite the withdrawal of the Whig proposal, the issue struck a chord with northern Democrats. They had been challenged by Representative White to join this cause, with which their constituents so fervently agreed. In an evening session that very day, Congressman David Wilmot, a Democrat from Pennsylvania, introduced his own amendment to the $2 million bill: "Provided, That, as an express and fundamental condition to the acquisition of any territory from the Republic of Mexico by the United States . . . neither slavery nor involuntary servitude shall ever exist in any part of said territory."[89] Wilmot was a most unlikely northern Democrat to accept White's challenge. His willingness to challenge the president and his southern colleagues on this issue, and the enthusiastic support he garnered from northern Democrats, is a strong indication of how much resonance this issue now had with northern voters. Wilmot was a staunch Polk Democrat who had supported the president on every issue that came before the Congress. He proudly proclaimed, "I am no croaker against the South. I have suffered abuse for her constitutional rights . . . I am not insensible to the claims of the South upon my affection and respect."[90] Indeed he had suffered for southern interests; most recently he supported the president's efforts to lower tariffs despite the fierce condemnation he received from his constituents. Wilmot's loyalty to Polk, and worse yet, the praise he received from southern newspapers and political leaders for his stand on the tariff, virtually guaranteed that his future political prospects were dead. His only hope was to champion a clearly northern issue that would demonstrate renewed loyalty to his northern constituents.[91]

While Wilmot offered his amendment primarily to save his own political future, the issue of slavery in any new U.S. territory instantly

---

[87] Brauer, *Cotton vs. Conscience*, 209.
[88] Schroeder, *Mr. Polk's War*, 44–46.
[89] Ibid., 46.
[90] Richard R. Stenberg, "The Motivation of the Wilmot Proviso," *The Mississippi Valley Historical Review* 18 (1931–1932), 537.
[91] Ibid., 538.

polarized Congress along North-South lines and changed the character of the debate on the Mexican War until its end. Of all issues in U.S. politics, slavery was the most intimately connected with rival territorial identities and interests within the United States. As long as the question of U.S. gains from the war was linked to slavery, U.S. policy would be shaped by new regional political alignments that were facilitated by the institutional mechanisms this federal system provides for regional competition. As Hietala notes, the regional polarization on Wilmot's amendment "stemmed largely from different expectations about how the adoption of the proviso would affect the North and South."[92] In each section the Wilmot Proviso was seen to have highly asymmetric political and economic implications that could not be ignored. Politically, the domestic balance of power between the North and South, and changes in this balance, were linked directly to sectional representation in the Senate and House. Therefore, the implications of adding states to the Union as either free-soil or slaveholding became crucial for the domestic balance of power and the ability of the North and South to protect and advance their particular policy issues.

Earlier it was argued that a political party may choose to oppose military force in a particular situation if its members expected such opposition to be rewarded with enhanced political strength relative to rival parties, or at least prevent the erosion of relative political strength.[93] Within the American federal system the political benefits of taking a position either in favor of or against the use of military force for certain objectives may be conceived in regional, and not partisan terms. That is, enhanced political strength may be desired for one's *section*, not necessarily for one's *party*. Under these conditions we find an incentive for members of rival political parties who happen to represent the same region to form interparty coalitions to protect or improve the political strength of their section within the larger Union.

For the North, the Wilmot Proviso was the easiest means to restrict what many northerners saw as the increasing dominance of slave-power in the United States.[94] Under this amendment, any new U.S.

[92] Hietala, *Manifest Design*, 167.

[93] William Mabe, Jr., and Jack S. Levy, "Opposing War for Political Gain: A Comparative Study of the U.S. in the Quasi-War and the War of 1812." Paper presented at the 1998 Annual Meeting of the American Political Science Association, Boston, Massachusetts, September 3–6, 1998.

[94] Morrison, *Democratic Politics and Sectionalism*, 161–63; Varg, *New England and Foreign Relations*, 210.

state carved from Mexican territory would join the roster of free states rather than slave in the federal Union. Stoking these fears of slave-power dominance were common sentiments expressed in the South about the importance of southwestern expansion for the role of this section in American politics. One representative editorial from a Milledgeville, Georgia, newspaper asked, "How could any true southerner oppose the war when its results would 'be to secure to the South the balance of power in the Confederacy, and, for all coming time, to give her the control in the operations of the Government?'"[95] According to the *Chicago Daily Journal*, the conquest of Mexico was "goaded on as it was by a *Southern spur* to perpetuate a peculiar institution ... blood flowed in streams that the brilliant achievements ... might redound to the credit of a purely Southern policy."[96]

In economic terms it was widely understood in the North that extending the slave system into the Southwest meant putting these new bountiful territories off-limits to free labor. According to Hietala, "white workers would refuse to migrate to areas where slaves and freed men would degrade white labor."[97] Wilmot himself defended his amendment in these terms, to "preserve a fair country, a rich inheritance, where the sons of toil, of my own race and color, can live without the disgrace which association with negro slavery brings upon free labor."[98] New York congressman Preston King made the same argument when he reintroduced the amendment in January 1847.[99] With these clear northern interests at stake, Van Buren Democrats in the Northeast had an easy time supporting the Wilmot Proviso.[100] Many northwestern Democrats, despite their strong penchant for U.S. expansion, joined northeastern Democrats to vote for Wilmot.[101] So popular were these views in the North that, in addition to congressional action on the issue, ten northern state legislatures passed resolutions supporting Wilmot.[102]

For the South, defeating the movement to restrict slavery in territory taken from Mexico was seen as a political imperative that would determine the future of the South within the Union and ultimately

---

[95] Schroeder, *Mr. Polk's War*, 55.
[96] Ibid., 56.
[97] Hietala, *Manifest Design*, 122.
[98] Haynes, *James K. Polk and the Expansionist Impulse*, 147.
[99] Hietala, *Manifest Design*, 126.
[100] Morrison, *Democratic Politics and Sectionalism*, 15–17; Schroeder, *Mr. Polk's War*, 46.
[101] Wiltse, *John C. Calhoun*, 288.
[102] Merk, "Dissent in the Mexican War," 52.

whether the social and economic order of slavery would survive in the United States. During the first year of the war the dominant assumption in both the North and the South was that Mexican territory could support the slavery system, which made the effort to restrict its expansion to the Southwest a legislative necessity for the North and a dire threat to the South. The opinion of most southerners, Democrats and Whigs alike, was that the Wilmot Proviso was a northern conspiracy to establish a cordon of free states to the west and south of the slave states, thus locking in the number of slave states as the number of free states increased. Within the U.S. federal system this would permanently put the South in a minority status. Ironically, by the end of 1847 it came to be widely believed by southerners that these Mexican territories would not support plantation agriculture and thus were not suitable for slavery on a wide scale. By default, any Mexican territory annexed by the United States would be free-soil. This actually became a prominent argument some southern Democrats directed toward their northern colleagues to convince them that the Wilmot Proviso was unnecessary.[103] Despite widespread acceptance that the proviso did not reflect a practical political problem for the South, southerners of both political parties, at the popular and elite levels, slaveholders and nonslaveholders alike, united around the view that the precedent set by the amendment had to be treated as if it were a practical political problem.[104]

The strong territorial division on the question of slavery in new territories was most clearly evident in the votes on the Wilmot Proviso, which "revealed a clear North-South sectional pattern which overrode previous party commitments."[105] This was true not only in the Demo-

[103] Fuller, "The Slavery Question and the Movement to Acquire Mexico." Polk himself held this view on the unsuitability of these territories for slavery, so he fumed that the link made by Wilmot and his northern supporters between slavery and the "Mexican War is not only mischievous but wicked." Polk, *Diary*, vol. 2, 308.

[104] Wiltse, *John C. Calhoun*, 296. Calhoun worried, "If this aggressive policy be followed . . . and we are to be entirely excluded from the territories which we already possess, or may possess . . . what will be the situation hereafter? . . . There will be but fourteen [states] on the part of the South—we are to be fixed, limited and forever—and twenty-eight on the part of the non-slaveholding states . . . . The Government, Sir, will be entirely in the hands of the non-slaveholding states, overwhelmingly." Morrison, *Democratic Politics and Sectionalism*, 52–61.

[105] Joel H. Silbey, *The Shrine of Party: Congressional Voting Behavior 1841–1852* (Pittsburgh, Pa.: University of Pittsburgh Press, 1967), 90–96. For another voting pattern study that confirms Silbey's findings, see Thomas B. Alexander, *Sectional Stress and Party Strength: A Study of Roll-Call Voting Patterns in the United States House of Representatives 1836–1860* (Nashville, Tenn.: Vanderbilt University Press, 1967), 111.

cratic party but in the Whig party as well, that up to this time had been
united in its opposition to Polk's war. In the final vote, the House majority in favor of prohibiting slavery in territory taken from Mexico
came from a regional coalition of 53 northern Democrats and 28 northern Whigs, with only two nonnorthern congressmen, both from Kentucky, voting with the majority.[106] Horace Greeley, writing in the *New
York Tribune*, called the vote "a solemn declaration of a United North
against the further extension of slavery under the protection of the
American Flag."[107] In the Senate, while Wilmot's proviso was defeated
31 to 21, the vote here also split along clear North-South lines, with 8
northern Democrats joining 13 northern Whigs in favor of restricting
slavery, and 10 southern Whigs aligning with 21 Democrats (a handful
of extreme expansionists from the North with the remainder from the
South)[108] to provide the majority for rejecting the amendment. In January 1847 the Wilmot Proviso was again introduced as an amendment
to a special war appropriation submitted by Polk, his "$3 million bill."
As in the previous vote, a coalition that included the majority of northern Democrats and all northern Whigs in the House passed the
amendment 115 to 105. In fact, every vote for the amendment was
from the North. In the Senate, the Wilmot Proviso to the $3 million bill
was defeated 32 to 21, again along territorial lines, the majority of the
nay votes coming from the South, with four votes from extreme expansionists in the North to seal the proviso's defeat.[109]

As legislation, the Wilmot Proviso alone did not impose institutional constraints on President Polk's efforts to exact a larger territorial
indemnity from Mexico. The amendment was not written to restrict
territorial expansion, but to put conditions on how territory taken
from Mexico would be regulated concerning slavery. More important,
the amendment was defeated in the Senate each time it was introduced, so the Wilmot Proviso never became U.S. law. Despite the fact
that the proviso failed as legislation, it precipitated a bitter and dangerous sectional split. It forced the Whig party and important regional
factions within the Democratic party to rethink the question at the

---

[106] Connor and Faulk, *North America Divided*, 146; Pletcher, *Diplomacy of Annexation*,
460–61; Merk, *Manifest Destiny and Mission*, 175.

[107] Schroeder, *Mr. Polk's War*, 49.

[108] These northern Senate votes against the Wilmot Proviso came from extreme expansionists who realized that putting antislavery conditions on territorial expansion
might actually prevent territorial expansion altogether. Morrison, *Democratic Politics and
Sectionalism*, 36–37.

[109] Merk, *Manifest Destiny and Mission*, 175.

heart of the political struggle over territorial expansion and the Mexican War. As a result, these opponents of Polk's policy imposed a new question on the national debate. After the Wilmot amendment was defeated for a second time the dispute was no longer over whether slavery would be permitted in territory taken from Mexico, but whether the United States should expand into Mexican territory at all. For Whigs and Democrats, both northern and southern, the debate over the Wilmot Proviso demonstrated how destructive the issue of slavery could be to party unity and to national politics in the Union. One Virginia Democrat explained that the party split was so serious that "all around is dissension and distrust. Gloom overspreads the party."[110] According to a Georgia Whig journal, "Nothing appears plainer to us than that the North is united on the Wilmot proviso. The South is united against it. Hence raises a question of lurid and fearful portent."[111] Whig congressman Solomon Foote of Vermont warned his colleagues that by wrestling with the issue of territorial expansion and slavery, "You are rushing headlong and blindfolded upon appalling dangers . . . You are rekindling the slumbering fires of a volcano."[112] As debate on the amendment flared in Congress it became plain to northern and southern Whigs that avoiding the issue of slavery altogether was the only solution. But to avoid the problem of slavery in connection with territorial expansion meant that the United States must not pursue territorial expansion in the first place. Caleb Smith of Indiana argued that "the only ground of safety—the only ground that will secure the peace and harmony of the country—the welfare and prosperity of the Union, is to keep the territory, with all the distracting questions connected with it, out of the Union."[113] As Pletcher explains, the Whigs' answer to this problem "was as simple as the omission of one word from the Wilmot prescription of 'No more slave territory.' The new prescription was 'No more territory.' The omission of the word 'slave' was designed to quiet the disruptive moral overtones of the Wilmot Proviso and to draw the sting that offended the Southern slaveholding society. 'No more territory' was neutral on slavery and held northern and southern Whigs together."[114]

---

[110] Graebner, *Empire on the Pacific*, 179; Weems, *To Conquer a Peace*, 441.
[111] Schroeder, *Mr. Polk's War*, 124.
[112] Ibid., 77.
[113] Ibid.
[114] Pletcher, *Diplomacy of Annexation*, 54. Haynes, *James K. Polk and the Expansionist Impulse*, 168; Schroeder, *Mr. Polk's War*, 77–86; Fuller, "The Slavery Question and the Movement to Acquire Mexico," 33; Morrison, *Democratic Politics and Sectionalism*, 173.

By the end of 1847, John Calhoun was firmly convinced that Mexican territory would not support the slave system. If Polk were allowed to force Mexico to concede a huge territorial indemnity, the South would suffer from the addition of U.S. states that would become free-soil by default. In a vigorous speech to a packed Senate chamber in January 1848, Calhoun railed against the All Mexico movement and the dangers to the U.S. political system inherent in this objective. To Calhoun, the danger came from either holding territory with a heterogeneous alien people as an imperial appendage of the United States, or in trying to absorb an alien people who he argued were totally unfit for democracy. Calhoun's speech rallied southeasterners against U.S. expansion beyond the thinly populated provinces of California and New Mexico.[115] The Van Buren Democrats and Calhoun Democrats were bitterly split on the question of slavery and had thus been rivals during the political wrangling over the Wilmot Proviso. In a larger sense they also were rivals in the developing conflict over the future of the Democratic party. Even so, these two factions had a common position on expansion into territory south of 32 degrees latitude. The reasons for their opposition to Polk's territorial expansion were, of course, radically different, yet together with the Whig party these factions posed a formidable challenge to the extreme expansionists. Van Buren Democrats had pegged their political fortunes and evolving position on the Mexican War to the increasing antislavery sentiment in the North. Despite the growing belief that Mexican territory would not support slavery, Van Buren Democrats were most concerned that southwestern expansion would be perceived by the northern electorate as an initiative meant to strengthen the South and in turn strengthen the power of slave interests in the Union. If northeastern Democrats failed to oppose Polk's ambitions, the Whigs would portray these Democrats as sympathetic to southern interests. The safest political position to take then, and

[115] Calhoun's argument had less appeal in the Southwest (in Texas, Louisiana, Mississippi, Missouri, Tennessee, and Alabama), which was dominated by a spirit of Manifest Destiny and nationalism. This nationalist sentiment made expansion more important than a possible shift in the North-South balance. Fuller, "The Slavery Question and the Movement to Acquire Mexico," 41. On southeastern opposition to a larger territorial indemnity and the potential of a southeastern Democrat/Whig party alignment, see Lander, *Reluctant Imperialists*, 160–61; Morrison, *Democratic Politics and Sectionalism*, 46–51; Wiltse, *John C. Calhoun*, 328–29; Merk, "Dissent in the Mexican War," 52, and *Manifest Destiny and Mission*, 150–51; Graebner, *Empire on the Pacific*, 204; Schroeder, *Mr. Polk's War*, 68–71, 130, 152.

one that still did not violate their commitment to free-soil, was to oppose All Mexico and other territorial goals below 32 degrees North.[116] In a coalition with the Whigs, southeastern and northeastern Democrats had the votes in both houses of Congress to block the president's desired gains from the war.

Despite the legislative majority that stood ready to oppose the Polk administration, diversity among the Whigs and regional Democratic factions prevented Polk's opponents from settling on a specific legislative initiative that would force the president to accept a specific alternative to his open-ended territorial goals. The best this legislative majority could do was vote down Polk's efforts to obtain congressional support for continuing the war. The longer Polk fought the war, the harsher the territorial settlement could be. Denying Polk the resources to prosecute the war became an important institutional point of constraint that undermined the war effort. For the president, this was troubling enough; his frustrations with the lack of congressional support and his concerns for carrying the war into the coming year are reflected throughout his diary in the early months of 1847. Increasingly distraught over the divisions in his own party, in January he complained that despite "a large nominal majority in both Houses, I am practically in a minority."[117] At the beginning of February 1847, with no congressional decision on his request for a $3 million war appropriation after weeks of debate, Polk derided Congress and his party for their inability to reach a consensus. "It is now in the third month of the Session," Polk observes,

> and none of my war measures have yet been acted upon. There is no harmony in the Democratic Party . . . . In truth faction rules the hour, while principle and patriotism is forgotten. While the Democratic Party are thus distracted and divided and are playing this foolish and suicidal game, the Federal party [which is how Polk always referred to the Whigs] are united and never fail to unite with the minority of the Democratic Party, or any faction of it who may break off from the body of their party, and thus postpone and defeat all my measures.[118]

Congress finally approved the $3 million war bill in March and the Wilmot Proviso was defeated for the second time. Even so, the persistent

---

[116] Hietala, *Manifest Design*, 217; Schroeder, *Mr. Polk's War*, 5, 67, 131; Varg, *New England and Foreign Relations*, 205.

[117] Polk, *Diary*, vol. 2, January 15, 1847, 328.

[118] Ibid., February 5, 1847, 368.

regional tension created by the war and by the link between slavery and territorial expansion compelled Polk to seek an early peace in the spring of 1847 before the United States had fully subdued Mexico. His diary entry for January 23, 1847, recounts a conversation with Whig congressmen John Crittendon of Kentucky, during which Polk admits that the debate in Congress was forcing him to moderate his war goals. "I told him I deprecated the agitation of the slavery question in Congress, and though a South-Western man and from a slave-holding State as well as himself, I did not desire to acquire a more Southern Territory . . . because I did not desire by doing so to give occasion for the agitation of a question which might sever and endanger the Union itself."[119] To end this agitation, Polk realized, he not only had to moderate his territorial goals, he had to end the war as well: "I am the more solicitous to open negotiations and to concluding a peace with Mexico because of the extraordinary delay of Congress to act upon War measures which I have recommended to them."[120] It was then, after consulting with his cabinet, that Polk dispatched Nicholas Trist to Mexico in April 1847 with broad powers to negotiate an end to the war. Trist's instructions allowed him to accept a territorial settlement that fell far short of what Polk, his cabinet, and his congressional supporters had previously thought possible to obtain. The effort to obtain a border at 26 degrees North or all Mexican territory east of the Sierra Madre mountains was dropped. The All Mexico movement and administration demands for exacting a higher indemnity did enjoy a revival when U.S. troops occupied Mexico City in the fall of 1847 and the Mexican government resisted negotiations despite the total defeat of its army. Military success in Mexico, however, did little to blunt the antiexpansionist position of the Whig party and the dissident Democrats.

In the meantime, despite his orders to return to Washington, Trist had successfully negotiated the treaty that secured California and New Mexico for the United States. The Treaty of Guadalupe Hidalgo, which reached Polk on February 19, 1848, put the president in a serious bind. Secretary of State Buchanan and Treasury Secretary Walker argued fervently that Polk should reject the treaty because it ceded far too little territory to the United States, a sentiment Polk agreed with. Buchanan was again demanding all territory east of the Sierra Madres while Walker pushed the All Mexico option. Yet the president's diary

[119] Ibid., January 23, 1847, 350.
[120] Graebner, *Empire on the Pacific*, 191.

from February 21 reveals Polk's fears of the serious consequences he would face if he refused to end the war and settle for more moderate war gains. One option, Polk wrote, was that "I should demand more, perhaps, to make the Sierra Madres the line." The problem with this option though, was that "it was doubtful whether this could be ever obtained by the consent of Mexico." To achieve this goal the United States would have to continue its occupation of Mexico and use its military resources to inflict greater costs, thereby forcing Mexico to eventually concede these terms. At the domestic level, however, Polk realized he could never sustain this policy.

The first problem was ensuring he would have the resources to continue the occupation of Mexico. Polk writes,

> A majority of one branch of Congress [the House] is opposed to my Administration . . . . If I were now to reject a treaty made upon my own terms, as authorized in April last, with the unanimous approbation of the Cabinet, the probability is that Congress would not grant either men or money to prosecute the war. Should this be the result, the army now in Mexico would be constantly wasting and diminishing in numbers, and I might at last be compelled to withdraw them, and then lose the two provinces of New Mexico and Upper California which were ceded to the United States by this treaty.[121]

The second problem was that even if Polk managed to coerce Mexico into accepting different treaty terms, Polk was certain he could never win a two-thirds Senate majority for a treaty that ceded all the territory the United States was in a position to take. In fact, Calhoun's proposal for the withdrawal of U.S. troops from Mexican territory south of 32 degrees North, and the formation of a defensive line along the southern border, was gaining ground in the Senate. A journal in New York indicated that Whigs were prepared to rally around Calhoun on this position.[122] The final problem was that unless Polk eliminated the regionally divisive questions raised by his Mexico policy from U.S. politics, the Democratic party was likely to suffer a permanent rupture or at least lose the upcoming presidential and congressional elections. Polk worried that "should the opponents of my Administration succeed in carrying the next Presidential election, the great probability is that the country would lose all the advantages secured by this treaty." In his

121 Polk, *Diary*, vol. 3, February 21, 1848, 347–48.
122 Lander, *Reluctant Imperialists*, 166–67.

final analysis Polk conceded, "If I were now to reject my own terms offered in April last I did not see how it was possible for my Administration to be sustained."[123] With no hope for overcoming these federal institutional constraints on his preferred outcome, Polk submitted the treaty to the Senate, which ratified it by a vote of 38 to 14 on March 10, 1848.[124] While Polk was reluctant to give up the great territorial gains within his grasp, Democratic senator Benton noted that "peace was the only escape from so many dangers, and it was gladly seized upon to end the war which had disappointed all calculations."[125]

Conclusion

Like the War of 1812, the Mexican conflict stands in marked contrast to other international crises before the Civil War in which the United States backed away from armed conflict. But it differs in one important respect from the earlier war. In 1812 a majority of senators and representatives legitimately supported war with Great Britain, yet in 1846 a majority in Congress actually opposed this war while voting to carry it forward. The Mexican War seems to represent a distortion of the conflict decision process and the logic of federal democratic peace envisaged by the U.S. founders. Not only was the president able to increase the risk of war dramatically on his own authority by deploying a military force into disputed territory, members of Congress ultimately sanctioned what most did not actually support. In this way the Mexican War is a complete failure of America's federal structure to constrain the use of military force, and it offers an excellent opportunity to consider conditions that might reduce the likelihood that democratic institutions will have this constraining effect.

President Polk's ability to create this crisis with Mexico and almost guarantee a military clash is among the best examples in U.S. history of what Alexander Hamilton noted about presidential power in 1794. In an exchange of letters with James Madison debating President Washington's right to declare U.S. neutrality on his own authority as chief executive, Hamilton conceded that certain presidential actions

---

[123] Polk, *Diary*, vol. 3, February 21, 1848, 348.

[124] Merk, *The Monroe Doctrine and American Expansionism*, 192; Schroeder, *Mr. Polk's War*, 157.

[125] Norman A. Graebner, "Party Politics and the Trist Mission," *The Journal of Southern History* 19 (May 1953), 156.

would have the effect of creating an "antecedent state of things" to which Congress had no choice but to react. In other words, the president could pursue actions on his own authority that would limit Congress' options once the possibility of international conflict emerged. The *timing* of congressional involvement in the chain of events that may lead to war then becomes critical for determining how much the president can shape the problem free from congressional involvement, and how much latitude Congress has to address that problem once it does get involved. As an international dispute intensifies, the most obvious point at which the legislature may exert a constraining influence on events is when the executive requests a formal declaration of war. Yet as this case makes clear, if Congress waits until this final moment to exercise some role in shaping the state's policy in an evolving crisis, events may progress to the point at which the legislature's freedom of action is severely restricted. President Polk's own authority allowed him to deploy a military force in a way that, while certainly short of outright war, created a dangerous military standoff that was more likely to result in an armed clash than in a peaceful resolution. With such a high probability of war inherent in his actions, the time to impose constraints to prevent war was before U.S. soldiers marched to the Rio Grande. Even if Congress had taken the initiative after General Taylor's forces were deployed to the Rio Grande, in the three-month period between the president's order to move south and the actual border clash, opponents of this coercive and volatile policy could have demanded through legislation that the president withdraw U.S. forces to reduce the likelihood of conflict initiated by either Mexican or U.S. military commanders in the field.

For his part, Polk had no legal obligation, in strict institutional terms, to initiate congressional action on his policy because he was not ordering this force into battle. He did not require additional resources to support the deployment, and there was no preexisting proscription from Congress on deploying a force into this disputed region. Congress itself had the prerogative and the obligation to initiate action on Polk's policy before he militarized the dispute or once it was recognized that the dispute was intensifying. Polk was preparing to ask Congress for a declaration of war, as he was obligated to do, before taking further military action against Mexico to achieve his objectives. Had the chain of events on the Rio Grande and in Washington provided enough time for Polk to submit this request and thereby initiate congressional action on Mexico policy before a border clash occurred, it is most likely that Congress would have rejected a declaration of war and initiated steps to defuse the tense standoff. This would have forced Polk to rely solely on diplomatic means to resolve U.S.–Mexican issues. This case demonstrates that in spite of the potent institutional mechanisms available for controlling executive branch aggression, in spite of the large majority in Congress that would have united in opposition, not just to war with Mexico, but to coercive, militarized diplomacy as well, the necessary initiative from within Congress never materialized. Polk filled the void with actions pursued on his own authority and his actions drove the timing and outcome of the dispute.

Despite Polk's ability to create a war crisis with Mexico as an "antecedent state of things," the logic of federal democratic peace failed on a second level. Once Mexican and U.S. troops had their first violent contact Congress was given another opportunity to pull the United States back from full-scale war. As Whigs and dissident Democrats argued at the time, an isolated border skirmish is not a war, nor does it impose an obligation to escalate the conflict to war. Referring to the *Chesapeake* crisis of 1807, which inflamed U.S. passions for war with Great Britain yet did not escalate into a wider conflict, one Whig pointed out that the United States again could avoid escalation of an isolated clash. Yet in overwhelming numbers Whigs and Democrats supported Polk's war bill, despite their vigorous opposition to the policy these congressmen were now endorsing.

This second failure provides insight into a dimension of political decision-making that rarely, if ever, receives treatment in democratic peace research. The dominant assumption in this literature, held by both proponents and critics of democratic peace theory, is that the question of using force in foreign policy will be bifurcated in all cases. In other words, the policy choice is assumed to be limited to either voting for war or voting against war. But the voluminous public choice literature clearly demonstrates that political decision-making, particularly in legislative bodies, is almost never this straightforward and simple.[126] More often, the structure of political choices can be manipulated to drastically alter the options available and the incentives political actors have for choosing among them. Riker calls this open manipulation of political choices the "art of heresthetics," and its pur-

---

[126] For example, see Kenneth Arrow, *Social Choice and Individual Values* (New Haven: Yale University Press, 1963); William H. Riker, *Liberalism Against Populism: A Confrontation Between the Theory of Democracy and the Theory of Social Choice* (San Francisco: W. H. Freeman, 1982).

pose is to improve the chances that a given policy preference will win.[127] The Mexican War case provides an excellent example of the effects of heresthetics on legislative choice and how this can confound the theoretical expectations of many variants of democratic peace theory.

President Polk knew that if he gave Congress a chance to vote yes or no on a straightforward declaration of war against Mexico, a winning coalition of Whigs and dissident Democrats could form around this question to defeat his policy. His solution was to use a strategy described by Riker: "Those who expect their preferred alternative to lose initially may introduce new alternatives" that, because of the different incentives involved in the choices available, are more likely to attract a winning coalition.[128] Polk's war bill did not ask for a vote for or against war, it asked for supplies and reinforcements for General Taylor's army that was engaged in a war that already existed by an act of Mexico. Through manipulation of the question posed, Polk and his congressional allies confronted their opponents with the choice of taking a patriotic stand behind an American force slugging it out with an enemy on a distant frontier, or leaving that U.S. force stranded. While the federal democratic arrangement of the U.S. political system provided the institutional mechanisms necessary for Polk's opponents to prevent conflict escalation, this became moot due to the priority Whigs and dissident Democrats had to place on supporting the national-level identities and concerns activated by this crisis and Polk's portrayal of it. Only by manipulating the choice before Congress was the president able to circumvent the political hazards presented by the federal system and attract a winning coalition that would serve his goals. The role of heresthetics in the outcome of other cases must be given greater attention in democratic peace literature.

The final puzzle, and the one in which we actually find a robust role for democratic institutions as a constraint on foreign policy, asked why the United States failed to obtain the amount of territory from this war that its victory would permit. Several significant findings emerge from the study of this puzzle. Meinig argues that with the immense potential for U.S. expansion in this period "it is not difficult to imagine a considerably more extensive framework [for the country]: a Greater United States." He notes, however, that "such imagination must force

---

[127] William H. Riker, "Political Theory and the Art of Heresthetics," in *Political Science: State of the Discipline*, ed. Ada Finfter (Washington, D.C.: American Political Science Association, 1983), 47–67.

[128] Ibid., 64.

a whole series of 'might-have-beens' through the intense struggles of American domestic politics."[129] In Frederick Merk's words, in the absence of domestic dissent the treaty "would have been even harsher. Much more of Mexico would have been taken. Dissent moderated the treaty by revealing the dangers of the programs of All Mexico and Manifest Destiny."[130]

We need to take this insight on the effects of domestic opposition one step further. As argued in chapter 1, a major weakness of the institutional democratic peace literature is that rarely do we find satisfactory explanations for why divided institutions and electoral accountability necessarily push toward peace or otherwise limit the use of military force in foreign policy. Just because such institutional mechanisms are in place does not also mean that there will be opposition to aggressive foreign policy or that latent opposition will make use of institutional mechanisms. Nor is it enough to simply explain the outcome as the result of majority opposition in Congress to the president's objectives, the separation of powers, and Congress' ability to influence such matters. The real insight comes from understanding why there was opposition to this policy in the first place, the nature of this opposition, how the distinctive institutional arrangement of federal democracy facilitated this opposition, and how the specific policy choices formed. Opposition to Polk was more pronounced, active, and effective on the expansion question than on the origins of war with Mexico because of the tight connection between expansion and the asymmetric regional interests that would be affected by the outcome. While opposition to the war bill was pronounced, in practical political terms there was only a loose link between regional identities and interests and the question of going to war with Mexico. With slavery linked to expansion, however, the strong regional implications of this policy choice reversed the political incentives, which now favored regional concerns, and set the stage for robust competition on this dimension of the conflict.

We can see from this case that there is no reason to expect opposition to a particular foreign policy choice to be unidimensional in nature, as many democratic peace theorists treat it. There was no general popular view on the costs of continuing the war to seek various expan-

[129] Meinig, *Shaping of America*, 214.
[130] Merk, "Dissent in the Mexican War," 63.

sionist options. There was no unified opposition party view on the war and expansion. Nor was there one dominant regional view that carried the day in the effort to limit U.S. territorial gains. The reasons various groups opposed Polk's expansionist plans were highly diverse and often contradicted one another. Van Buren Democrats and Calhoun Democrats broke with the administration because of the political implications of southwestern expansion for the slavery issue, yet their fears contrasted markedly. Calhoun's southeastern Democrats were convinced that adding Mexican territory to the Union would further tip the political balance away from slaveholding states. In contrast, Van Buren Democrats believed that southwestern expansion would be perceived by the northern electorate as a southern-oriented goal and thus politically damaging to the North. Southern Whigs were sympathetic to Calhoun's concerns, while northern Whigs were apt to agree with Van Buren Democrats, yet each regional group of Whigs was also motivated by ideological or normative opposition to rapid expansion and the use of military force to achieve it. Whigs also opposed territorial expansion for political reasons, fearing that expansion would split the party on regional lines and jeopardize their common partisan efforts on issues such as tariffs, the national bank, and internal improvements. These various groups did not need a common reason to oppose Polk's agenda. The common denominator was simply that expansion came to be seen as detrimental to their individual interests, both regional and partisan.

6

CUBA AND MEXICO IN THE 1850s

In just three years, from the annexation of Texas in 1845 to the cession of California and New Mexico at the end of the Mexican War, the United States grew in size by 64 percent. James Debow, the superintendent of the U.S. Census, observed, "The territorial extent of the Republic is . . . nearly ten times as large as the whole of France, Britain, Austria, Prussia, Spain, Portugal, Belgium, Holland, and Denmark, together; one-and-a-half as large as the Russian empire in Europe."[1] Despite this phenomenal territorial growth, expansionist appetites in the United States were hardly sated. In fact, to the enthusiasts of Manifest Destiny success in the war with Mexico seemed to demonstrate that there were few external constraints to a policy of continual growth in the Western Hemisphere and into the Pacific. In August 1850, *DeBow's Review* declared, "The military spirit of the country has been aroused, and is rife for anything, and woe to the power that shall endeavor to stay it . . . . The cry of war is flattering to our pride and our power, and they are either of them equal to that of any other nation, ancient or modern."[2] The Democratic administrations of Franklin Pierce, elected

[1] Donald W. Meinig, *The Shaping of America: A Geographical Perspective on 500 Years of History*, vol. 2 (New Haven: Yale University Press, 1993), 159.
[2] Norman A. Graebner, ed., *Manifest Destiny* (Indianapolis, Ind.: Bobbs-Merrill, 1968), 248–49.

in 1852, and James Buchanan, elected in 1856, embodied the expansionist spirit that the Democratic party had championed for several decades. Territorial and commercial expansion became top foreign policy priorities for both presidents.

The neighbors of the United States certainly recognized the threat posed by its confidence and ambitions after the Mexican War. The Mexican press, in particular, sounded repeated warnings that even generated interest in an alliance of Latin American republics to hold off the United States. In the early 1850s the *Correo do Espana* "likened [America] to a Russia unrestrained by the balance of power."[3] Interestingly, this comparison with imperial Russia seemed appropriate to American expansionists themselves. In a report from the Senate Foreign Relations Committee, the influential Senator John Slidell of Louisiana saw little difference between the empire building of European states and the expansion that the United States was undertaking in its own part of the world. Nor did Senator Slidell find this conquest normatively problematic. Slidell argued,

> The tendency of the age is the expansion of the great powers of the world. England, France, Russia, all demonstrate the existence of this pervading principle. Their growth, it is true, only operates by the absorption, partial or total, of weaker powers—generally, of inferior races. So long as this extension of territory is the result of geographic position, a higher civilization, and greater aptitude for government, and is not pursued in a direction to endanger our safety or impede our progress, we have neither the right nor the disposition to find fault with it. Let England pursue her march of conquest and annex India, France extend her dominions on the southern shores of the Mediterranean, and advance her frontiers to the Rhine, or Russia subjugate her barbarous neighbors in Asia; we shall look upon their progress, if not with favor, at least with indifference. *We claim on this hemisphere the same privilege that they exercise on the other.*[4]

In the 1850s U.S. expansionists looked first to the acquisition of Cuba from Spain, by purchase if possible, by force if given a pretext. Expansionists also targeted Mexico in renewed efforts to absorb territory denied them at the end of the Mexican War and to extend U.S. influence over Mexican domestic affairs through military intervention.

---

[3] J. Fred Rippy, *The United States and Mexico* (New York: F. S. Crofts, 1971), 39–40.
[4] Graebner, *Manifest Destiny*, 298–99; emphasis added.

Despite the expansionist fervor in the United States in the 1850s, the enthusiasm with which the Pierce and Buchanan administrations embraced the expansionist agenda, the confidence in U.S. capabilities, and the absence of significant external resistance to these projects, the United States did not resort to armed force in response to several crises in this period. Moreover, the absence of the use of force is contrary to what we might expect considering the interests at stake and the perceived risks of not meeting policy objectives for Cuba and Mexico. In the context of democratic peace theory, three crisis periods in the 1850s offer the chance to test competing explanations for restraints on the use of military force by the United States. The first foreign policy crisis and related theoretical puzzle explored in this chapter involves U.S.–Mexican relations. Territorial conflict between these two continental neighbors was certainly not resolved by their recent war. Lingering confusion over which state rightfully owned the Mesilla Valley along the southern border of New Mexico brought the United States and Mexico to the brink of war again, with military force mobilized by both sides to enforce their conflicting claims. Despite U.S. military superiority in this face-off, President Pierce chose to back down and rely on diplomacy to attain America's objective. As expected, diplomacy ultimately yielded disappointing territorial gains that fell far short of what the United States was in a position to obtain through force. The second crisis period and theoretical puzzle involves U.S. interests in Cuba. From the earliest years of the republic, the annexation of Cuba was an objective that had widespread political support across parties and regions. In 1852 President Pierce declared the acquisition of Cuba to be his number-one foreign policy priority, despite Spain's long-standing refusal to even discuss its purchase by the United States. Even when a string of crises emerged between the United States and Spain over Cuba, crises serious enough to make the most cautious members of Pierce's cabinet talk openly of war, Pierce let these opportunities slip away without the bold action he had promised. With time, the crises passed peacefully. What held the president back from using force when the pretext for war appeared?

The third crisis period emerged during the presidency of James Buchanan and renewed the possibility that the United States would use military force in Mexico. Over the course of the 1850s the Mexican government slipped into violent civil conflict between conservative and liberal factions. In the midst of the chaos created by this conflict, a series of U.S. grievances began to mount, including unpaid debts and atrocities committed against U.S. citizens and property in Mexico and raids into U.S. territory by bandits and Native Americans operating from Mexican territory. Buchanan declared that such instability was intolerable and that the United States was obligated to intervene with military force to provide order. The puzzle this crisis poses stems from the anticlimactic outcome: why, despite the serious nature of this problem, the apparently clear justification for using force to protect U.S. interests, and President Buchanan's insistence on intervention, did the United States fail to act?

The Mesilla Valley Dispute

President Franklin Pierce faced his first foreign policy crisis just months after taking office. A dispute with Mexico over possession of a strip of land in southern New Mexico had resulted in such a dangerous level of militarization that a second Mexican-American war appeared imminent, just five years after their first war had ended. For many in the United States, the disputed Mesilla Valley was vital for U.S. security and economic development. Most important, it was considered the best route for a transcontinental railroad to link the eastern United States with its new possessions in the Southwest and on the Pacific coast. For Mexico, defending this territory against U.S. encroachment was a matter of national honor, particularly after losing so much territory to the United States so recently in the past. The dispute began with heated rhetoric and threats from both sides, and by early 1853 U.S. and Mexican military forces were being mobilized to occupy and defend the valley. Events in the region had progressed to a point at which President Pierce was compelled to decide whether or not he would sanction the use of military force to resolve the dispute in America's favor. Despite the many features of the crisis that seemed to push the president toward using force, the dispute did not produce a military clash. Instead, Pierce initiated negotiations that produced the Gadsden Treaty, in which the United States actually agreed to pay for territory that the administration and Congress had declared already belonged to the United States.

Pierce's decision to rely on negotiations to secure U.S. interests here is even more surprising considering that Mexico's willingness to sell the territory was highly uncertain. This doubt was a serious concern to Secretary of State William Marcy. In a letter to James Gadsden, the U.S. minister in Mexico, Marcy downplayed the chances of diplomatic success. Marcy admits that the

questions now pending between the two countries [are] of grave importance and conceded difficulty; and it is apprehended that you will find
the government and people of Mexico not favorably disposed to fair adjustment of them. The hostile feelings engendered by the late war with
Mexico, embittered by the severe wounds inflicted on her national
pride, have not wholly subsided; and it is feared that the degree of irritation yet remaining will embarrass our negotiations with her."[5]

Moreover, Pierce's territorial ambitions were much grander than just
the Mesilla Valley. His ultimate objective was to secure a territorial
cession that included a large portion of Tamaulipas, Nuevo Leon,
Coahuila, Chihuahua, and Sonora, and all of Baja California.[6] Despite
the likelihood that Pierce would fail to obtain not only the large swath
of northern Mexico he desired, but the Mesilla Valley as well, he was
in Marcy's words, "determined . . . to take a liberal course."[7] Why this
expansionist president (who just months earlier had declared that he
would not accept any timidity in U.S. foreign policy) rejected the use
of military force, which clearly was the more certain option for obtaining his territorial goals, is the puzzle.

The Origins of the Crisis

The origins of this crisis lie in the Treaty of Guadalupe Hidalgo that
ended the Mexican-American War in 1848. An error in the map used
by the treaty negotiators to describe the new border between the
United States and Mexico had placed the town of El Paso, a critical
landmark for the boundary line, thirty-four miles too far north and
more than a hundred miles too far east. The joint Mexican-American
boundary commission thus had to decide whether to use the actual location of El Paso or the geographic position for the town from the erro-
neous map as the point from which to run the boundary west from the
Rio Grande River. This was an important decision. If the boundary
commission used the actual location of El Paso to run the line, the
United States would gain control of 6,000 additional square miles of

---

[5] Secretary of State William L. Marcy to James Gadsden, United States Minister to
Mexico, July 15, 1853, in *Diplomatic Correspondence of the United States: Inter-American Affairs, 1831–1860*, ed. William R. Manning (Washington, D.C.: 1937), 134.

[6] Rippy, *United States and Mexico*, 138; Roy Franklin Nichols, *Franklin Pierce: Young
Hickory of the Granite Hills* (Philadelphia: University of Pennsylvania Press, 1931), 325.

[7] Marcy to Gadsden, in *Diplomatic Correspondence*, 134.

territory, the Mesilla Valley, which would otherwise remain with Mexico. The Mexican commissioner argued, however, that the treaty negotiators never intended for the United States to obtain this territory. Believing that the territory in dispute was worthless and that Mexico would never agree to use the actual location of El Paso for the boundary line, the U.S. commissioner accepted Mexico's position. In his view, aside from a 1.5 mile strip immediately adjacent to the Rio Grande River, the Mesilla Valley "is a desert without water, food, or grass, where not one acre can ever be cultivated, where no military post can be sustained, and which can never be inhabited." The one small village in the valley was composed "of mud or chiefly stick houses" and populated by Mexicans who had left Santa Fe rather than become U.S. citizens.[8]

Had the joint commissioners been granted sole authority to strike such a compromise the issue might have been resolved at this point. Yet the boundary provision in the peace treaty explicitly stated that the surveyors from each party also had to agree with all decisions. Lieutenant Gray, the U.S. surveyor, refused to agree with this solution to the problem. First, Gray argued, the value of the land had no bearing on the United States right to it under the treaty, and second, the land actually had immense value to the United States. Gray characterized the Mesilla Valley as "one of the most beautiful and fertile along the course of the Rio Grande," stating that its soil was "proverbial for its productivity and would grow most varieties of fruits and vegetables."[9] Most important of all, the territory provided the best route for a transcontinental railroad through a natural break in the Rocky Mountains that was free of snow throughout the year.[10] With this final argument Lieutenant Gray had pinpointed the reason that the prospects of losing the territory to Mexico became such a great source of agitation in the United States.

When the Mexican-American boundary commission was first organized in January 1849, the U.S. commissioner was explicitly instructed by Secretary of State James Buchanan to collect information necessary for planning a rail route along the southern border.[11] Between 1851 and 1853, developing a transcontinental railroad became a subject of

---

[8] Odie B. Faulk, *Too Far North . . . Too Far South* (Los Angeles: Westernlore Press, 1967), 75.
[9] Ibid.
[10] Paul Neff Garber, *The Gadsden Treaty* (Glouster, Mass.: Peter Smith, 1959), 22.
[11] Rippy, *United States and Mexico*, 114.

intense interest in the United States. In the second session of the Thirty-second Congress, from 1852 to 1853, the Senate devoted more time to this topic than to any other issue.[12] The addition of California as a new state in 1850, the discovery of gold, mass migration to the west, and the tremendous potential for economic growth offered by the new state convinced Americans across regions and political parties that a transcontinental railroad was also a vital interest. It was essential for moving troops quickly to the new territory of the Southwest and the Pacific to defend these distant possessions against foreign armies.[13] The railroad was necessary to protect the emigrant trails against Native Americans, to provide rapid and reliable mail delivery, and to facilitate commerce. Many argued that without a rail link to bind California to the rest of the Union, this great state would drift in its political loyalties and eventually seek independence.[14] To its southern promoters, a southern route for this transcontinental railroad was the key to arresting what was being called the "Southern decline," a sense that the South was not keeping pace economically with the industrial North. Business and political leaders from the South had great interest in the commercial advantages of a link to California, so it is not surprising that southerners took the initiative to spur its construction. Southerners also believed that if a southern route were selected for the Pacific railroad, California and the southwestern territory would be populated primarily by southern people. This would bind the far Southwest and the Pacific coast to the Old South as natural political and economic allies.[15] For southern leaders, the best route was through the Mesilla Valley.

By June 1852 the controversy over the boundary commission agreement that adjusted the El Paso map error in Mexico's favor reached the Senate Foreign Relations Committee. Under Chairman James Mason of Virginia the committee adopted a resolution repudiating the terms of the agreement and censuring the U.S. commissioner for conceding this point to his Mexican colleague. In July, Representative Volney Howard of Texas argued vociferously in the House against surrender-

[12] Garber, *Gadsden Treaty*, 23.

[13] Secretary of War Jefferson Davis repeatedly spoke of the military necessity of a transcontinental railroad in 1853. For example, see Dunbar Rowland, ed., "Jefferson Davis and the Pacific Railway," in *Jefferson Davis, Constitutionalist, His Letters, Papers and Speeches*, vol. 2 (New York: J. J. Little and Ives, 1923), 256–61.

[14] Robert R. Russel, "The Pacific Railway Issue in Politics Prior to the Civil War," *Mississippi Valley Historical Review* 12 (1925–1926), 189–90.

[15] Ibid., 192.

ing the Mesilla Valley and the southern rail route that could run through it, while another Texan, Thomas Rusk, led the charge in the Senate. Texas had the most immediate interests at stake in whether the Mesilla Valley was secured for a southern rail line; either San Antonio, Galveston, or Houston would be the natural eastern terminus for such a line.[16] Any city through which the enormous transcontinental trade would pass was expected to grow into a great metropolis.[17] While Texas would gain the most from this route, the Texans' position attracted support throughout the South because the entire section was expected to benefit. Howard's leadership in the House and Rusk's leadership in the Senate produced two crucial amendments that put Congress on record in opposition to the boundary commission compromise on the Mesilla Valley. The most important amendment, passed in August 1852, declared that "no part of the appropriation [for running the boundary line] should be used until it should be made to appear to the President of the United States that the southern boundary of New Mexico had not been established further north of El Paso than is laid down in the Disternell map."[18] In effect, this amendment shut down the boundary commission and negated its compromise solution to the Mesilla Valley problem. President Fillmore, realizing that the Mexican government would not accept the more southerly boundary line for New Mexico demanded by Congress, was forced to order the commission to stop its work and disband immediately. By October 1852, possession of the Mesilla Valley was left unresolved with no existing forum for a peaceful solution. In the meantime, events in the region militated against benign neglect by either side and pushed the United States and Mexico closer to war.

Militarization of the Dispute

Despite the anxiety expressed in Washington over the prospects of losing the Mesilla Valley to Mexico, the initiative for militarizing the dispute did not come from either the president or congressional pressure. The initiative came from Governor William Lane of New Mexico, who issued a provocative proclamation asserting U.S.

---

16 Faulk, *Too Far North*, 106; Garber, *Gadsden Treaty*, 23.
17 Russel, "Pacific Railway Issue," 190.
18 Rippy, *United States and Mexico*, 113; Faulk, *Too Far North*, 106–7.

ownership of the valley and prepared a military force to occupy it. This was exactly the type of situation envisioned by John Jay in *Federalist 3*, when he noted that citizens in the border regions who had immediate interests in local grievances would most likely initiate disputes on borders of the United States.[19] Although members of the national government supported Lane's ultimate objective, they were removed from local pressures that seemed to demand vigorous action, even violence, to secure local interests in the region. Governor Lane's decision was a reaction to several features of the dispute. First, he felt compelled to take possession of the valley to preempt a similar move by Mexico that was already underway. Soon after the U.S. and Mexican boundary commissioners agreed to the border compromise that put the Mesilla Valley in the Mexican state of Chihuahua, Governor Angel Trias declared that he would extend his government's protection over the inhabitants of the region. The Mexican government saw its legal possession of the valley as inevitable, so, it was argued, Trias was right to extend his authority here. Besides, Mexican officials claimed, all residents of the valley desired annexation to Chihuahua. Lane disputed both assertions. He was further incensed when Governor Trias declared that only Mexicans could own land in the valley and then proceeded to strip Americans of their property claims without compensation. The threat became more palpable and unacceptable when Governor Trias sent five hundred men and six pieces of artillery to back up this plan in the fall of 1852. While Trias had to withdraw these troops after a short occupation because of the lack of funds, to Lane this was a clear violation of U.S. sovereignty that, if left unchecked, could lead to permanent Mexican possession of the territory. Second, Governor Lane was influenced by a petition he received from a group of residents of the Mesilla Valley who strongly protested Mexican efforts to assert authority over the region. Third, Americans in New Mexico firmly supported U.S. claims to the valley. Before Lane was sworn in as governor in September 1852 he had been "urged by the territorial delegates to Congress from New Mexico to occupy the disputed ground by force."[20] Finally, when news reached Lane that Congress had rejected the more northerly compromise border in favor of maintaining

---

[19] John Jay, *Federalist 3* in *The Federalist Papers*, ed. Clinton Rossiter (New York: Penguin, 1961), 44–45.
[20] Rippy, *United States and Mexico*, 116.

the U.S. claim to the Mesilla Valley, he believed he now had the political opening to take action for its defense.[21]

On March 13, 1853, Governor Lane rode into the town of Dona Anna with a volunteer force from New Mexico and Texas and issued this proclamation: "I, William Carr Lane, Governor of the Territory of New Mexico (upon my own official responsibility—without orders from the cabinet in Washington) do hereby, in behalf of the United States, retake possession of the said disputed territory."[22] To make the claim official, he mailed the proclamation, along with a list of points to justify his action, to Governor Trias in Chihuahua. In response, Trias issued a counterdeclaration insisting that not only did the Mesilla Valley belong to Chihuahua, but that the Mexican-U.S. border was even further north than that as well.[23] Included in Trias's declaration was a clear warning: "I shall use the means unquestionably necessary for its defence and conservation, in case it is attacked, and upon Your Excellency alone shall rest the responsibility for the consequences."[24] Lane also received a warning from a representative of the Mexican central government who urged him "to abandon your present resolution; because, if you do not . . . it becomes my duty . . . not to permit any occupation of territory which would be prejudicial to the national honor."[25]

On orders from Mexican president Santa Anna to march troops into the Mesilla Valley and resist the Americans,[26] Trias raised money, assembled troops and supplies, and marched nearly a thousand men to El Paso by the end of April. The state legislature of Chihuahua declared a state of emergency, the Mexican national government deployed a contingent of the army with artillery to Chihuahua, the governor of the state of Durango was ordered to assist Trias, and the

[21] Ibid., 115–16; Garber, *Gadsden Treaty*, 71; Faulk, *Too Far North*, 119; George Griggs, *History of the Mesilla Valley, or the Gadsden Purchase* (Las Cruces, N.M.: Bronson, 1930), 30. Governor Lane's willingness to use force to defend the U.S. claim here is evident in a letter to his wife, dated February 15, 1853: "Be not surprised if I should take possession of the disputed territory, which I dare say I will find to be without adequate protection, against internal and external violence . . . if duty calls upon me to occupy and protect this country . . . I will do it." Calvin Horn, *New Mexico's Troubled Years: The Story of the Early Territorial Governors* (Albuquerque, N.M.: Horn and Wallace, 1963), 47.

[22] Horn, *New Mexico's Troubled Years*, 46; Griggs, *History of the Mesilla Valley*, 38–39.

[23] For a summary of the points made by both Lane and Trias to justify their rival claims, see Rippy, *United States and Mexico*, 117.

[24] Ibid.

[25] Ibid., 118.

[26] Horn, *New Mexico's Troubled Years*, 47; Griggs, *History of the Mesilla Valley*, 37.

governor of Zacatecas sent two hundred troops to the frontier.[27] As a final measure, the Mexican government instructed its diplomats abroad "to secure aid, direct or indirect," from England, France, and Spain for the effort to "restrain the ambitious designs of the United States."[28] On the U.S. side, the Pierce administration ordered a significant increase in military preparations on the southwestern frontier in case war did result from the local standoff. The New Orleans *Picayune* reported that six companies of infantry were sent from Texas to New Mexico and two companies of light artillery in New Mexico would receive fresh horses. Three hundred men from Fort Leavenworth in Kansas left on June 20 for Santa Fe. Through the summer and fall of 1853 these troops made preparations for a new military post opposite El Paso, and more infantry and artillery troops were dispatched to western Texas and ordered to erect defensive bulwarks along the Rio Grande.[29]

Why No Second Mexican-American War?

President Pierce himself was not responsible for initiating the political or military steps that created this crisis with Mexico. Yet by the spring of 1853 he could not avoid the responsibility of deciding how to resolve it. The military standoff in the region limited his options. He could support Governor Lane's efforts to coerce Mexico into accepting U.S. claims with this show of force or fight to secure the valley if necessary. Or he could restrain further military escalation and seek a peaceful resolution. Given the interests at stake here and the militant character of his administration, we might expect that Pierce would have used military force to guarantee U.S. possession of the Mesilla Valley. Not only was this particular territory considered a vital interest by the administration, the administration itself was overwhelmingly staffed with Democrats committed to aggressive U.S. expansion. This was particularly true of Secretary of War Jefferson Davis and Attorney General Caleb Cushing, the most influential members of his cabinet.[30]

[27] Rippy, *United States and Mexico*, 121–22; Garber, *Gadsden Treaty*, 73; Faulk, *Too Far North*, 121.
[28] Seymour V. Connor and Odie B. Faulk, *North America Divided: the Mexican-American War 1846–1848* (New York: Oxford University Press, 1971), 176–78.
[29] Rippy, *United States and Mexico*, 123, 145–46.
[30] Larry Gara, *The Presidency of Franklin Pierce* (Lawrence: University Press of Kansas, 1991), 44, 70.

Even Pierce's more moderate secretary of state, William Marcy, believed that securing more territory from Mexico in this region was essential for a transcontinental railroad.[31] And as noted, the administration had little faith that Mexico would entertain U.S. proposals to negotiate a purchase agreement to resolve the dispute. Despite these aspects of the case, Pierce did not pursue the military option. The president did firmly support Governor Lane's contention that the Mesilla Valley belonged to the United States.[32] Yet he repudiated Lane's methods as too aggressive and likely to lead to war, a course the president was determined to avoid. As a result, Lane was replaced as governor of New Mexico by David Meriwether, who was instructed by Marcy to "abstain from taking forcible possession of the tract, *even if on your arrival in New Mexico you find it held adversely to the claim of the United States* by Mexico or the authorities of Chihuahua." Similarly, Jefferson Davis ordered the military commander of New Mexico to "avoid, as far as you consistently can, any collision with the troops or civil authority of the Republic of Mexico or the State of Chihuahua."[33] In essence, the Pierce administration was so insistent on avoiding military conflict that it would overlook Mexican occupation of this U.S. territory and put its faith in diplomacy to gain possession of it.

Marcy explained that the United States would comply with standard provisions in international law for the resolution of this dispute. He wrote, "Where a dispute as to territorial limits arises between two nations, the ordinary course is to leave the territory claimed by them . . . in the same condition . . . in which it was when the difficulty first occurred, until an amicable arrangement can be made . . . . It has not been the intention of the United States to deviate from this course."[34] Yet this alleged willingness to comply with international law in 1853 does not reflect a pattern of U.S. compliance with such provisions in earlier

[31] Ivor Spencer, *The Victor and the Spoils: A Life of William L. Marcy* (Providence, R.I.: Brown University Press, 1959), 256.

[32] Nichols, *Franklin Pierce*, 266. In a letter to Alfred Conkling, the U.S. minister in Mexico, Marcy affirmed that "very little doubt exists here as to the fact that the disputed territory . . . was within the limits of New Mexico at the date of the Treaty of Guadeloupe Hidalgo; and that nothing has since taken place to transfer it to the State of Chihuahua . . . Governor Lane is justified in claiming the disputed territory as part of New Mexico and in denying that the acts of the boundary commission had in any manner effected a transfer of that territory from New Mexico to Chihuahua." Marcy to Alfred Conkling, United States Minister to Mexico, May 18, 1853, in *Diplomatic Correspondence*, 131–32.

[33] Rippy, *United States and Mexico*, 119–20; emphasis added.

[34] Marcy to Conkling, May 18, 1853, in *Diplomatic Correspondence*, 131.

territorial disputes. President Polk certainly felt no obligation to let diplomacy have the last word in the Rio Grande boundary dispute of 1846. Polk took it upon himself to resolve that border problem with coercive force, similar to President Madison in 1813, who pursued possession of East Florida from Spain through military occupation. Why did Pierce, the avowed expansionist, choose not to follow the example set by his predecessors for territorial expansion? A quote from a contemporary Mexican newspaper, *El Universal*, phrases the puzzle well: "President Polk invaded us because his country desired... more territory. Today there exists the same desire.... Why does not Mr. Pierce satisfy the democrats? Why does he not extend, as thpey say, the *area of liberty*... . Ah! it would be worthy of the Model republic to *emancipate* the new world by the same system which it had employed in Texas, California and New Mexico."[35] What was different in 1853 to produce such a different course of action in U.S. foreign policy and stifle the president's willingness to use military force to achieve his territorial objectives?

The first explanation we must consider is the possibility that U.S. decision-makers were deterred by the expected costs of Mexican military opposition or by the possible intervention of European states for the defense of Mexico. Despite the apparently vigorous Mexican military response to Governor Lane's declaration concerning the Mesilla Valley, and Mexico's appeal to Europe, there is no evidence to suggest that President Pierce or any member of his cabinet was concerned about external military opposition, by Mexico or by a European ally. It was clear to both the United States and Mexico that Mexico's military response to the crisis was a hollow show of force. Mexico was in no shape to defend the Mesilla Valley against the force assembled by the United States on the southwestern frontier. In the spring of 1853 the Mexican treasury was bankrupt and frontier posts had been abandoned because the army was in disarray and poorly equipped.[36] As President Santa Anna described it several years later,

> a considerable Anglo-American force was threatening the Department of Chihuahua, and to evade the war into which we were being provoked was a most urgent matter. The Commandante General in fulfillment of his duty, had collected all the troops at his disposition and was already advancing upon the Americans; but being insufficient to resist successfully, I ordered him to be warned that under no circumstances was he to

35 Rippy, *United States and Mexico*, 124; emphasis in original.
36 Ibid., 105, 127.

make any hostile demonstration against the troops of the United States, and that with prudence . . . he should fall back to the capital of the Department.[37]

In contrast, of the eleven thousand soldiers in the army of the United States, eight thousand were deployed in the southwest, five thousand of these being stationed solely for the defense of the southern border of Texas and New Mexico.[38] The stark contrast between U.S. and Mexican military capabilities was clearly evident to the Pierce administration, so there was no reason to fear an armed clash as the means to secure U.S. interests here. Additionally, there was virtually no concern for European intervention. Despite Mexico's appeal for European assistance, France and Great Britain had no interest in becoming embroiled in a war in North America as the Crimean crisis developed in the east.[39] Domestic instability and financial crisis would also prevent Spain from providing assistance to Mexico.

In the absence of external resistance to U.S. pressure in this crisis, it is necessary to turn next to the domestic level for an explanation of restraints on the use of force by the United States. As in the *Chesapeake* crisis of 1807, this is a case in which the president exercised self-restraint, while Congress never had a direct role. Pierce never requested congressional approval to support Governor Lane with military force, nor did Congress intervene on its own initiative. In the case of the Mesilla Valley dispute, Pierce made an independent decision to de-escalate the crisis. In short, the evidence in this case indicates two domestic factors that compelled Pierce to exercise self-restraint: (1) his overriding concern about *latent* domestic opposition that he believed would be activated if he initiated congressional action on this issue; and (2) the fear that the use of force would jeopardize the Democrats' hold on Congress and the White House in the next elections. In other words, he faced the double-barreled institutional risk of both long-term debilitating political penalties against his own political future and his party's, and the more immediate likelihood that Congress would refuse to sanction armed conflict. Most important, his calculations of the political consequences of war in this case were rooted in

---

[37] Griggs, *History of the Mesilla Valley*, 44.

[38] Garber, *Gadsden Treaty*, 30.

[39] J. B. Conacher, *Britain and the Crimea, 1855–1856: Problems of War and Peace* (New York: St. Martin's Press, 1987); Alan Dowty, *The Limits of Isolation: the United States and the Crimea* (New York: New York University Press, 1971).

federal asymmetry over the question of using military force to secure additional Mexican territory. For Pierce, federal asymmetry made this a no-win situation because this foreign policy problem could not escape the larger context of regionalism within U.S. domestic politics of this period.

In U.S. domestic politics, the 1850s was a decade marked by both great triumphs for national vitality and by turmoil over the extension of the slavery system to new territories. With the admission of California as a state in 1850 the United States had secured a continental span, while the decade brought a period of unprecedented economic growth. The divisive debate over slavery extension raised by the Wilmot Proviso during the Mexican War flared again during the debate over whether California would be admitted as a free state. The Compromise of 1850, however, a plan crafted by Whig Henry Clay and Democrat Stephen Douglas, seemed to resolve this controversy and soothe sectional irritation with provisions meant to satisfy North and South.[40] The compromise allowed California to enter the Union as a free state and abolished the slave trade in the District of Columbia. Yet it also enacted a potent fugitive slave law that required "northern citizens to assist in the capture or transport of fugitive slaves, regardless of moral objections."[41] Although many in the North and South were unhappy with particular dimensions of the compromise, the majority of U.S. citizens were committed to the stability of the Union, so compromise supporters hoped that it would help the United States weather this controversy, end the acrimonious divide created by slavery, and foster unity across the republic. Aside from small groups of secessionists in the South, primarily in South Carolina, until the very eve of civil war most observers believed that the Union would survive the disagreement. Opinion leaders in both regions wanted the Democratic and Whig parties to regroup on a national basis and challenge each other on older national issues.[42] In this political climate it was more important than ever before that any president or presidential contender appeal explicitly to both sections to sustain support for national office. The Democrats had nominated Franklin Pierce of New

[40] Michael P. Riccards, *The Ferocious Engine of Democracy: A History of the American Presidency* (New York: Madison Books, 1995), 181–82.

[41] Keith Polakoff, *Political Parties in American History* (New York: John Wiley and Sons, 1981), 168.

[42] Joel H. Silbey, *The Shrine of Party: Congressional Voting Behavior, 1841–1852* (Pittsburgh, Pa.: University of Pittsburgh Press, 1967), 122.

Hampshire in 1852 as a compromise candidate who could appeal to both North and South. In fact, he became a symbol of Democratic party unity.[43] Jefferson Davis of Mississippi, Pierce's secretary of war and the future president of the Confederacy, predicted that the United States was entering a period of domestic peace, expanded trade, and greater prosperity. President Pierce, he declared, knew "no North, no South, no East, no West."[44] As a northerner, Pierce was notable for his southern sympathies. According to one biographer, "Pierce undoubtedly believed that the South had always been the victim of aggression from certain northern interests."[45] As a result, he would not tolerate northern interference in the slavery system. Despite this perspective, he was also extremely sensitive to the danger of championing issues other northerners would see as enhancing southern interests. The only way to protect both the Union and the Democratic party from the dangers of sectionalism was to firmly avoid the slavery controversy. Pierce elevated this to a core principle of his administration that framed how he addressed both domestic and foreign problems. His strongest statement of this principle is found in his first annual message to Congress in the fall of 1853, which he prepared in the midst of the Mesilla Valley controversy. Referring to the relative political stability in the Union following the Compromise of 1850, Pierce declared, "This repose is to suffer no shock during my official term, if I have power to avert it." He continues by explicitly acknowledging that federal asymmetry on whatever public issue may arise posed the greatest danger to this repose, and his goal was to pursue those programs that could generate national consensus. "While men inhabiting different parts of this vast continent can not be expected to hold the same opinions . . . they can unite in a common object and sustain common principles essential to the maintenance of" domestic peace.[46] Pierce concluded this discussion by applying the principle to U.S. territorial expansion, which he viewed as the "fundamental problem of the republic."[47] Pierce outlined a vision of U.S. growth that would include "the probable accession of the populations already existing in other parts of our hemisphere." While his inaugural address had declared

[43] Roy Franklin Nichols, *The Democratic Machine, 1850–1854* (New York: Columbia University, 1923); Gara, *Presidency of Franklin Pierce,* 21–35.

[44] Davis, "Speech of Jefferson Davis" at Wilmington, Delaware, July 15, 1853 in *Jefferson Davis,* 238.

[45] Gara, *Presidency of Franklin Pierce,* 79.

[46] Nichols, *Franklin Pierce,* 299–300.

[47] Ibid.

that "my administration will not be controlled by any timid forebodings of evil from expansion,"[48] as his first foreign policy crisis raised
the danger of war on the southern border, his message to Congress
presented a much more cautionary view rooted in regional diversity
over expansionist opportunities. The United States "could only be
kept in national cohesion by . . . strict deference to the sovereign rights
and dignity of every state," which ultimately demanded avoiding the
problem of slavery as the United States expanded.[49]

The Democrats' superior ability to minimize intraparty disruptions
in the early 1850s over slavery was rewarded in 1852 with a huge win
in Congress and allowed Democrats to take back the presidency.[50] With
such large majorities in the legislature (61 percent in the Senate and 67
percent in the House) and with control of the executive branch it appeared that the Democratic party was in a position to dominate U.S.
politics and the policy process with little organized opposition. President Pierce was aware, however, of the underlying regional tensions
within the party and the fragile consensus on which his presidency
rested. The administration of Franklin Pierce demonstrates vividly
how the effects of federal institutional divisions emerge as a potent
source of policy constraints when party loyalty breaks down and when
party leaders lack a solid base for holding members together. The Democrats nominated Pierce in 1852 as a compromise candidate who
raised the fewest objections with party members across the country.
Once in office, however, Pierce lacked the broad-based, firm party support necessary for binding the members together in the midst of lingering sectional distrust. While Pierce considered himself the leader of the

[48] Basil Rauch, *American Interests in Cuba, 1848–1855* (New York: Columbia University
Press, 1948), 254.
[49] Nichols, *Franklin Pierce*, 300. The Democratic party platform of 1852 also resolved to
"resist all attempts at renewing . . . the agitation of the slavery question." Nichols, *Democratic Machine*, 229. Jefferson Davis, while a strong southern rights supporter, also acknowledged that the "democratic party is pledged in all time to prevent from revival
domestic division over slavery." Jefferson Davis to B. Tucker, October 8, 1853, in *Jefferson
Davis*, 271.
[50] Polakoff, *Political Parties*, 170. In 1852, northern and southern Whigs were deeply
divided over their presidential nominee, Winfield Scott. Although Scott was a slave
owner, southern Whigs feared that his administration would be dominated by free soilers, while many northern Whigs were unsatisfied because of his pledge to fully enforce
the fugitive slave act and his refusal to countenance any agitation on slavery. A number
of southern Whigs either supported Franklin Pierce or refused to vote. Gara, *Presidency
of Franklin Pierce*, 37. For many southerners, the Democrats were more trustworthy because this party presented itself as the stalwart defender of southern rights. Avery O.
Craven, *The Growth of Southern Nationalism, 1848–1861* (Baton Rouge: Louisiana State
University Press, 1953), 240.

Democratic party, loyalty to his administration was virtually nonexistent.[51] Secretary of War Jefferson Davis was the only member of his cabinet with any standing in Congress, yet his supporters were purely southern in orientation. According to Senator Slidell of Louisiana,

> While there is a general disposition [among the Democrats] to give [Pierce] a fair and frank support I do not believe that there is one man upon whose personal devotion he can count. Every measure proposed by him will be received with the respect due to the official chief of the party but there is probably not a member of the Senate who does not consider his own individual opinions in every other respect entitled to quite as much consideration as that of the President, in other words, he is the 'de jure' not the 'de facto' head of the party.[52]

This lack of personal connections and loyalties from members of Congress made it even more difficult for him to bridge the institutional divide between the executive and legislative branches. Pierce's efforts to carefully distribute patronage offices to rival factions in the party only antagonized sectional jealousies; his appointments convinced many in the South that Pierce would support the Free Soil cause, while others made northerners believe he was caving in to the extreme states-rights members of the party.[53] Under conditions of such sharp regional tensions it is hard to imagine the most skillful of political leaders holding the party or his nation together to support a contentious war policy.

Pierce's decision to forgo the use of military force and to rely on the pessimistic prospects of diplomacy to achieve his expansionist goals during the Mesilla Valley crisis can only be understood in this broader domestic context. While we do not have direct textual evidence on exactly what Pierce himself was thinking when he ordered U.S. officials to avoid a clash with Mexico,[54] all historians of this incident and Pierce's biographers agree that this decision was based on his belief that a move toward war would produce intense regional divisions. These divisions would in turn prevent congressional support for war

[51] Gara, *Presidency of Franklin Pierce*, 76.

[52] Louis Martin Sears, "Slidell and Buchanan," *American Historical Review* 27 (October–July 1922), 719–20; Nichols, *Franklin Pierce*, 308–9.

[53] Nichols, *Franklin Pierce*, 292.

[54] Nichols notes that Pierce destroyed his personal papers from the presidency and all White House correspondence has disappeared. The papers of his cabinet officers and departmental files provide the best information on decision making in this administration. Ibid., 547. Gara reports that Franklin Pierce's manuscripts are scarce. Gara, *Presidency of Franklin Pierce*, 201.

and posed a serious political danger to both Pierce and his party.[55] Unlike the debate over expansion during the Mexican-American War, there was no direct link to slavery in the Mesilla Valley dispute. New Mexico was a nonslave territory, so adding the Mesilla Valley alone would make no direct difference to the slavery issue. But a second war fought to take territory from Mexico, particularly given the much larger territorial objectives entertained by the president, could not escape this earlier context. Northern congressmen would perceive any effort to seize the Mesilla Valley with force as a policy oriented explicitly toward southern interests. The sectional divergence on such a war would be intensified by the asymmetric regional benefits to be derived from securing the Mesilla Valley for a southern transcontinental railroad route. The United States Army at this time was actively surveying alternative northern and southern routes. The ultimate decision on where the transcontinental line would run would be based not only on practical engineering considerations, however. This question had already become an intense political issue dividing members of Congress on geographic lines. A good indicator of the sectional rivalry that would be produced if Pierce fought a war to secure territory for a southern route is the debate over the transcontinental railroad during the Thirty-third Congress (1852–1853). This debate on whether the United States should build either a northerly or southerly route became so intense between members of each section that Congress was unable to take any action on the project at all.[56] It was clear to Pierce that a cross-party coalition of northern representatives and senators, which would be numerically larger than a similar coalition of southerners, would stand united against the use of force to establish control over the disputed Mesilla Valley.[57]

Pierce was also held in check by the fear that if he took the United States to war with Mexico the Democrats would suffer in the next congressional elections and he would probably lose the White House in

---

[55] Rippy, United States and Mexico, 127; Nichols, Franklin Pierce, 300; Nichols, Democratic Machine, chap. 1; Gara, Presidency of Franklin Pierce, 79; Faulk, Too Far North, 124; Odie B. Faulk, Land of Many Frontiers: A History of the American Southwest (New York: Oxford University Press, 1968), 55; Odie B. Faulk, Destiny Road: The Gila Trail and the Opening of the Southwest (New York: Oxford University Press, 1973), 50.

[56] Polakoff, Political Parties, 23.

[57] Of the 38 Democratic senators in 1853, 22 were from free states, 16 from slave states. In the House, the Democrats had 85 representatives from the North compared to 60 from the South. Overall in the House, northern representatives had a majority of 146 to 88 from the South. Overall in the Senate, northern states sent 34 senators to Washington, while southern states sent 28. Nichols, Franklin Pierce, 305.

1856. Critics of the electoral accountability argument in the democratic peace literature note that the potential penalties imposed on political leaders by the electorate for a risky foreign policy can come only after the policy is pursued. Despite the political risks, these critics argue, in the absence of immediate penalties political leaders may be willing to pursue an aggressive foreign policy and hope that success will actually produce rewards at election time, or, as a minimum, political leaders might hope that they will have time to rehabilitate their image before the next election. Under these conditions we would expect electoral accountability to have little effect as a constraint on the use of military force.[58]

In the Mesilla Valley dispute, however, electoral accountability had a strong *ex ante* effect on Pierce's decision-making because of the electoral costs the Democrats had paid so recently in the past, after the Mexican-American War. In the presidential election of 1848 the Democratic candidate, Lewis Cass, was defeated by his Whig opponent Zachary Taylor. Democrats blamed this loss purely on the sectional divisions within the party caused by the war with Mexico and the debate over territorial expansion and slavery. One southern Democrat at the time complained that "the rank and file [in the party] have rebelled by regiments," voting for Taylor because he was a southerner, while rejecting Cass because he was from Michigan. Many Democrats from the Old Northwest deserted Cass too, despite his past influence in the region, because he refused to support the Free Soil cause. The Democrats also lost the huge number of electoral college votes from New York because of the party split in the state between Free Soilers and conservative Democrats.[59] President Pierce was very sensitive to the lesson of 1848: northern sectionalism leads to Democratic defeats.[60] He was also certain that another war with Mexico would have the same effects, and this was an outcome he was determined to avoid. Not only would the federal arrangement of the U.S. political system facilitate a sectional split in the party that would deny him congressional support for war, the state-based system for electing presidents and members of Congress provided another outlet for the expression of regional interests in national politics. Because this system rewarded

---

[58] For example, see the discussion in Bruce Russett, *Controlling the Sword: The Democratic Governance of National Security* (Cambridge: Harvard University Press, 1990), 87–117.

[59] Craven, *Growth of Southern Nationalism*, 50–51.

[60] Gara, *Presidency of Franklin Pierce*, 79; Faulk, *Destiny Road*, 50.

the increasingly more numerous and populous northern states with
more electoral votes and representation in the House, any president or
party closely associated with a southern policy that adversely affected
northern interests could suffer a fatal blow.[61] In spite of Pierce's inaugural promise that he would not shrink from expansionist opportunities, the use of military force in response to the Mesilla Valley dispute
was a political loser in the short-term and would impose long-term
political costs that Pierce was unwilling to pay. Moderation in the
Mesilla Valley crisis was the only option he had for avoiding the political dangers presented by the federal system.

The Crisis over Cuba

Soon after the Pierce administration initiated negotiations with Mexico
to resolve the Mesilla Valley dispute, a sense of crisis emerged within
the United States over the future of Cuba. The strategic position of
Cuba, its commercial value, and the problems created by its internal social structure made the island a perpetual source of anxiety to the
United States as long as it remained in foreign hands. Cuba was also
seen as a great prize if the United States could gain possession for itself.
The early 1850s was a period of serious agitation in U.S.-Spanish relations, marked by specific crisis points that might have been used by the
United States as a pretext for taking military action to advance long-
standing U.S. interests. Upon entering office, Franklin Pierce declared
that attaining Cuba would be the administration's number-one foreign
policy priority. His cabinet and diplomatic corps, dominated by committed expansionists, fully supported this goal and the use of U.S.
power to achieve it. What is surprising, however, is that during the
most dangerous periods of the crisis (when U.S. anxiety over conditions in Cuba had peaked, just as harassment of U.S. ships around
Cuba aroused a war spirit in the country) the Pierce administration

---

[61] The magnitude of northern dominance in the U.S. federal system is most vividly il-
lustrated by comparing the political representation of large northern states to large
southern states. For example, in the 1850s New York alone sent 33 representatives to the
House, while Virginia, the most populous southern state, sent only 13 representatives.
The next most populous northern states, Pennsylvania and Ohio, had 25 and 21 representatives respectively. In contrast, the next most populous southern states, Kentucky
and Tennessee, had only 10 representatives apiece. Kenneth C. Martis, *The Historical
Atlas of Political Parties in the United States Congress, 1789–1989* (New York: Macmillan,
1989), 106–7.

failed to take military action, either limited action in response to these specific incidents, or a larger effort to seize Cuba from Spain. The task in this section is to determine why the United States was restrained from using force as a response to this crisis in Cuba by evaluating alternative explanations based on possible external or domestic opposition.

Traditional U.S. Interests in Cuba

Cuba was certainly not a new concern to the United States of the 1850s. In fact, U.S. statesmen of the founding period had a clear appreciation for Cuba's strategic importance to the new republic. Geographically, Cuba's position in the Caribbean creates two relatively narrow passages into the Gulf of Mexico: to the north between Cuba and the Florida Keys, to the south between Cuba and the Yucatan Peninsula. Interest by the United States in Cuba grew progressively as the United States increased its territorial holdings along the Gulf of Mexico in the first half of the nineteenth century. This was particularly true with the Louisiana Purchase in 1803, when the United States gained control of the Mississippi River delta, and the annexation of Texas in 1845, which expanded the U.S. gulf shoreline to the Rio Grande. Thomas Jefferson was the first president to formally announce the "no transfer" policy, which stated that the United States would never tolerate a transfer of Cuba from Spain to another European power.[62] American statesmen considered Spain too weak to use Cuba effectively to threaten the United States, particularly as its Latin American empire crumbled in the early part of the century. Yet in the hands of Great Britain or France, Cuba could serve as a potent base for controlling U.S. access by sea to its own territory along the gulf. Great Britain had taken control of Cuba in 1763 during the Seven Years War and held it until 1783, so the possibility of such a transfer occurring again was not far-fetched.[63] Every administration from Jefferson on supported the no transfer policy.[64]

America's interests in the future of Cuba did not rest with merely preventing its transfer to another power; many Americans believed

[62] Thomas A. Bailey, *A Diplomatic History of the American People* (Englewood Cliffs, N.J.: Prentice-Hall, 1980), 286.

[63] Frederick Merk, *The Monroe Doctrine and American Expansion, 1843–1849* (New York: Alfred A. Knopf, 1966), 235.

[64] Sidney Webster, "Mr. Marcy, The Cuban Question, and the Ostend Manifesto," *Political Science Quarterly* (March 1893), 1.

that Cuba was destined to become a U.S. possession. In 1823, John Quincy Adams was the first secretary of state to assert openly that "the annexation of Cuba to our federal republic will be indispensable to the continuance and integrity of the Union itself." He did not advocate an aggressive policy to seize Cuba from Spain. Instead, he believed that the time would come when Cuba's attachment to Spain would be severed, possibly by the same revolutionary spirit that had severed its other colonies in the Western Hemisphere. When this happened, he argued, Cuba "can gravitate only towards the North American Union . . . which cannot cast her off from its bosom."[65] While Adams's vision of future U.S. annexation of Cuba would require patience, in the 1840s momentum was building among prominent Democrats to hasten this process. In 1845, David Yulee, a Democratic senator from Florida, introduced a resolution urging the Polk administration to make an offer to purchase Cuba from Spain. In 1847, the influential expansionist editors John L. O'Sullivan and Moses Beech lobbied President Polk and Secretary of State Buchanan hard on a purchase of Cuba, and Vice President Dallas spoke openly of Cuban annexation to the United States.[66] This coincided with a real fear that Britain was preparing to seize Cuba as payment for the 46-million-pound debt Spain owed to British creditors.[67] With Texas now part of the United States and Americans pursuing various ventures to develop a canal or railroad across the isthmus at Tehauntepec, Mexico, Cuba's strategic location was more important than ever. By the late 1840s an Anglo-French rapprochement in Europe freed Britain to devote greater diplomatic attention and more resources to other parts of the world, including the Western Hemisphere. In this period Britain attempted to expand its territorial base in Central America and the Caribbean—which was currently limited to Belize and Jamaica—by extending a protectorate over the Mosquito Indians on the Gulf coast of Nicaragua and Honduras. This protectorate would give Britain possession of the most likely point on the Gulf of Mexico for a future canal to the Pacific. It would also allow this commercial giant to preempt U.S. efforts to control an isthmian canal itself, which would put the

[65] Secretary of State John Quincy Adams to Mr. Nelson, U.S. Minister to Spain, April 28, 1823, in *House Executive Documents*, 32 Congress, 1 Session, no. 121, p. 7.

[66] Frederick Binder, *James Buchanan and the American Empire* (Selinsgrove, Pa.: Susquehanna University Press, 1994), 134–35.

[67] Rauch, *American Interests in Cuba*, 56–60; James Callahan, *Cuba and International Relations: A Historical Study in American Diplomacy* (Baltimore: Johns Hopkins University Press, 1899), 199–200.

United States in a position to rival Britain's maritime commercial supremacy. By 1853, Great Britain was still the only state that had the ability to project sufficient power to truly threaten U.S. security and its interests in territorial and commercial expansion.[68] Moreover, throughout the 1850s it was widely feared that Britain and France together were scheming to impose a balance of power on the Western Hemisphere, to take control of Cuba to prevent it from falling to private adventurers from the United States, and to intervene in the worsening political situation in Mexico.[69]

British possession of Cuba was not only seen as a direct threat to U.S. security from a national perspective, southerners were becoming increasingly agitated over the threat British possession would pose to their sectional interests as well. This fear was heightened by British agitation for the emancipation of slaves in Spain's colonies of Cuba and Puerto Rico and aggressive antislavery patrols in the waters around the United States.[70] Democratic Senator Wescott of Florida argued that Britain

> seeks to emancipate the slaves in Cuba, and to strike the southern position of the Confederacy through its domestic institutions. . . . Are the southern States . . . prepared to see the slaves in Cuba emancipated . . . and then to see [Britain] in possession of Yucatan, and populate it with a colony of manumitted negroes from Jamaica? My State will not assent to such a state of things . . . Florida would be surrounded by a cordon of foreign colonial governments, the population of which would be emancipated slaves, under the control of the worst enemy of the United States.[71]

Senator John Calhoun of South Carolina would also support war with Great Britain to prevent its acquisition of Cuba. Calhoun had been Polk's greatest opponent in the Democratic party and in the Senate during the war with Mexico and the struggle over the Oregon Territory. Yet the prospect of the emancipation of slaves in Cuba should Britain gain control of the island was a nightmare for Calhoun, and one over which he was willing to fight to prevent.[72]

---

[68] Richard W. Van Alstyne, "The Significance of the Mississippi Valley in American Diplomatic History, 1686–1890," *Mississippi Valley Historical Review* 36 (September 1949), 215–38.

[69] Rippy, *United States and Mexico*, 198–99. John Clarke, *British Diplomacy and Foreign Policy, 1782–1865: the National Interest* (London: Unwin Hyman, 1989).

[70] Suzanne Miers, *Britain and the Ending of the Slave Trade* (New York: Africana, 1974); Howard Temperley, *British Antislavery, 1833–1870* (London: Longman, 1972).

[71] Rauch, *American Interests in Cuba*, 70.

[72] Ibid.

During his administration, President Polk saw the logic of each of these arguments, so he proposed that the United States purchase Cuba from Spain.[73] This would not only prevent the strategic and domestic dangers of British possession, it would also provide an opportunity to make up for lost territorial expansion in Mexico, an opportunity that had been missed because of domestic divisions over slavery expansion.[74] Polk's annexationist project was stillborn, however, before a purchase offer could be made. When the Spanish government learned of the interest of the United States in Cuba, it was so offended that it vowed pointedly that Spain would never give up its Caribbean possessions.[75]

The Pierce Administration and the Renewed Quest for Cuban Annexation

After a four-year lull in U.S. efforts to obtain Cuba from Spain during the presidency of Whigs Zachary Taylor and his successor Millard Fillmore (following Taylor's death in office),[76] 1853 marked the beginning of what one historian calls the "climax of U.S. interest in Cuba."[77] It is no surprise that the Pierce administration made the acquisition of Cuba its number-one foreign policy priority. Like the Polk administration before it, these Democrats embodied the enthusiasm of U.S. Manifest Destiny, with an ideological commitment to territorial expansion and a growing fixation on Cuba as the most desirable and reasonable objective. Two powerful sources of expansionist zeal had the greatest influence on President Pierce during the first years of his administration. The first was a political faction within the Democratic party

---

[73] Merk, *Monroe Doctrine*, 258–68.

[74] Rauch, *American Interests in Cuba*, 71.

[75] Binder, *James Buchanan*, 141.

[76] While the Whigs firmly supported the U.S. "no transfer" policy for Cuba, they refused to pursue even peaceful annexation. According to Edward Everett, secretary of state under Fillmore, both Taylor and Fillmore saw no reason to stir up sectional antagonism by incorporating a slaveholding territory into the Union. Everett also noted that these administrations would never use military force to acquire Cuba for normative reasons. The president would consider this a "disgrace to the civilization of the age." Graebner, *Manifest Destiny*, 254–59. The Whig administrations also took action to prevent private filibusters from seizing Cuba. Tom Chaffin, *Fatal Glory: Narciso Lopez and the First Clandestine U.S. War Against Cuba* (Charlottesville: University of Virginia Press, 1996).

[77] Rauch, *American Interests in Cuba*, 181. See also Merk, *Monroe Doctrine*, 270–71.

called "Young America." This faction was composed of those northern and southern extreme expansionists who advocated U.S. support, even intervention, on behalf of liberal revolutionary movements in Europe and territorial expansion in Cuba and Central America. Although the faction's candidate could not secure the Democratic nomination in 1852, Young America had a strong influence on the party's platform and President Pierce felt obligated to respect the faction's influence. One Pierce biographer argues that the views of Young America overshadowed all other factions during his presidency.[78] Young America also had the sympathy and active support of key members of Pierce's administration, including Attorney General Caleb Cushing, who often had more influence on foreign policy than the secretary of state.[79] Young America was also championed by Assistant Secretary of State A. Dudley Mann, whose appointment was made as a concession to Young America,[80] and by the U.S. minister to Spain, Pierre Soule. Soule, the most aggressive and militant of the southern expansionists, would be charged with representing the United States' interest in obtaining Cuba to the Spanish government.[81] James Buchanan, now U.S. minister in London, also shared Young America's expansionist vision.[82] At the end of the Polk administration, Buchanan declared, "We must have Cuba. We can't do without Cuba, and above all we must not suffer its transfer to Great Britain. We shall acquire it by a coup at some propitious moment . . . Cuba is already ours. I feel it in my finger tips."[83] The second source of expansionist pressure on Pierce came from the strong southern influence on his own thinking and within his administration. As noted earlier, his sympathies were with the South when issues affecting sectional interests were raised in U.S. politics, and foreign policy was no exception.[84] Jefferson Davis, the secretary of war, was the most prominent southerner in the cabinet. He was a man who was almost singularly sectional in his political views, and as a close friend of Pierce, the most influential of the president's advisors.[85]

---

[78] Gara, *Presidency of Franklin Pierce*, 127.

[79] Ibid., 44, 70; Rauch, *American Interests in Cuba*, 257.

[80] M. E. Curti, "Young America," *American Historical Review* 32 (October 1926), 34–55.

[81] J. Preston Moore, "Pierre Soule: Southern Expansionist and Promoter," *The Journal of Southern History* 21 (May 1955), 203–23.

[82] Binder, *James Buchanan*, 166; Gara, *Presidency of Franklin Pierce*, 56.

[83] Binder, *James Buchanan*, 142.

[84] Gara, *Presidency of Franklin Pierce*, 79; Meinig, *Shaping of America*, 157.

[85] Gara, *Presidency of Franklin Pierce*, 62.

Although there was sporadic support in the North for the annexation of Cuba, this effort was almost solely a southern-driven enterprise. From the early decades of U.S. independence, obtaining Cuba
could be defended as a truly national interest, which some still did. Its
importance as a strategic chokepoint made threats by foreign powers
from Cuba a genuine concern, not only for southerners but also for
westerners who relied on the Mississippi River outlet to gain access to
external markets and for those on the Atlantic seaboard who had
heavy stakes in maritime trade. While these national-level interests in
Cuba never lost their importance, in the 1850s the sectional interests of
the South came to dominate U.S. policy. For southerners, U.S. possession of Cuba would satisfy both offensive and defensive goals. In an
offensive sense, Cuba was new territory for expanding the slave-plan-
tation system that was then facing a crisis. Bringing new territory
under cultivation was seen as the only solution to a current drop in
cotton prices, the rise in slave labor costs, and soil depletion that resulted from growing just one crop. By this time cotton cultivation had
spread as far westward as possible, so moving south was the only option for plantation owners.[86] In a defensive sense, U.S. acquisition of
Cuba would prevent the emancipation of Cuba's large slave population. This was certain if Great Britain took control of the island or if
Spain gave way to persistent British pressure on this issue. Adding
Cuba to the Union as one or more slave states would also help restore
the political balance between North and South.

While the annexation of Cuba had stronger and more widespread
support in the South, Pierce saw this objective as one means to unite
Union Democrats in the North with States-Rights Democrats in the
South, and thus solidify the party. In a reference to Cuba in his inaugural address he cast annexation in broad national terms: "It is not to
be disguised that . . . our position on the globe, render[s] the acquisition of certain possessions . . . eminently important for our protection
. . . essential for the preservation of the rights of commerce and the
peace of the world."[87] So from the beginning of the Pierce administration the national and sectional-level interests raised by Cuba provided
the rationale for bold action to take possession of the island. If Spain refused to sell, eager annexationists believed that all Pierce needed was a
specific insult against the United States that could serve as a pretext for

[86] Rauch, *American Interests in Cuba*, 196–99.
[87] Ibid., 254.

seizing it. Over the next two years, events in Cuba and a series of critical incidents directed against the United States offered the opportunity expansionists were looking for.

Crisis and Opportunity for Military Action

From 1853 to 1855, U.S.-Spanish relations were dominated by a combustible mix of features that presented unambiguous conditions for war. A militant U.S. executive branch consumed by a growing sense of urgency over the future of Cuba, goaded by consistent domestic pressure to take decisive action against Spain's obstinate refusal to sell the colony, was given the pretext for military action. The crisis was touched off when Cuban officials seized a U.S. ship in Havana harbor. While this could serve as a proximate cause for war, the underlying sense of urgency was compelled by the so-called "Africanization scare" of 1854 to 1855. This was a reform period in Cuba, driven by the new governor-general, Juan Pezuela, meant to prepare for full emancipation of the slave population and the integration of emancipated slaves into the general affairs of the colony.[88] Pezuela's reforms included an edict allowing slaves to hire themselves out to individuals other than their masters. The money they earned could then be used to purchase their freedom. Pezuela freed fifteen thousand slaves in May 1854 and introduced a large number of free black apprentices from Africa. He announced that the government would arm free mulattos and blacks to help protect Cuba, who, while enlisted, would enjoy the same status as regular Spanish soldiers. There were also efforts to provide free schools for blacks, to increase their birth rate, and permit interracial marriages.[89]

For southerners, emancipation in Cuba was intolerable. First, these reforms would prevent U.S. annexation. No southerner would agree to add the island to the Union after its black population was free, even to acquire the strategic benefits of Cuba's geographic position and the economic benefits of its natural resources. Emancipation would obviously eliminate Cuba as the solution to the crisis in plantation agriculture in the United States. Second, and perhaps most worrisome, an

---

[88] Ibid., 285.
[89] C. Stanley Urban, "The Africanization of Cuba Scare, 1853–1855," *Hispanic American Historical Review* 37 (February 1957), 29–38; Callahan, *Cuba and International Relations*, 274.

emancipated black population in Cuba would serve as a constant inspiration to slaves in the United States, just as free blacks in other parts of the West Indies inspired slaves in Cuba. Great Britain had freed 668,000 slaves in its West Indian colonies in 1834, and France freed 161,000 slaves in its West Indian colonies in 1848.[90] The result in Cuba had been a string of violent slave revolts from 1832 through the 1840s, and southern Americans feared the same fate.[91]

The sense of urgency provoked by Pezuela's "Africanization" reforms was shared widely within the Pierce administration, even by those like Secretary of State Marcy who were not southern sympathizers. This urgency was caused by strong evidence to support a key assumption of the Pierce-Marcy foreign policy, that Britain and France were cooperating in a long-term effort to contain U.S. territorial and commercial expansion. Lord Clarendon, the British foreign secretary, confirmed this assumption in a speech in February 1854. While discussing Britain's alliance with France for the coming war with Russia, Clarendon pointed out that with regard to affairs in the Western Hemisphere, the policies of England and France were "in entire harmony."[92] Both Britain and France had a strong interest in eliminating the competitive advantages of slave-based production enjoyed by tropical agriculture in slaveholding colonies. It was clear that abolitionist pressure from Britain and France was behind Spain's toleration for Pezuela's reforms in Cuba. Much more insidious to the United States, however, was evidence that Great Britain also sought emancipation in Cuba as the most effective means to prevent U.S. annexation of the island. In 1851, British foreign secretary Palmerston admitted that a free black population "would create a most powerful element of resistance to any scheme for annexing Cuba to the United States, where slavery exists."[93] In a letter to Buchanan, Marcy described the growing sentiment that ultimately Britain and France intended to establish a joint protectorate over Cuba, but as far as he was concerned, "This assumed guardianship over affairs in this part of the world will not be acquiesced in by the United States."[94] This outside interference in Cuban affairs had the important effect of uniting moderates and ex-

[90] Urban, "Africanization of Cuba Scare," 31; Merk, *Monroe Doctrine*, 255.

[91] Rauch, *American Interests in Cuba*, 38–44.

[92] Nichols, *Franklin Pierce*, 326.

[93] Urban, "Africanization of Cuba Scare," 30–31; Callahan, *Cuba and International Relations*, 275.

[94] Callahan, *Cuba and International Relations*, 276.

tremists in the Pierce administration behind the belief that U.S. acquisition of Cuba was the only solution to the various problems created
for the United States.

The Pierce administration realized that, despite the charged atmo-
sphere created by the Africanization scare and European meddling,
any military initiative for wresting Cuba from Spain could be justified
only if Spain gave the United States a specific pretext for war.[95] On
February 28, 1854, just such a crisis emerged. On this date the U.S.
steamer *Black Warrior* pulled into Havana harbor on a routine stop to
deliver mail and passengers. Following a dispute over the ship's manifest, Cuban officials seized the *Black Warrior* and arrested the captain.[96] In the United States, this incident was treated as a grave insult
that could not go unanswered, not only by Young Americans and
southern imperialists hungry for Cuba, but by moderates in the Democratic party and among the general public as well.[97] As it became
clear that the Spanish government would not acknowledge any
wrongdoing on the part of its officials in Havana,[98] the demand for
some form of retaliatory action grew, fanned by the more militant
members of the cabinet, Congress, and the press.[99] Secretary of War
Jefferson Davis and Attorney General Caleb Cushing quickly resolved
that the United States should impose a blockade against Cuba and use
the incident as an opportunity to seize it for the United States. With
time, a general war spirit swept the Pierce administration.[100]

In his March 15 response to Congress' request for information on
the incident, Pierce chose threatening language to describe the tenu-
ous state of U.S.–Spanish relations and the gravity of the *Black Warrior*
affair. This was to prepare Congress for the likelihood that the United
States would ultimately use force to compel Spanish restitution. He

[95] Ibid., 266.

[96] Henry Lorenzo Janes, "The Black Warrior Affair," *American Historical Review* 12
(January 1907), 280–98.

[97] Nichols, *Franklin Pierce*, 327; Binder, *James Buchanan*, 203; Webster, "Mr. Marcy,"
11–12.

[98] The Spanish government argued that detention of the ship was mere enforcement
of legitimate harbor regulations and a fiscal matter between the ship's owner and officials in Havana. Webster, "Mr. Marcy," 16–17.

[99] Press coverage of the crisis intensified the general sense that the *Black Warrior* affair
could at some point produce war between the United States and Spain. The *Washington
Union*, connected closely to the administration, was persistent in its demand that the
United States seize Cuba as indemnity for a long list of grievances against Spain. Ibid.,
25–26; Janes, "Black Warrior Affair," 294.

[100] Callahan, *Cuba and International Relations*, 274, 277; Janes, "Black Warrior Affair,"
291.

declared in the message that Spain's action was "so clear a case of wrong that it would be reasonable to expect full indemnity . . . but similar expectations in other cases have not been realized." Therefore, Pierce concluded, it would be "vain to expect that a series of un-friendly acts . . . can long be consistent with peaceful relations." If Spain refused to make amends, the president affirmed, he would "not hesitate to use the authority and means which Congress may grant to insure the observance of our just rights, to obtain redress for injuries received, and to vindicate the honor of our flag."[101]

The best indication of how serious this incident was treated by the administration is the reaction of Secretary of State Marcy and Postmas-ter General Campbell, the two most moderate members of the cabinet. Marcy, who had been reluctant to antagonize Spain over Cuba, was fu-rious over the seizure of the *Black Warrior*, which he believed was a de-liberate effort to provoke the United States and to force Britain and France to come to Spain's aid.[102] In a letter to Soule in Madrid, Marcy declared that "the outrage is of such a marked character that this gov-ernment would be justified in demanding immediate satisfaction for the wrong-doers in Havana, and ought in case of refusal to take a re-dress into its own hands."[103] The normally cautious Campbell blamed Britain for masterminding Spain's insults against the United States, which, he argued, must be stopped "even at the cannon's mouth." If the problem grew, Campbell promised, "Our people will be in arms from Maine to Texas."[104]

As Pierce deliberated over how to respond to the Spanish insults against the United States and the persistent domestic demands for ac-tion against Cuba, Marcy instructed Soule to renew the offer to pur-chase the island. Yet with little hope that Spain would actually accept the offer, Marcy instructed his principal diplomats in Europe, James Mason in France, Buchanan in Great Britain, and Soule in Spain, to meet in confidence and develop recommendations for the president on the best course of action should Spain refuse to sell. In October 1854, Mason, Buchanan, and Soule produced a report that provided the strongest argument yet in support of military action to remove the Cuba problem from U.S. foreign policy. After reviewing the familiar ar-guments on the importance of Cuba for U.S. security and the dangers

---

[101] Nichols, *Franklin Pierce*, 328; Gara, *Presidency of Franklin Pierce*, 150–51.
[102] Spencer, *Victor and the Spoils*, 319; Callahan, *Cuba and International Relations*, 269.
[103] Webster, "Mr. Marcy," 16.
[104] Binder, *James Buchanan*, 203–4; Nichols, *Franklin Pierce*, 327.

of "Africanization," the "Ostend Manifesto" declared that "the Union can never enjoy repose, nor possess reliable security, as long as Cuba is not embraced within its borders." The goal then, was annexation. The report continued, "But if Spain, dead to the voice of her own interests, and activated by stubborn pride and a false sense of honor, should refuse to sell Cuba to the United States, then the question will arise, what ought to be the course of the American government under such circumstances?" Buchanan, Mason and Soule argue that military action to obtain Cuba is justified by nothing less than the general principle of self-preservation, "the first law of nature, with States as well as with individuals." "We should . . . be unworthy of our gallant forefathers, and commit base treason against posterity, should we permit Cuba to be Africanized and become a second St. Domingo, with all the attendant horrors to the white race, . . . seriously to endanger or actually to consume the fair fabric of our Union." From this dire scenario they concluded, "By every law, human and divine, we shall be justified in wresting [Cuba] from Spain if we possess the power; and this upon the very same principle that would justify an individual in tearing down the burning house of his neighbor if there were no other means of preventing the flames from destroying his own house." Finally, on top of this general principle that justified U.S. action against Cuba, they contend that the specific insults committed by Spain give the pretext for taking such action.

> A long series of injuries to our people have been committed in Cuba by Spanish officials and are unredressed. But recently a most flagrant outrage on the rights of American citizens and on the flag of the United States was perpetrated in the harbor of Havana under circumstances which, without immediate redress, would have justified a resort to measures of war in vindication of national honor. That outrage is not only unatoned, but the Spanish government has deliberately sanctioned the acts of its subordinates.[105]

While the Spanish government did release the *Black Warrior* and pay damages to its owner, U.S.–Spanish relations actually worsened following new incidents in early 1855. The U.S. merchant ship *Eldorado* was fired on by a Spanish frigate in March, and the press carried reports that the U.S. vice-consul in Cuba had been arrested for conspiring with Cuban revolutionaries and that the U.S. flag was torn down

---

[105] James Buchanan, Pierre Soule, and James Mason, "Ostend Manifesto," October 18, 1854, in *Manifest Destiny*, 287–93.

at the consulate.[106] In response, Pierce ordered "that as many of our ships of war as could be made available should be ordered to rendezvous near Havana."[107] The secretary of state agreed with this decision, although he stated he was "entirely opposed to *getting up a war* for the purpose of Seizing Cuba," that is, opposed to instigating war. However, he continued, "if the Conduct of Spain should be such as to justify a war, I should not hesitate to meet that state of things."[108]

Explaining America's Failure to Act during the Cuba Crisis

Despite the underlying and proximate causes for war between the United States and Spain from 1854 to 1855, the Pierce administration failed to act with military force to secure its objectives in Cuba. By June 1854 Pierce had retreated from the opportunity to use the *Black Warrior* affair as a cause of war, and by the summer of 1855 he had fully rejected the use of force to achieve annexation or to punish Spain for harassing U.S. ships. As in the Mesilla Valley dispute with Mexico, the institutional point of constraint on the use of U.S. force was the president himself. Congress never imposed a legislative impediment to his Cuba policy. In fact, aside from the request for information on the *Black Warrior* incident and U.S. negotiations with Spain for the purchase of Cuba, the only official communication from Congress came from a Senate Foreign Relations Committee delegation that wanted Pierce to seek the suspension of U.S. neutrality laws. This would have allowed private filibusters to seize Cuba without U.S. government interference (this too Pierce rejected).[109] The task then is to explain why Pierce made the decision not to use military force when so many elements of the crisis seemed to compel him in the other direction.

One explanation we can discount for this decision is that the Pierce administration was deterred by the expected costs of military conflict with Spain or by the possibility of British or French intervention against the United States. First, at no time in the crisis did U.S. decision-makers express any concern for Spanish power. The widespread belief was that Cuba was so weakly defended that a U.S. force would

---

[106] Spencer, *Victor and the Spoils*, 322; Nichols, *Franklin Pierce*, 394.
[107] Webster, "Mr. Marcy," 26–28.
[108] Spencer, *Victor and the Spoils*, 388–89; emphasis in original.
[109] Gara, *Presidency of Franklin Pierce*, 152; Nichols, *Franklin Pierce*, 342.

encounter little resistance. Cuba was the prime target for U.S. expansion not only because of the offensive and defensive advantages of obtaining the island, but because it was considered the territory most easily obtained through military force as well.[110] In 1854 and 1855 the Spanish government was paralyzed by internal revolt and financial distress, and it appeared that the monarchy was near collapse.[111] Second, with Great Britain and France already fighting Russia in the Crimea, U.S. decision-makers were confident that neither country would be willing to come to Spain's aid. The Anglo-French commitment in the east not only provided security against wider European intervention in a struggle over Cuba, it was a compelling reason to strike Cuba now, before the European war ended.[112] At the height of tensions over the *Black Warrior*, Marcy wrote to James Buchanan in London that even if European intervention were likely, Spain's insults against the United States were so egregious that the United States would still press ahead with a vigorous course of action for obtaining justice in the case.[113] During this same period the most militant members of the cabinet, Jefferson Davis and Caleb Cushing, argued that the United States should defy European opinion and seize Cuba.[114] The administration also believed that the Crimean War would prevent Britain and France from sending naval forces for the much simpler task of helping Spain defend against mere filibusters.[115]

The best explanation for Pierce's decision not to use military force is found in domestic politics. Specifically, constraints on U.S. power were rooted in strong regional differences over the most basic questions of whether the United States should seek annexation of Cuba and use force to achieve this goal. As we have seen, both northerners and southerners mainly viewed the annexation of Cuba as a sectional interest favoring the South, not as a national interest affecting all states equally. Even though Cuba did have general strategic value, which extreme expansionists in the North pointed out, the vast majority in the North saw Cuba simply as a slaveholding colony that, if added to the Union, would strengthen the "slave power" in U.S. politics. These territorially asymmetric perspectives became even more salient for U.S.

---

[110] Graebner, *Manifest Destiny*, 245–46.
[111] Gavin B. Henderson, "Southern Designs on Cuba, 1854–1857 and Some European Opinions," *The Journal of Southern History* 5 (1939), 373.
[112] Nichols, *Franklin Pierce*, 329.
[113] Callahan, *Cuba and International Relations*, 270.
[114] Ibid., 274.
[115] Rauch, *American Interests in Cuba*, 283.

behavior over Cuba than the Mesilla Valley dispute because the Africanization scare and the *Black Warrior* affair coincided in time with the sectional fury over the Kansas-Nebraska Act. While the Compromise of 1850 brought relative stability to U.S. politics, by the spring of 1854 sectionalism flared to its most dangerous level yet. Senator Stephen Douglas, hoping to improve his chances of winning southern support for the Democratic presidential nomination in 1856, proposed that slavery be permitted in states carved from the Nebraska Territory. This would, in effect, abrogate the great Missouri Compromise of 1820 that prohibited slavery north of 36–30 degrees latitude. Douglas himself admitted that he had antagonized the North so severely with this plan that "I could travel from Boston to Chicago by the light of my own [burning] effigy."[116] The ensuing debate on the Kansas-Nebraska bill further divided the sections and hardened their regional identities and political loyalties. The traditional alignment of the Old Northwest and the South across a range of political issues broke down for good due to growing antislavery sentiment in the Old Northwest and the lack of southern support for a recently defeated rivers and harbors bill that the Northwest considered vital for its development.[117] The Old Northwest and the Northeast were converging in their political identities and finding enough common ground in the great questions of the day to align consistently on national issues. While few thought seriously about disunion at this point, North-South antagonism now framed every issue that had some link to the rival political interests of the sections. Because Cuba policy had such clearly asymmetric effects on territorially distributed interests in the United States, the politics of the issue were dominated by this rivalry.[118]

This was the situation President Pierce faced in the spring and summer of 1854 as his administration wrestled with the question of how to

[116] Polakoff, *Political Parties*, 172.

[117] Ibid. See also Craven, *Growth of Southern Nationalism*, 21–32.

[118] Gara, *Presidency of Franklin Pierce*, 128, 155; Meinig, *Shaping of America*, 158; Nichols, *Franklin Pierce*, 340; Rauch, *American Interests in Cuba*, 280. While there was variation across the South in economic, social and geographic characteristics, the slavery controversy made southerners acutely aware of their common interests in this system. Even though a minority of them actually owned slaves, the social structure created by slavery was one that all southerners shared. Considering the fact that 35 percent of the total southern population in 1850 was black, even nonslaveholders had a stake in preventing the future emancipation of such a large bloc to prevent the perceived problems this would create for the region. For their part, northerners began to think of all southerners as slaveholders, even though this view was far from reality. And while the percentage of abolitionists in the North was quite small, support for free-soil principles was strong. Craven, *Growth of Southern Nationalism*.

respond to Spanish insults and whether to take advantage of the opportunity to seize Cuba that was now at hand. Pierce was constrained in this case by the same features of U.S. politics that constrained him during the Mesilla Valley crisis: asymmetry in territorial views on the policy problem combined with the federal arrangement of the U.S. political system. Despite the strength of the Democratic party in both the House and the Senate, party unity was an instant casualty of competitive territorial interests. As Secretary of State Marcy explained in a letter to James Mason in France, the Kansas-Nebraska question had "sadly shattered our party in all the free states and deprived it of the strength which was needed and could have been much more profitably used for the acquisition of Cuba."[119] The difficulty of holding a Democratic majority together to support the use of force was foreshadowed by the debate over Cuba annexation in early 1853. In this debate, northern and southern Democrats portrayed even peaceful annexation through purchase in starkly different terms. Southern Democrats argued that the United States could not survive without Cuba and the goal justified the costs of war. Most northern Democrats argued that the only way to obtain Cuba was through war, which they would never permit, and even if Spain agreed to sell the island, northern Democrats would not allow this slave territory into the Union.[120]

This pattern of sectional disagreement, played out in the Senate and House, is found at every point in the crisis, particularly when it appeared that the Pierce administration was leaning toward military action. Each time northern opposition flared over some particular initiative, Pierce backed down, refusing to sustain any move that further split the Democratic party, hardened the Free Soil position, and forced northern Democrats to align with members of other parties in this region of the country.[121] Because of the numerical superiority in both the number of states and the total population in the North, Pierce quickly recognized that it would be impossible to build a congressional coalition large enough to sustain any military action against Spain.[122] Secretary of State Marcy must be credited with having a decisive moderating influence in the administration. A veteran of the struggle in New York between Free Soil and conservative Democrats, Marcy was particularly sensitive to the bitterness of the split in the party caused by the

[119] Gara, *Presidency of Franklin Pierce*, 152.
[120] Graebner, *Manifest Destiny*, 267–68.
[121] Spencer, *Victor and the Spoils*, 319.
[122] Nichols, *Franklin Pierce*, 341; Callahan, *Cuba and International Relations*, 278.

slavery issue, and he saw clearly how quickly antislavery views were unifying the North. While Marcy was not a Free Soil Democrat, his anger over Spain's actions in the *Black Warrior* affair and other insulting incidents was tempered by his lack of enthusiasm for the annexation of Cuba, which was a product of his northern background. When he agreed to join the Pierce cabinet, Marcy was dismayed by the militant character of other members of the administration and their expansionist and southern sympathies. Yet he proved to be a consistent representative of moderate northern sentiment on foreign policy and thus a voice of caution that kept Pierce attuned to northern opposition in Congress and its effects on the party.[123]

Pierce's reaction to several specific opportunities to advance his objectives for Cuba illustrate his readiness to back down from vigorous action to avoid stoking northern animosity. The first opportunity came soon after the *Black Warrior* incident. Several southern congressmen initiated a resolution to provide the president with $10 million and the authority to prepare the navy and army for military action against Cuba if he should decide this was necessary. Senator James Mason, still a member of Congress at this time, polled the Senate and discovered that northern opposition in this body made such a resolution impossible. Pierce actually intervened with members of the Senate Foreign Relations Committee to squelch this effort to give him congressional approval and the funds for military action. Following the president's intervention, the measure died.[124] The second opportunity came on May 30, 1854, during a White House visit from John Slidell of Louisiana, James Mason of Virginia, and Stephen Douglas of Illinois, the members of the Democratic majority on the Senate Foreign Relations Committee. They had come to convince Pierce to support Slidell's proposal that the neutrality laws be suspended. This would allow the filibuster expedition of General John Quitman, a former governor of Mississippi, to sail from New York and New Orleans to seize Cuba. During this meeting Pierce proposed the creation of a three-man commission that would present the U.S. case for Cuba to the Spanish government. Pierce also suggested that the commission could then issue a subtle threat that the only way to prevent the filibuster invasion was to cede Cuba peacefully to the United States. Pierce also

---

[123] Spencer, *Victor and the Spoils*, 223, 261, 332; Gara, *Presidency of Franklin Pierce*, 128; Callahan, *Cuba and International Relations*, 278.

[124] Callahan, *Cuba and International Relations*, 273; Spencer, *Victor and the Spoils*, 324; Nichols, *Franklin Pierce*, 340, 353.

promised to ask for a large appropriation from Congress to support U.S. military action if the filibuster failed. Yet instead of following through on his promise, which was made to placate this delegation for the short-term, Pierce issued a proclamation the next day that made clear his intentions to enforce the neutrality laws against any filibuster from the United States. In the words of Marcy's biographer, "Pierce had not dared to send Congress the proposal for the commission."[125] Such a bold proposal for war would never win congressional support and would needlessly antagonize the North so soon after the Kansas-Nebraska Act was signed.[126]

The third opportunity came with the Ostend Manifesto from Buchanan, Mason, and Soule in Europe. Instead of embracing their argument about self-preservation and the national interests at stake, Pierce and Marcy repudiated the diplomats for such a brazen proposal. Pierce's reaction had little to do with any serious disagreement with the view expressed in the report. His reaction was the result of the tremendous northern condemnation he received because of the Ostend suggestions, which leaked to the public soon after the report arrived in Washington in November 1854.[127] The Free Soil party took great offense at what was interpreted to be a purely southern policy couched in terms of national interest, and Pierce could not afford to be associated with such a blatantly southern orientation.[128] Even to America's opponents it was clear how domestic politics were affecting the Pierce administration's policy on Cuba. In the summer of 1854 the Spanish minister to the U.S. reported to his government that in the midst of internal strife "all the questions promoted by the hostile policy of this government against us remain as if paralyzed; the press is silenced and the affair of the *Black Warrior* almost forgotten."[129]

In the congressional elections of 1854, any presidential hope that Democratic unity in Congress could sustain some portion of his Cuba

---

[125] Spencer, *Victor and the Spoils*, 324.

[126] Rauch, *American Interests in Cuba*, 286; Gara, *Presidency of Franklin Pierce*, 152. In an effort to placate the expansionists after this setback, the administration proceeded with another offer to purchase Cuba from Spain, yet northern opposition in Congress blocked an appropriation to support Soule's negotiations for a purchase. Nichols, *Franklin Pierce*, 353; Urban, "Africanization of Cuba Scare," 40.

[127] Polakoff, *Political Parties*, 173; Nichols, *Franklin Pierce*, 368; Binder, *James Buchanan*, 213.

[128] Henderson, "Southern Designs on Cuba," 374. Indignant over this rejection, Soule resigned his diplomatic post in Madrid, and Mann resigned as assistant secretary of state. Webster, "Mr. Marcy," 24; Binder, *James Buchanan*, 214.

[129] Janes, "Black Warrior Affair," 297.

policy suffered a fatal blow. As a result of the Democratic party's association with the Kansas-Nebraska Act and the policy to acquire Cuba,
northern voters turned away from the party in droves to hand the Democrats a terrible electoral defeat in this section. In the process, the huge
margin of control the Democrats had in the House was erased as anti-
Nebraska Republicans and Know-Nothings were elected in overwhelming numbers. In 1852 the Pierce ticket had won every northern
state but two, in 1854 the Democrats lost every northern state except
two (New Hampshire and California).[130] Overall, the Democratic
party's strength in the House decreased from a two-third majority to a
one-third minority. While the Democrats still controlled the Senate,
northern Democratic senators were more conscious of their constituents' antislavery views than ever before. The state-based electoral
system of this federal polity had rewarded those candidates whose loyalty to northern antislavery interests was unchallenged. As a result of
the loss of Democratic dominance in the North and the subsequent rise
of opposition parties there, northern unity would be quicker to coalesce
on national issues that intersected with strong regional interests. This
meant that the strength of the coalition representing northern opposition in Congress was even more formidable. If the president had lacked
the ability to generate support for Cuba policy from the Thirty-third
Congress, he was sure that such support was out of the question from
the Thirty-fourth Congress. Accepting this fact, Pierce abandoned all efforts to acquire Cuba, by both peaceful and militant means. This was
true even in early 1855 when Spain again antagonized the United States
by firing at a U.S. merchant ship. While Pierce sent a naval squadron to
the region in response, he had no choice but to take steps to quickly de-
escalate the crisis before having to face the prospects of taking military
action on a larger scale without congressional backing.[131]

Chaos in Mexico and the Proposed U.S. Intervention

The Origins of the Crisis

With the Gadsden Treaty of 1853, President Pierce had managed to
extricate the United States from a violent clash with Mexico over the

---

[130] Merk, *Monroe Doctrine*, 273–74; Rauch, *American Interests in Cuba*, 293–94; Nichols,
Franklin Pierce, 365.
[131] Nichols, *Franklin Pierce*, 394–96; Spencer, *Victor and the Spoils*, 338–40; Rauch, *American Interests in Cuba*, 295; Urban, "Africanization of Cuba Scare," 45.

disputed Mesilla Valley. While the United States failed to obtain the large swath of Mexican territory demanded in these negotiations, the treaty did stabilize U.S.–Mexican relations, allowing the Pierce administration to turn its attention to Cuba. Unfortunately, stability in Mexican–U.S. relations was fleeting. By the time James Buchanan entered the White House in 1857, Mexico was again the United States number-one foreign policy problem. During the course of his administration, Buchanan presented Congress with three separate requests for authority to intervene in Mexico with military force. To Buchanan, there were three compelling reasons for the United States to pursue this policy.

First, President Buchanan and his secretary of state, Lewis Cass, were firmly committed to the Democratic party's long-term policy of perpetual territorial expansion. This commitment stemmed from the personal belief they shared in the importance of territorial growth for the country's continuing prosperity and national power. Despite the phenomenal territorial growth of the United States during the previous decade, Cass declared in 1858, "It is idle to tell me we have land enough . . . . [The] constant torrent [of immigrants] requires more land, more territory upon which to settle, and just as fast as our interests and our destiny require additional territory in the North, or in the South, or on the islands of the Ocean, I am for it."[132] This commitment also helped these two northerners placate southern Democrats who now dominated the party following the successive defeats suffered by the Democrats in the North.[133] Southern Democrats continued to insist that territorial growth southward provided their only hope to retain sufficient political power within the Union to safeguard their interests. The recent failure of Pierce's efforts to acquire Cuba meant that further expansion into Mexico was the best option for Buchanan and Cass to satisfy their southern supporters. The Gadsden Treaty, like the 1848 Treaty of Guadalupe Hidalgo before it, was a huge disappointment for U.S. expansionists.[134] Buchanan set his sights on obtaining Baja California and large parts of Sonora and Chihuahua during his administration. He also committed himself to securing a perpetual right of

[132] William Carl Klunder, *Lewis Cass and the Politics of Moderation* (Kent, Ohio: Kent State University Press, 1996), 289–90.

[133] In the Thirty-fifth Congress, elected in 1856, of the 41 Democrats in the Senate, 23 were from the South, 18 from the North. Of the 132 Democrats in the House, 83 were southern, 49 were northern. In the Thirty-sixth Congress, elected in 1858, of the 38 Democrats in the Senate, only 12 were from northern states, while 26 were from southern states. Of the 91 Democrats in the House, only 28 were northern, while 63 were southern.

[134] James Callahan, "The Mexican Policy of Southern Leaders under Buchanan's Administration," *Annual Report of the American Historical Association* (1910), 136.

way across the isthmus at Tehauntepec for transportation of U.S. goods to the Pacific Ocean. Buchanan made an offer to purchase this territory at the beginning of his term, yet it was rebuffed.

Despite Mexico's desperate need for money, no Mexican leader could withstand the domestic outrage that would result from ceding any more land to the United States. Mexico's refusal made it clear that any territorial cession would most likely require the use of U.S. military force.[135] Two successive U.S. ministers to Mexico, frustrated by the firm resistance of the Mexican government, urged the president to use military force to achieve this important goal. In April 1855, James Gadsden had recommended to President Pierce that "if property, extension of territory, or other grants or commercial privileges are not acceptable [to Mexico] . . . resort must be had to the sword, which will end in the absorption of the whole Republic."[136] Gadsden's successor, John Forsyth, was convinced that Mexico would never negotiate this issue, so he made a similar recommendation three years later to President Buchanan. "You want Sonora?" he asked ominously.

> The American blood spilled near its line would justify you in seizing it. . . . You want other territory? Send me the power to make an ultimate demand for the several millions Mexico owes our people for spoliations and personal wrongs. . . . You want the Tehauntepec transit? Say to Mexico, "Nature has placed that shortest highway between the two oceans, so necessary to the commerce of the world, in your keeping. You will not open it yourself nor allow others to open it to the wants of mankind. . . . Give us what we ask for. . . or we will take it."[137]

These recommendations found a sympathetic audience with Buchanan and Cass.

The second compelling reason for U.S. military intervention in Mexico was the collapse of the Mexican political system in 1858. Mexican politics had long been dominated by a struggle between two factions, a conservative monarchical faction under the influence of the clerical party, and a liberal faction that resisted the conservatives' efforts to subvert Mexico's republican system. In the summer and fall of 1858 this struggle turned violent. The country was divided into rival regions

---

[135] Rippy, *United States and Mexico*, 212–14, 218; Callahan, "Mexican Policy of Southern Leaders," 135.

[136] Callahan, "Mexican Policy of Southern Leaders," 137.

[137] Rippy, *United States and Mexico*, 216.

controlled by each faction, with the conservative government of General Miramon remaining in Mexico City, while his rival, General Benito Juarez, established his capital in Veracruz to control the eastern part of Mexico.[138] For the Buchanan administration, the ensuing chaos created by this civil conflict and its effects on U.S. interests within Mexico and along the U.S.–Mexican border were simply intolerable. In his third message to Congress in December 1859, Buchanan described the situation in foreboding terms: "Outrages of the worst description are committed both upon persons and property. There is scarcely any form of injury which has not been suffered by our citizens in Mexico during the last few years . . . . Life has been insecure, property unprotected, and trade impossible except at a risk of loss which prudent men can not be expected to incur."[139] According to the U.S. minister gross abuses of U.S. citizens in Mexico were being perpetrated by government officials and bandits alike. Several Americans had been murdered in the midst of the civil unrest and a number of Americans had been imprisoned or executed by the Miramon government for protesting abuses or for trying to protect their property, which was being seized without compensation. The government had seized U.S. merchant ships in Mexican harbors while U.S. consular officials who protested were being imprisoned. Robbery and murder throughout the country were becoming common and unchecked by a government unable to provide domestic security. In the absence of law enforcement along the Mexican-U.S. border, the southwestern portion of the United States was in a perpetual state of insecurity. Mexican bandits and Indians from Chihuahua and Sonora raided U.S. settlements in Arizona and New Mexico and intercepted coaches and U.S. postal delivery throughout the Southwest.[140] The Miramon government's refusal to even consider indemnity claims for American lives and property served to antagonize the administration further. In his second annual message in December 1858, Buchanan declared that the problems caused by the events in Mexico and along the border gave the United States ample cause for hostilities against the Conservative government.[141]

[138] Donald Stevens, *Origins of Instability in Early Republican Mexico* (Durham, N.C.: Duke University Press, 1991).
[139] Howard Lafayette Wilson, "President Buchanan's Proposed Intervention in Mexico," *The American Historical Review* 5 (July 1900), 688.
[140] Ibid., 689.
[141] Ibid., 690–91.

Perhaps even more unsettling to the Buchanan administration was the mounting evidence that Spain, Great Britain, and France were preparing to intervene in Mexico to restore order. This became the third compelling reason for the United States to use military force here. Buchanan considered intervention in Mexico by some outside power as inevitable. In a message to Congress he declared, "Mexico ought to be a rich and prosperous and powerful republic. . . . Is it possible that such a country as this can be given up to anarchy and ruin without an effort from any quarter for its rescue and its safety? Will the commercial nations of the world, which have so many interests connected with it, remain wholly indifferent to such a result?" But Buchanan also held firmly to the view he had first expressed when still secretary of state in 1846: the United States could not tolerate European intervention in Mexico. "Should Great Britain and France attempt to place a Spanish or any other European prince upon the throne of Mexico, this would be resisted by all the power of the United States." Such a gross violation of the Monroe Doctrine would demand a military response from the United States. His message to Congress continued, "The aid which [Mexico] requires . . . belongs to this government to render, not only by virtue of our neighborhood to Mexico . . . but by virtue, also, of our established policy, which is inconsistent with the intervention of any European power in the domestic concerns of that republic."[142] With the end of the Crimean War in 1856, the threat of European intervention in Mexico became acute. Napoleon III of France was increasingly influential with the conservative government of General Miramon and he pressured Mexico to accept a European monarch.[143] In October 1858, Cass learned that Spain was preparing for a naval assault and military intervention against the liberal government in eastern Mexico in response to abuses inflicted on Spaniards and to compel the payment of Mexican debts to Spanish bondholders.[144] Spain was also urging Britain and France to mount a joint intervention to help the Miramon government defeat its liberal challenger and restore domestic stability to Mexico.[145] Buchanan knew that the only way to prevent the impending European intervention, and thus avoid military conflict with Great Britain, France, and Spain,

---

[142] Rippy, *United States and Mexico*, 211, 222.
[143] Wilson, "President Buchanan's Proposed Intervention," 692; Binder, *James Buchanan*, 247–48.
[144] Callahan, *Cuba and International Relations*, 299–300.
[145] Wilson, "President Buchanan's Proposed Intervention," 700.

was for the United States to intervene first. "If we do not [lend aid to Mexico]" he warned Congress, "it would not be surprising should some other nation undertake the task, and thus force us to interfere . . . under circumstances of increased difficulty, for the maintenance of our established policy."[146]

Buchanan Demands Authority for Military Intervention

In response to the expansionist demand for additional Mexican territory, the civil chaos in Mexico, and the looming possibility of European intervention, President Buchanan requested authorization from Congress on three separate occasions to intervene with military force. The first request came in the form of his second annual message to Congress in December 1858. In this message, Buchanan argued that the United States had an obligation to protect U.S. citizens from the rampant violence in Mexico, from abuse by the Mexican government, and from the predatory raids across the uncontrolled border. The best way to do this, he declared, was to establish a protectorate over the northern parts of Sonora and Chihuahua, to build military posts within Mexico to control violence in the northern regions, and to deploy military forces in other parts of Mexico, particularly along the Tehauntepec isthmus transit routes. Buchanan followed up on his message with a bill submitted to the Senate Foreign Relations Committee on January 11, 1859, that authorized the president to use military force for the purposes outlined in the previous message. The Senate ignored this bill until Buchanan sent another message to Congress on February 18 asking the Senate to consider his request. After a vigorous debate, the Senate rejected his request by a vote of 31 to 25.[147]

Buchanan's second request for congressional authorization to use military force in Mexico came in his third annual message to Congress in December 1859. In this message, Buchanan proposed an even more audacious plan for U.S. force. He was not merely asking Congress to approve of protective military services for American citizens, although he repeated his recommendation to establish a protectorate over Sonora and Chihuahua. Buchanan was now asking Congress to authorize an

---

[146] Rippy, *United States and Mexico*, 222.
[147] Ibid., 217–19.

intervention to tip the scales in Mexico's civil war by actively bringing down the conservative Miramon government. In its place, Buchanan intended to form an alliance with Juarez's faction and support its efforts to assert control over the entire country, bring an end to domestic insecurity, and stop the cross-border incursions into the U.S. Southwest. Despite the desperate situation in Mexico and Buchanan's call to arms, Congress completely ignored his recommendation and took no action. Neither the House nor the Senate even debated the Mexican problem.[148]

Buchanan made one final bid to force Congress to acknowledge the need for U.S. military action in Mexico and to establish an authoritative basis for the president to deploy forces as necessary. He ordered his envoy Robert McLane to negotiate and sign a protectorate treaty with the Juarez government that the president could present to the Senate for ratification. After recognizing the Juarez faction as the de facto government of Mexico, McLane negotiated a treaty with Foreign Minister Ocampo in which Mexico virtually ceded away its sovereign rights against external interference to the United States. The McLane-Ocampo Treaty of December 14, 1859, established Mexico as one big protectorate of the United States. This would allow the United States to treat any attack on Mexico or threats to its domestic tranquility as an attack on itself. The United States thus had the right to intervene in Mexico at will whenever its interests were jeopardized by either foreign powers or by domestic disturbance. The treaty would also give the United States the exclusive right to maintain security over the Tehauntepec isthmus to protect U.S. commerce. Buchanan submitted the treaty to the Senate on January 4, 1860, with McLane's exhortation about the dire consequences for the United States if the treaty were rejected: "If the United States should decline the responsibility of the convention, the continuation of anarchy in Mexico would result in direct intervention from some quarter and perhaps expose the United States to the 'responsibility of a general war and a conquest that few would desire to undertake or consummate.'"[149] After a four-month delay, the Senate finally debated the treaty in earnest, and then rejected it on May 31 by a vote of 27 to 18.[150]

[148] Ibid., 222–23; Binder, *James Buchanan*, 248.
[149] Callahan, "Mexican Policy of Southern Leaders," 148.
[150] Binder, *James Buchanan*, 248–50; Rippy, *United States and Mexico*, 219–26; Wilson, "President Buchanan's Proposed Intervention," 696; Callahan, "Mexican Policy of Southern Leaders," 144.

Explaining the Absence of U.S. Military Intervention in Mexico

Constraints on President Buchanan's ability to use military force in response to the crisis in Mexico differ in one clear way from the constraints on his predecessor. President Pierce exercised self-restraint,
never allowing his Mexico and Cuba policies to develop to the point at
which Congress would trump his military initiatives. Buchanan, on the
other hand, was ready to use military force in Mexico and eagerly
pushed his military proposals into Congress for approval. In this case,
Buchanan gave Congress the chance to exercise its institutional prerog-
atives. As a result, the potential opposition from northerners that Pierce
sought to avoid became formal legislative opposition that derailed
Buchanan's plans and effectively constrained the use of force. As in
previous cases, the important question concerns the nature of congressional opposition and how this opposition may have been shaped by
the federal institutional arrangement of the U.S. political system.

By the late 1850s, the territorial nature of political opposition to the
use of military force for expansion, particularly southward expansion, had become a familiar feature of U.S. foreign policy. The regional split on the expansion question in the United States, with its
origins in the slavery debate and the Wilmot Proviso of 1846, had
only strengthened through the 1850s, exacerbated by the domestic rift
caused by the Kansas-Nebraska Act of 1854. The question of intervention in Mexico, therefore, was seen in almost strictly sectional terms.
For the North, expanding U.S. control over America's southern neighbor could only result in greater political strength for the slave states.
This is evident in the sectional character of the two Senate votes taken
on Buchanan's policy. In the first Senate vote, of the 31 senators voting in opposition to Buchanan's requested intervention, 20 were from
the North. Only 4 northern senators voted with Buchanan. The South
was more evenly divided, but the majority of southern senators supported Buchanan. Among southerners who voted against intervention, they did so primarily for constitutional, not sectional reasons;
they were uncomfortable giving the executive such open-ended authority for using military force.[151] In the vote that rejected the
McLane-Ocampo treaty, which gave the United States the right to
intervene in Mexico at will, we find an even sharper sectional distribution. Of the 27 votes against the treaty, 23 were from northern

---

[151] Rippy, *United States and Mexico*, 218–19.

senators. Of the 18 votes in favor of the treaty, 14 came from the South. Only 4 senators from the North approved of the treaty, and only 4 senators from the South voted to reject it.[152]

Interestingly, the opposition to Buchanan's policy reflected in these votes was largely partisan in character as well. This is seen most vividly in the vote on the protectorate treaty. Of the 27 votes against the treaty, 21 were from Republicans, while only 6 Democrats voted against the Democratic president. Of the 18 Senators who voted to ratify the Democratic president's treaty, all were Democrats themselves. Not a single Republican voted with Buchanan. The distinctive sectional-partisan alignment on these votes reflects the underlying change in the regional distribution of the dominant political parties in the United States. While one could argue that this was a partisan vote by Republicans in Congress against the Democratic president and his congressional supporters, this argument would neglect the fact that each of the main parties now primarily represented one of the U.S. territorial sections. The Republican party, which had emerged in just a few years to become a major force in U.S. politics, was a purely northern party representing the antislavery position held by the majority of northerners. Most of the Republicans' supporters were former northern Whigs and Free Soil Democrats. While the Democratic party held some Senate and House seats from the North in the late 1850s, its greatest strength was in the South and it was dominated by southern-leaning political leaders.

The most important feature of political opposition in Congress in this period is that sectional priorities and partisan politics were more closely aligned than at any time in U.S. history. Under these conditions there was very little tension between party and sectional interests. In effect, Republican strength in the North, like Democratic strength in the South, made it easier to organize and sustain political coalitions representing sectional views in Congress. In previous periods, when the dominant political parties were truly national in scope, rival territorial views were often constrained in the best interests of party unity. In the late 1850s, however, territorial views did not compete with partisan interest, so they received their fullest expression in national politics. With the slavery debate dominating national politics during the Buchanan administration, sectional perspectives dominated national politics. This was the milieu in which the president attempted to generate con-

---

[152] Wilson, "President Buchanan's Proposed Intervention," 696; Rippy, *United States and Mexico*, 226.

gressional support for military action in Mexico. Buchanan tried to stimulate national-level convergence on the view that the United States interests demanded action by framing his policy as a corollary to the Monroe Doctrine. Despite the real danger of a joint European effort to install a European monarch in Mexico (which actually materialized during the U.S. Civil War), sectional identities were too polarized by this point for Buchanan's arguments to be persuasive. With northerners dominating legislative decisions, Buchanan's hands were tied.[153]

Conclusion

The three cases examined in this chapter on the 1850s provide a valuable complement to the earlier cases discussed in this book. While the use of military force by the United States to pursue foreign policy goals throughout the first half of the nineteenth century was shaped in important ways by U.S. federal institutions, the 1850s demonstrate the institutional logic of federal union taken to an extreme. The conditions in this period came as close as one is likely to find to the hypothesized institutional logic discussed in chapter 2. Federalism can be distinguished from other democratic systems by how easily this institutional arrangement can accommodate territorial interests. It does so through the political incentives of a state-based electoral system and the opportunity for territorial perspectives to penetrate national-level decision-making through the legislature. Yet even in this prototypical federal state, the politics of the early nineteenth century were not always dominated by competition among rival territorial interests; national-level identities and interests often competed with the local. Political parties could serve as a mechanism for centralizing decision-making on issues that were national in character. Political competition, even within specific regions of the country, was often dominated by ideological, economic, or social concerns that were distributed evenly across the territorial subunits that compose the federal state. The distinctive features of federalism have their most decisive impact on policymaking when these nationalizing features break down and strong territorial identities and interests fill the void.

---

[153] Frederick Merk, *Manifest Destiny and Mission in American History: A Reinterpretation* (Cambridge: Harvard University Press, 1963), 208; Binder, *James Buchanan*, 248; Klunder, *Lewis Cass*, 290; Rippy, *United States and Mexico*, 223–26; Callahan, "Mexican Policy of Southern Leaders," 149.

According to the logic of federal union discussed in chapter 2, asymmetry in regional views and interests on national issues is what provides the basis for the type of political competition that coincides with an institutional arrangement that privileges territorial communities, their identities, and goals. This is exactly what we find in the United States of the 1850s. The catalyst, of course, was the emergence of the debate over the role of slavery in the future development of the United States. Here was a single issue that set the dominant context for both domestic and foreign policy. More important, it did so in a way that brought sectional identities and interests to the foreground because of the geographic character of slavery within the United States. As a result, the traditional national-level issues that had characterized much of U.S. politics in previous decades receded in importance. As sectional tension intensified with the increasing bitterness of the struggle over slavery, national political parties found it increasingly difficult, if not impossible, to remain unified on a set of national-level policy positions. As a result, the Democratic-Whig two-party system, which had been responsible for nationalizing U.S. politics, broke down. By 1853 national-level parties had been pushed aside or weakened by regional parties and sectional identities that took full advantage of the U.S. federal arrangement to organize territorial coalitions that dominated political competition.

The consequence of taking federal logic to its extreme in national-level decision-making was the clear pattern of constraints we find in the foreign policy of presidents Pierce and Buchanan. As noted in this chapter, the specific mechanisms for constraints on the use of force were different; Pierce exercised self-restraint, while Buchanan had restraints imposed on him by Congress. Yet the source of these constraints was ultimately the same: sectional rivalry over U.S. policy toward Mexico and Cuba played out in Congress and in party politics. Pierce acknowledged the nature of this sectional competition and the dominance of the northern coalition that would oppose him. Not wanting to incite the destructive sectional antagonism that would emerge if he aggressively pursued his expansionist goals for Mexico and Cuba, for which he would inevitably face legislative and/or electoral defeat, Pierce chose moderation in his policy. In contrast, Buchanan believed that Congress would unite behind the national importance of intervention in Mexico, so he urged Congress to back his ambitious plans for deploying U.S. forces. The northern coalition that intimidated Pierce into moderation denied Buchanan the support he needed. The "colossus of the North," while unrestrained by an external balance of power, was held firmly in check by the internal logic of its domestic political system.

7

A FEDERAL DEMOCRATIC PEACE

A primary objective of this book has been to revive interest in the rich history of American foreign relations before the Civil War. Unfortunately, this period has been largely ignored by students of international relations, even by those scholars interested in the link between the domestic politics of democratic states and international conflict behavior. Both realist and liberal scholars of international relations have failed to appreciate how often the early American republic faced foreign adversaries and the prospect of armed conflict to defend its interests or fulfill expansionist opportunities. Contrary to the prevailing characterization of the United States in this period, the early American republic did not exist in "splendid isolation" from the competitive international politics so familiar to the Europeans. While the Atlantic Ocean certainly reduced the immediacy of security pressure on the United States compared to states in Europe itself, America could not escape the ripple effects of great power conflict in Europe or the insecurities and temptations produced by an elastic geographic periphery. As a result, the United States was involved in a large set of international crises in the early nineteenth century that clearly held the potential for war.

More important than America's mere involvement in a string of international crises is the fact that the United States backed down repeatedly in those disputes resolved short of war, as the previous chapters have shown. Moreover, in several cases we see America accepting much smaller territorial gains from war than we would expect given its material capabilities relative to its adversaries. This history of militarized conflict and America's tendency to seek de-escalation to avoid war makes the United States an ideal case for testing the rival arguments in international relations theory that attempt to explain why states avoid military conflict in an anarchical state system. Was America forced to retreat over and over again by stronger adversaries that could inflict unacceptable costs on this relatively weak state? Or is this pattern in American behavior rooted in the logic of American democracy that increased the difficulties of using military force as a tool of foreign policy?

The overall conclusion of this book is that not a single case in which America backed down from war can be explained without an appreciation for the vision of American domestic politics produced by James Madison and John Jay in *The Federalist Papers*. Like other Enlightenment students of republican government, Madison and Jay firmly believed that domestic institutions, if properly arranged, could check the war-prone impulses of states, their leaders, and their citizens. Madison was quick to point out, however, that among republics America was sui generis. Americans were taking a step that Machiavelli, Montesquieu, and Rousseau would consider audacious; they were constituting a republic across a vast territorial expanse, something earlier theorists considered impossible for republican government. What made this possible, Madison argued, was federal union among smaller republics that would constitute the United States. Not only would federal union be reflected in the basic building blocks of America, it was reflected by the internal composition of the Senate, the House of Representatives, and the presidential electoral system. A first principle of the institutional structure of the United States would be its territorial base. In turn, it was federal union that Madison and Jay expected to have the most consistent constraining effect on America's use of military force.

Madison's and Jay's beliefs about federal union and American foreign policy relied on more than federal institutions alone. In *The Federalist Papers* we find a clear appreciation for the broader social, economic, and geographic context over which these institutions of federal union were laid. This social context would produce the actual substance or content of American politics and was central to the logic of republican constraints they articulated. A feature of American politics produced by this diverse social, economic, and geographic milieu would be the proliferation of diverse interests, beliefs, worries, and ambitions gathered within the broad physical limits of the United States. In a more centralized political system, such geographic diversity and contending political perspectives might be irrelevant for decision-making. Centralized political institutions can deny various domestic groups access to the policy process or minimize their influence over the electoral incentives of key leaders. Madison and Jay argued, however, that when the diversity among the various territorial communities of the Union were combined with federal institutions, institutions that made it possible to protect and advance asymmetric interests, American leaders would find it immensely difficult to go to war in any situation that failed to generate widespread consensus. And consensus generation in the diverse American republic would never be easy.

Of course, as the U.S. Constitution was being debated by state legislatures and as Madison, Hamilton, and Jay wrote their famous letters in the Constitution's defense, their vision of American domestic politics and foreign policy was merely deductive conjecture. Because America would be the first federal republic, they had no empirical record on which to base their arguments or to bolster their confidence that American conflict behavior would actually reflect their logic. What the empirical chapters of this book demonstrate, however, is just how prescient Madison and Jay were, and how powerfully their nascent theory of federal democratic peace captures the actual American experience before the Civil War. Federal union is a much more useful framework for understanding the institutional sources of constraints on America's use of force than the separation of powers alone. Clearly, the separation of powers was a necessary constraining mechanism in a number of cases, such as the war crisis with Great Britain of 1809, the efforts to seize East Florida from Spain in 1813, to seize Canada during the War of 1812, to annex All Oregon in 1846 and larger parts of Mexico in 1847–1848, and to use military force in Mexico in the late 1850s. In each of these cases Congress actually denied the president the authority to pursue these objectives. However, the separation of powers fails to explain why Congress opposed the use of force for these purposes in the first place. Federal union, on the other hand, provides insight into the politics within Congress that explains congressional behavior. Likewise, the incentives produced by federal asymmetry and federal institutions explain why presidents have on occasion exercised self-restraint, in the absence of an overt congressional role, such as Jefferson's decision not to request war during the *Chesapeake* crisis of 1807, and Pierce's reluctance to use force to settle the Mesilla Valley dispute with Mexico and the Cuba crisis with Spain.

Federal democratic peace links the broader social context of American politics to executive and legislative decision-making in a way that separation of powers analysis cannot.

The focus on federal asymmetry in this book has also demonstrated the value of avoiding unitary actor assumptions or the search for a dominant set of incentives when looking for sources of restraint on the use of force, whether from the realist or liberal tradition. For realists, if a state exercised restraint, particularly in a crisis situation, it is assumed that the distribution of power led state leaders to calculate the risks of using force as outweighing the possible benefits. Realists tend to assert that state leaders will conceive of the potential costs of military force in terms of the aggregate interests of the state as a whole. No matter how much domestic diversity there is within a state, realist calculations of aggregate costs and benefits are expected to be the dominant concern in external relations and applicable to all interests within the state. From this theoretical perspective, opposition to the use of force is not expressed by particular groups or political actors in the domestic political system, opposition to using force is a policy choice rationally derived by state leaders. Like realists, Kant makes similar assumptions concerning a unitary set of interests that motivate domestic opposition to war. It is not the state that is unitary, of course; Kant recommends dividing state institutions into executive and legislative bodies with separate functions. Yet for Kant, all citizens within a republic will tend to share an aversion to war because, in an aggregate sense, all citizens will pay the costs of war. His argument about republican constraints on military force depends on popular consensus on avoiding war. In other liberal theories on opposition to the use of force it is common to find one particular set of incentives that are expected to be dominant in the decision process, such as normative limits on using force or the preservation of important commercial ties that might be jeopardized if the state were to use force against a particular adversary. In many of the studies that follow these approaches, other possible sources of opposition to the use of force are rarely taken into consideration.

The case studies presented here, however, demonstrate that the decision process is not necessarily dominated by any one source of opposition: realist, Kantian, normative, or commercial, for example. Instead we find a complex mix of motives that combined to keep the use of force in check. Most important, it is possible for both realist and liberal motives to be active simultaneously among those political actors with some influence on the decision process. For each of the crises examined in this book, recognizing that domestic opposition would not be unidimensional was essential for discovering how America's federal arrangement made constraints on the use of force possible. For example, northeastern opposition to war with Great Britain in 1807, 1809, and 1812 was motivated by both economic and normative considerations, neither of which was shared by the Northwest and the South. The Northwest had strong security concerns motivating its plea for war, particularly the increasing threat posed by the Native American confederation that northwesterners believed was receiving encouragement and support from Great Britain. For the Northwest, this threat justified the risks of war. Yet the majority in the Northeast simply did not share this sense of external threat from Great Britain. War with Great Britain might actually bring devastation to coastal regions of the Northeast (while leaving the insulated Northwest unscathed), and the interests at stake in this conflict did not justify paying this cost.

Economic and normative motives also produced opposition in the Northeast to territorial expansion into Upper and Lower Canada. And while the South did not share the Northeast's economic perspective on British maritime policy, and certainly did not join the Northeast in its normative affinity for Great Britain, the South joined the Northeast in opposition to northward territorial expansion. Southerners did so, however, for very different reasons. The concern in the South was that new states carved from British territory would naturally be nonslave-holding and thus tip the political balance between slave and nonslave states in favor of the North. As a result, the majority of southern legislators, including members of the president's party, withheld support for several initiatives to provide the material resources to take the fight into Canada. While the Northeast and the South were motivated to oppose this war aim for very different reasons, together this multidimensional domestic opposition proved fatal for President Madison's goals.

While the interpretation of American conflict behavior presented in this book focuses on domestic explanations, it does not deny the role of realist logic as a potential part of state decision-making in any of these cases. This runs against the tendency of other literature on democracy and war, from both realist and liberal scholars, that treats explanations for constraints on armed conflict as either exclusively external in origin, produced by strategic calculations of relative power, or exclusively internal in origin, produced by competition among domestic actors or normative prohibitions against using force against certain states or for certain objectives. In each of the cases presented in this book it has been argued that realist logic was not the overriding cause of American restraint. However, in several cases it was shown that certain political actors opposed war because of concerns about America's power disadvantage and the likely costs of armed conflict. Yet in no case was this the sole motive for opposition to war or a consensus position among key American leaders. Moreover, we have seen that federal asymmetry actually produced rival definitions within the United States of what America's interests were, how to define threats and what to do about them, and rival calculations of the costs and benefits of using military force in particular cases. These rival realist perspectives most often emerged from different geographic regions of the United States, as the logic of federal democratic peace anticipated. These rival realist views often combined with other sources of opposition to war, from commercial, normative, and political perspectives, to reduce the likelihood of consensus on using military force.

Of all the cases examined in this book, the Oregon dispute demonstrates most clearly why realist logic must not be written off by students of the democratic peace. While democratic peace is firmly rooted in the liberal theoretical tradition, the insights of realism, in cases like the Oregon dispute, provide an essential part of the explanation for opposition to the use of military force. What makes the peaceful resolution of the Oregon dispute a case of democratic peace and not simply realist deterrence is that the realist logic in this case was relevant only because America's federal democratic structure provided an institutional outlet for certain political leaders to act on these realist motives in the decision process. What the Oregon dispute also shows is that realist logic will not produce one monolithic set of calculations on relative power and the costs and benefits of using force in a particular situation. As seen in this case, the different regional perspectives on the value of All Oregon to the United States and the likely effects of war produced dramatically different calculations of the distribution of power between the United States and Great Britain and the costs the United States would suffer if it went to war.

The Old Northwest was "nearly mad" for Oregon, according to one contemporary observer, and the region was geographically insulated from where an actual war with Britain would most likely take place. As a result, political leaders from this region minimized British power and the risks of military conflict. Furthermore, they were the most aggressive in their demands that President Polk maintain his provocative policy toward Great Britain over Oregon, even if this increased the risk of sparking a military clash. In contrast, political leaders from the entire length of the Atlantic seaboard recognized that war with Great

Britain would be fought primarily along the coast, and would most likely bring naval assaults on coastal cities and possibly invasion of coastal regions. Without the same interests in pursuing All Oregon, political leaders from these regions calculated the costs of war in substantially different terms from their northwestern colleagues. Whigs and Democrats from the Northeast and the Southeast spoke of British power in menacing terms and argued that war would be a disaster for the United States. These dire realist calculations were not shared by the executive branch, and Polk was ready to continue with his risky policy toward Great Britain even if the potential for war was much greater as a result. While northeasterners and southerners tended to firmly believe Britain would fight for Oregon, Polk just as firmly believed that Britain would not. In the absence of the federal structure that provided institutional access for alternative realist calculations to enter the policy process, Polk might have pushed Great Britain into a military conflict based on his own calculations of the costs and benefits involved in this issue and the actual likelihood of war.

Of course, these realist calculations were not the only reasons for opposition to war with Great Britain. To fully explain the motives of Polk's opponents in the Northeast, the Southeast, and even the interior parts of the South, it is also necessary to include the commercial interests at stake for these regions. Not only would war impose physical costs on the Atlantic coast, it would sever the commercial link between these regions and Britain that was vital for their economic well-being. As argued previously, these commercial motives for opposing force were not dominant in American decision-making, and certainly not of greatest concern to the president. But the role of commercial interests as one of the motives for domestic opposition cannot be overlooked.

In the case of expansion into Mexican territory after the Mexican War and the crises of the 1850s over Cuba, the Mesilla Valley, and Mexican political chaos, realist calculations had no role in America's behavior whatsoever. Nor did general Kantian concerns over the costs and miseries of war or the commercial implications of using military force to address these problems. The normative implications of using force for these purposes, while part of the general Whig opposition to the Mexican War, were not apparent in domestic opposition in the Cuban and Mexican crises of the 1850s. In each of these cases, opposition to the use of military force was generated by the domestic political implications of southward expansion. Northern opposition was produced by the asymmetric consequences of adding new territory that might strengthen the southern states politically as a section within

the Union. While a sectional balance of power between the slave and
nonslave portions of the United States had been an objective shared by
most northerners and southerners for decades, by the late 1840s the
North was tempted to take advantage of opportunities to tip the political balance in its favor. Southerners increasingly saw their section in a
desperate struggle to maintain its political strength and protect its interests. Despite the absence of realist, Kantian, commercial, and normative reasons for restraints on the use of force in these cases, the
domestic political struggle alone was enough to produce fierce northern opposition to efforts to forcibly expand further south.

This book added another institution—political parties—to the
analysis of the domestic politics of war and peace in the early American republic. In both the normative and institutional literature on
democratic peace, one of the most serious gaps is the neglect of political parties. In a competitive political system parties often represent alternative normative orientations toward a range of political issues,
including the conditions that justify the use of military force. Political
parties will often be the vehicles through which normative views on
state violence get access to the policy process. The normative democratic peace literature would be enriched by a better understanding of
how different kinds of electoral systems and the organization of political parties in different democratic states will affect the conditions
under which norms will be more likely to influence decisions on the
use of force. The same can be said for institutional democratic peace
theory. In institutional arguments, political actors may be motivated to
oppose the use of force by more than just normative reasons, as made
clear above. Yet political parties will still play a crucial role in aggre-
gating and articulating these various motives for domestic opposition.
The structure of the party system, and most important, the internal coherence and discipline of political parties, will have a profound effect
on the likelihood of structural constraints on the use of force. This is
evident in each of the cases in this book.

The most important potential impact of parties on the policy process
is that coherent, disciplined parties can negate the effects of divided political institutions. In the case of American federalism, if the executive
branch and Congress are controlled by the same party, and if that party
remains united on a particular policy problem, the separation of powers, the division between the Senate and the House, and the diffusion of
authority among individual legislators may be largely meaningless for
decision-making. As the case studies presented here demonstrate, however, party coherence may vary greatly from issue to issue and vary on

the same issue over time. Party coherence on particular issues, and in different political systems, will mainly depend on two things. First, it will depend on the nature of the electoral system and the organization of the political parties themselves. To a great extent, these features of the political system will determine the incentives that individual political actors face when taking a position on various policy questions. What matters is whether the electoral system tends to reward legislators for serving the interests and political orientations of the constituency that elected them, or whether they are rewarded for remaining loyal to national party positions, even when these clash with the interests of their constituents. These incentives are also shaped by whether party leaders have mechanisms for punishing members that dissent from the party line on the positions advanced by the leadership. In many parliamentary systems, for example, legislators must appease the party leadership, which controls candidate lists, just to stand for election, and low-ranking party members may be denied the opportunity to move up in the party ranks if they break with the leadership. In parliamentary systems party members also have an incentive to remain united in order to form a government in the first place and to keep it in power.

In the American federal system, the constitutionally state-based electoral process has produced state-based party organizations in which the parties tend to remain noncentralized. Party leaders lack the kinds of mechanisms enjoyed by leaders in other democratic systems for enforcing discipline among a diverse group of party members, which might be necessary to ensure unity on important, yet divisive, issues. In the American federal system, legislators are rewarded for remaining loyal to their constituents, even if they have to break with the party to do so. In this system, the president does not depend on strict party unity to remain in power, nor do the individual legislators. While a breakdown in party unity makes it much more difficult to advance a national political program, the short-term incumbency of the executive and legislators does not depend on party unity. This simply means that the loss of party unity in the American federal system imposes fewer costs on individual political actors than the costs that might be imposed in other democratic systems. The noncentralized character of the American party system then often prevents single party government, in which the presidency and Congress is held by one party, from overpowering the potential constraints built into the institutional arrangement of American federalism.

Even within the same political system, party coherence can also vary across different issues, depending on how particular issues affect the various interests represented within the party. Any large party, particularly those in plurality electoral systems, will include a diverse membership that may not share the same perspectives on a range of issues. While parties must be held together around some core set of interests or values, they may also include a heterogeneous combination of interests and values on other issues. When those issues on which there is little party consensus emerge in the political system, it is difficult for the party to remain united in the policy process.

The breakdown of party unity in each of the crises examined in this book was crucial for allowing the institutional arrangement of the American system to impose constraints on the use of force. In a number of these cases one party had a large majority in Congress and held the executive branch. This was true during the disputes with Great Britain and Spain from 1807 through the end of the War of 1812, in which the Republican party vastly outnumbered the Federalists. It was true during the Oregon crisis in which the Democrats controlled the government, and during the Mesilla Valley crisis with Mexico and the Cuba crisis with Spain in 1854–1855, when President Pierce's Democratic party controlled Congress. Despite single-party government in these cases, the majority party regularly split along territorial lines, thus preventing party unity from bridging the institutional gaps in the system. In 1807 and 1809, dissent from northeastern Republicans—potential or real—helped prevent the use of force against Great Britain and nearly scuttled the war movement in 1812. The defection of southern Republicans on key legislation that would have provided the resources for taking the war into Canada seriously undermined this effort, as did the unwillingness of northwestern and northeastern Republicans to sanction President Madison's efforts to use force to wrest East Florida from Spain. The split in the Democratic party between the Old Northwest and the Calhoun Democrats of the South and the Van Buren Democrats of the Northeast prevented party unity on Polk's provocative policy toward Great Britain over Oregon. While Democrats and Whigs supported Polk's Mexican war bill by overwhelming margins, the subsequent effort to annex larger portions of Mexican territory split the Democratic party along North-South lines, thus killing any hopes for forcing Mexico to relinquish territory south of 32 degrees latitude. The worsening North-South split in the Democratic party would have made it impossible for President Pierce to attain congressional support for war over the Mesilla Valley and Cuba. Interestingly, during Buchanan's term, the Democratic party was largely united behind his effort to intervene in Mexico with military force. Yet by the late 1850s the Democratic party was primarily a southern party, and the opposition Republicans were a northern party. Party unity, therefore, really reflected sectional interests on this issue, and the North's dominance in the federal union prevented Buchanan's pursuit of what was seen in the North as a southern-oriented initiative.

Among the cases examined in this book we find both divided institutions and electoral accountability producing constraints on the use of military force. We also find the two main institutional points of constraint: presidential self-restraint and congressional action that denies the authority or the resources necessary to pursue a particular foreign policy. Overall, the actual or potential role of Congress in the decision process was more prevalent and consistent than electoral accountability. Electoral accountability, as discussed in earlier chapters, is an *ex post* constraint. This means that political leaders can be punished for certain policy decisions only after the decisions are actually made. As a result, this version of institutional democratic peace has been criticized because it does not have the same direct *ex ante* effect on the decision process that divided institutions might have to halt a move toward war. Electoral constraints depend on the president's calculations of electoral vulnerability and the political risks he is willing to take for a particular issue. As a result, this particular structural constraint does not have a consistent effect on decision-making. However, we do find electoral accountability to have been an important motive for presidential self-restraint in two cases involving the same president: President Pierce's decision to negotiate over the disputed Mesilla Valley and to de-escalate the military standoff that had developed on the New Mexico border, and Pierce's decision not to use military force to gain possession of Cuba. In each case, the key to turning the potential *ex post* electoral effects of each crisis into *ex ante* decisions for moderation in state behavior was the immediate sense of electoral vulnerability felt by the president. In the elections of 1852 the Democrats won a huge majority in Congress and took back the executive branch from the Whigs. Despite this recent electoral success, Pierce knew that the North would strongly reject any effort to resolve either crisis with military force. His own sense of electoral vulnerability and the vulnerability of his party in the North was so acute because the elections of 1848 provided a recent example of the penalties the Democrats had paid for using military force in an attempt to expand southward, thus stoking North-South antagonism over slavery. Pierce was faced with the same kind of situation in the Mesilla Valley and Cuba crises. In 1848 the Whig Zachary Taylor defeated the Democrats' candidate,

Lewis Cass, because the Democratic party was accused of a southern orientation by many northern voters. The Whigs solidified their majority in the House of Representatives in that election as well. Pierce was simply unwilling to put his own electoral fate, and that of his party, at risk for the sake of meeting these expansionist objectives. Combined with a clear understanding that northerners in Congress were likely to block any effort to gain legislative authority for the use of force in either case, Pierce exercised self-restraint and never took these policies to Congress in the first place, nor did he act with military force on his own authority.

The most common institutional point of constraint among these cases was legislative action that imposed constraints on executive action. In 1809, a move by northwestern Republicans to replace the embargo against Great Britain with war was defeated in Congress by a coalition of Republicans and Whigs in the Northeast. Congress' rejection of key legislation to provide the resources necessary for prosecuting a war in Upper and Lower Canada, and Congress's refusal to approve of the forcible cession of East Florida, doomed each of these expansionist initiatives. In 1846, congressional debate on Polk's provocative stance on Oregon and the conciliatory language on the dispute that was passed by overwhelming margins in the Senate and the House forced the president to accept that he would have no support from Congress if he continued to risk war over this issue. Perpetual divisions in Congress over expansion into Mexican territory and the failure of Congress to act promptly on key war legislation during the Mexican conflict convinced Polk that the Senate would not ratify a peace treaty that took any Mexican territory below 32 degrees north. President Buchanan lost successive congressional votes in his effort to gain authority for an intervention in Mexico.

This book also suggests that there are two important questions raised in cases such as these that will affect the likelihood of constraints on military force. First, who initiates congressional action that might produce legislative constraints in these kinds of crises, the president or members of Congress? What we find from these cases is that congressional action really depends on the president approaching Congress for authority or resources for particular initiatives. Rarely do we find individual congressmen or congressional blocs initiating action on their own that eventually produces constraining legislation. In 1809, action of this kind did come from within Congress, specifically, from northwestern legislators seeking an end to the embargo and the initiation of armed hostilities. In every other case, however, Congress was responding to some presidential initiative. For example, while a congressional delegation urged President Madison to submit a declaration of war request in 1812, action by Congress as a body was motivated by Madison actually making this formal request. Also, Congress was reacting to specific requests from the president when it denied resources for war in Canada and the seizure of East Florida. In the Oregon dispute, Congress was responding to a specific request from Polk to terminate the joint occupation agreement with Great Britain. In the Mexican War, the Wilmot Proviso was raised as a congressional initiative to constrain the president only after Polk had submitted a request for $2 million that would support an effort to end the war, and it was raised again when Polk submitted his $3 million bill the next year. In the late 1850s, restraint on the use of force in Mexico came only after President Buchanan made specific requests to Congress for its approval. At the height of tensions over the *Chesapeake* affair in 1807 and the Mesilla Valley and Cuba crises during Pierce's term, Congress never stepped in on its own initiative to put restrictions on how the president could respond to these crises. Finally, at no time during the long period in which Polk progressively increased the danger of war with Mexico did Congress intervene to put limits on his risky behavior. Polk never went to Congress himself so he was able to maintain a free hand until the conflict actually erupted. Even then, he kept the initiative and framed the issue as a national cause in order to trump the strong domestic opposition to prosecuting this war that might have produced a legislative defeat. Despite the central role that an institutional division between legislative and executive authority may have in how democratic states use force, these cases suggest that the initiative will rarely come from the legislature itself.

The second important question on the role of legislative action as a constraint on the use of force concerns the timing of such legislative intervention. Specifically, at what point does the legislature actually become involved in the series of events that increase the chances that military conflict will occur? In 1807 and 1809, in the Oregon dispute, and in the late 1850s, legislative pressure and action occurred before any military mobilization in response to these crises had begun. In contrast, one of the most important dimensions of the Mexican War was that President Polk had deployed a sizable military force directly into a disputed region before Congress had any role in the decision-making process. Polk's actions not only posed a direct challenge to the Mexican government with a tangible threat in a region that Mexico claimed as its sovereign territory, he also created a standoff between

Mexican and American troops on each side of the Rio Grande River, thus dramatically increasing the potential for a physical clash. While Polk had decided to offer Congress a chance to exercise its institutional prerogative with a request for a declaration of war, his previous actions made it more likely that a conflict would occur before Congress could pass judgment on his policy. On the very day he was preparing his request for a declaration of war, news of the border skirmish reached Washington. Now Polk had the chance to define the conflict as Mexican aggression, and congressional opponents of war had to choose between either providing or withholding material support for an American force currently engaged in combat. In this case, the conflict had progressed too far for Congress to make a simple choice between war or no war with Mexico. Under these circumstances, decision-making within America's federal institutions was dominated by nationwide patriotic enthusiasm that altered the political incentives faced by the opponents of war. This allowed the executive to manipulate the policy choice and nullify the institutional divisions in the system that might otherwise have constrained his aggressive objectives.

The final question to consider is the changing significance of federal union for U.S. foreign policy after the period considered in this book. After the Civil War and with the coming of the twentieth century the kinds of institutional constraints on the use of force found in these cases became more rare. But this is not because of any major change in the institutional arrangement of the federal system. America is still distinguished by an entrenched, territorially organized distribution of authority that provides an outlet for regional interests within the national government. The electoral system is still organized at the state level, which keeps the organization of the main political parties noncentralized. Legislators still face potent incentives to represent the particular interests of their local constituents, and the president is still selected by state-based electors. Power in Congress is still diffused among autonomous individual representatives and the separation of powers between the executive and the legislature is still a central organizing principle of American politics.

Despite this continuity in the institutional arrangement of the American system, there have been two major changes that have decreased the potential for constraints on military force within this system. The first major change was the elimination of slavery in the United States. With the North's victory in the Civil War, slavery was removed as a feature of the American political system, which removed the territorial characteristic that most sharply divided the federal

system along territorial lines and that by the late 1840s produced fre-
quent asymmetric effects on the North and South over both domestic
and foreign issues. The significance of this change is that fewer policy
issues now have direct and dire effects on the divergent social and economic interests of the North and South, nor does the domestic balance
of power between the North and South have the same intense value as
it did before the Civil War. As a result, the intensity of the competitive
dynamics of federal asymmetry has dramatically decreased.

This is not to say that America's pre–Civil War foreign policy behavior was merely a product of North-South sectional tensions rooted
in the slavery system. As noted in chapter 2, regional divisions in the
United States before the early 1850s were not simply along North-
South lines. The most persistent division from the first decade of the
nineteenth century until the decade before the Civil War was defined
by the states of the Northeast, the Old Northwest, and the South.
Slave-holding states on the Atlantic coast and those in the interior
Southwest also divided over several issues. Moreover, slavery did not
appear as a defining issue until the late 1840s in the Mexican War.
Each of the previous cases in this book, including the Oregon crisis of
1846, show the constraining logic of federal union without the sectional antagonism produced later by slavery. The logic of federal
democratic peace helps us link the domestic politics of American conflict decision-making across a diverse time period and shifting regional
groupings, interests, and issues. With the elimination of slavery, one
potent, but not the sole, basis for regional asymmetry was removed
from American politics.

Aside from this clear domestic change that had distinguished territorial communities in the United States, the country is still marked by
important differences among regions in their social characteristics,
economic interests, and geographic features. Yet the importance of this
remaining federal asymmetry for political competition over foreign
policy issues has decreased because of a second major change since the
antebellum period. The nature of potential challenges to American security and the scope of its interactions with other states in the international system were fundamentally altered after America solidified its
continental position and looked further abroad in its foreign policy.
This is a change in the nature of the foreign policy issues confronted
by the United States, and one that has actually reduced the significance of America's federal system as a source of constraints on the use
of force. In the first half of the nineteenth century, the greatest foreign
policy challenges and opportunities were on the immediate periphery

of the United States—in British North America, Spanish East Florida, Oregon, Texas and Mexico, and Cuba. As a result, each of the crises involving these peripheral regions was more likely to have direct asymmetric consequences for the particular interests of different regions within the United States. After the Civil War, however, America entered a truly quiescent period in its foreign policy, particularly in terms of problems that could have led to armed conflict with foreign adversaries. Its northern border with Great Britain, and then an independent Canada after 1867, had been settled in 1846, and the pressures for southern expansion evaporated with the end of slavery. In effect, all questions of expansion on the periphery had been resolved or removed from the American agenda. Without a real threat in its immediate neighborhood, the United States did not face the bitter problems of war and peace until the late 1880s and 1890s when Spain's control of Cuba again became an issue. By the 1890s, however, Cuba did not produce the kind of federal asymmetry that paralyzed President Pierce over forty years earlier. By the end of the nineteenth century, with America's continental expansion complete, and as it faced new questions over its global role, specific foreign policy questions did not have the kind of clear asymmetric effects on territorial communities seen in the first half of the century.

This does not mean that the federal system had become irrelevant as a source of constraints by the early twentieth century; it just means that the intensity of the distinctive institutional constraints from this federal system has decreased. For example, Edward Chester notes that "most scholars are in agreement that there was a sectional division of opinion prior to World War II over the twin issues of isolationism and internationalism/intervention. [The] traditional interpretation" is that "there were isolationists in all parts of the country, but they were most powerful in the Middle West and least so in the South." Conversely, "support for the internationalist view came from all parts of the country, but the Northeast was the most consistently internationalist section and the south the most vehemently interventionist section."[1] The differences noted here have little to do with an asymmetric effect of using military force on the direct interests of these different parts of the country. These differences are primarily in ideological or commercial orientations over the question of American isolation and intervention. But these regional

---

[1] Edward W. Chester, *Sectionalism, Politics, and American Diplomacy* (Metuchen, N.J.: Scarecrow Press, 1975), 187.

ideological and commercial distinctions, in combination with America's federal arrangement that gave them an institutional outlet at the national level, as well as weak party discipline and partisan politics, produced a string of failed foreign policy initiatives, like the failed ratification of the Treaty of Versailles and rejection of membership in the League of Nations and the World Court. The federal asymmetry described by Chester and America's federal arrangement also facilitated specific legislative initiatives designed to prevent the United States from asserting itself as a global power, such as the restrictive naval armaments policy,[2] the Neutrality Act,[3] and the work of the peculiar and profoundly influential Senate Munitions Investigating Committee, chaired by Senator Gerald Nye of North Dakota.[4] More recently, Michael Lind has argued that there is a lingering North-South divide on basic beliefs about using military force that he connects to strong regional differences over America's war in Kosovo at the end of the twentieth century.[5] Perhaps the clearest remaining link between federal asymmetry, the federal arrangement of America's political system, and foreign policy problems involves international trade rather than war.[6] Despite the lingering effects we may find in federal asymmetry and America's federal structure, it is clear that the end of the Civil War and the close of the nineteenth century loosened the tight link between the domestic political forces rooted in federal union and conflict behavior that Madison and Jay laid out in 1787.

[2] Leonard C. Hoag, *Preface to Preparedness* (Washington, D.C.: American Council of Public Affairs, 1941).

[3] Selig Adler, *The Isolationist Impulse* (London: Abelard-Schuman, 1957).

[4] Wayne Cole, *Senator Gerald P. Nye and American Foreign Policy* (Minneapolis: University of Minnesota Press, 1962). Chester asserts that "Nye was unquestionably instrumental in strengthening the isolationist sentiment in this country and laying the ground work for neutrality legislation." Chester, *Sectionalism*, 206.

[5] Michael Lind, "Civil War by Other Means," *Foreign Affairs* 78 (September/October 1999), 124–42.

[6] For the best discussion see Peter Trubowitz, *Defining the National Interest: Conflict and Change in American Foreign Policy* (Chicago: University of Chicago Press, 1998).

INDEX

CORNELL STUDIES IN SECURITY AFFAIRS

A series edited by

Robert J. Art
Robert Jervis
Stephen M. Walt

The Purpose of Intervention: Changing Beliefs about the Use of Force
 by Martha Finnemore

A Substitute for Victory: The Politics of Peacemaking at the Korean Armistice Talks
 by Rosemary Foot

The Wrong War: American Policy and the Dimensions of the Korean Conflict, 1950–1953
 by Rosemary Foot

The Best Defense: Policy Alternatives for U.S. Nuclear Security from the 1950s to the 1990s
 by David Goldfischer

Storm of Steel: The Development of Armor Doctrine in Germany and the Soviet Union, 1919–1939
 By Mary R. Habeck

America Unrivaled: The Future of the Balance of Power
 Edited by G. John Ikenberry

The Meaning of the Nuclear Revolution: Statecraft and the Prospect of Armageddon
 by Robert Jervis

Fast Tanks and Heavy Bombers: Innovation in the U.S. Army, 1917–1945
 by David E. Johnson

Modern Hatreds: The Symbolic Politics of Ethnic War
 by Stuart J. Kaufman

The Vulnerability of Empire
 by Charles A. Kupchan

The Transformation of American Air Power
 by Benjamin S. Lambeth

Anatomy of Mistrust: U.S.–Soviet Relations during the Cold War
 by Deborah Welch Larson

Planning the Unthinkable: How New Powers Will Use Nuclear, Biological, and Chemical Weapons
 edited by Peter R. Lavoy, Scott D. Sagan, and James J. Wirtz

Cooperation under Fire: Anglo-German Restraint during World War II
 by Jeffrey W. Legro

Uncovering Ways of War: U.S. Intelligence and Foreign Military Innovation, 1918–1941
by Thomas Mahnken

No Exit: America and the German Problem, 1943–1954
by James McAllister

Liddell Hart and the Weight of History
by John J. Mearsheimer

Reputation and International Politics
by Jonathan Mercer

Undermining the Kremlin: America's Strategy to Subvert the Soviet Bloc, 1947–1956
by Gregory Mitrovich

Report to JFK: The Skybolt Crisis in Perspective
by Richard E. Neustadt

The Sacred Cause: Civil-Military Conflict over Soviet National Security, 1917–1992
by Thomas M. Nichols

Liberal Peace, Liberal War: American Politics and International Security
by John M. Owen IV

Bombing to Win: Air Power and Coercion in War
by Robert A. Pape

A Question of Loyalty: Military Manpower in Multiethnic States
by Alon Peled

Inadvertent Escalation: Conventional War and Nuclear Risks
by Barry R. Posen

The Sources of Military Doctrine: France, Britain, and Germany between the World Wars
by Barry Posen

Dilemmas of Appeasement: British Deterrence and Defense, 1934–1937
by Gaines Post, Jr.

Crucible of Beliefs: Learning, Alliances, and World Wars
by Dan Reiter

Eisenhower and the Missile Gap
by Peter J. Roman

The Domestic Bases of Grand Strategy
  edited by Richard Rosecrance and Arthur Stein

Societies and Military Power: India and Its Armies
  by Stephen Peter Rosen

Winning the Next War: Innovation and the Modern Military
  by Stephen Peter Rosen

*Vital Crossroads: Mediterranean Origins of the Second World War,
1935–1940*
  by Reynolds Salerno

*Fighting to a Finish: The Politics of War Termination in the United States
and Japan, 1945*
  by Leon V. Sigal

Corporate Warriors: The Rise of the Privatized Military Industry
  by P. W. Singer

Alliance Politics
  by Glenn H. Snyder

*The Ideology of the Offensive: Military Decision Making and the Disasters
of 1914*
  by Jack Snyder

Myths of Empire: Domestic Politics and International Ambition
  by Jack Snyder

The Militarization of Space: U.S. Policy, 1945–1984
  by Paul B. Stares

Balancing Risks: Great Power Intervention In the Periphery
  by Jeffrey W. Taliaferro

The Nixon Administration and the Making of U.S. Nuclear Strategy
  by Terry Terriff

The Ethics of Destruction: Norms and Force in International Relations
  by Ward Thomas

Causes of War: Power and the Roots of Conflict
  by Stephen Van Evera

*Mortal Friends, Best Enemies: German-Russian Cooperation after the
Cold War*
  by Celeste A. Wallander

The Origins of Alliances
by Stephen M. Walt

Revolution and War
by Stephen M. Walt

The Tet Offensive: Intelligence Failure in War
by James J. Wirtz

The Elusive Balance: Power and Perceptions during the Cold War
by William Curti Wohlforth

Deterrence and Strategic Culture: Chinese-American Confrontations, 1949–1958
by Shu Guang Zhang